THIS JOURNAL BELONGS TO:

....

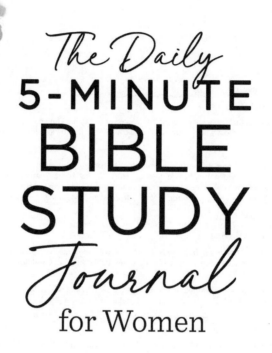

The Daily
5-MINUTE
BIBLE
STUDY
Journal
for Women

365
Encouraging
Readings

BARBOUR
PUBLISHING

Introduction

Do you find it hard to make time for Bible study? You intend to do it, but the hours turn into days, and before you know it, another week has passed and you have not picked up God's Word. This book provides an avenue for you to open the Bible regularly and dig into a passage—even if you only have five minutes!

MINUTES 1–2: *Read* carefully the scripture passage for each day's Bible study.

MINUTE 3: *Understand.* Answer a couple of prompts designed to help you apply the verses from the Bible to your own life.

MINUTE 4: *Apply.* Read a brief devotional based on the day's scripture. Think about what you are learning and how to apply the scriptural truths to your own life.

MINUTE 5: *Pray.* A prayer starter will help you to begin a time of conversation with God. Remember to allow time for Him to speak into your life as well.

May *The Daily 5-Minute Bible Study Journal for Women* help you to establish the discipline of studying God's Word. Pour yourself a cup of coffee and make that first five minutes of your day count, or use these studies to end your day strong. You will find that spending even five minutes focused on scripture and prayer has the power to make a huge difference. Soon you will want to make time for even more time in God's Word!

Day 1

CALL UPON THE LORD

—— READ PSALMS 86:1–87:7 ——

KEY VERSES: *Give ear, O Lord, to my prayer; and attend to the voice of my supplications. In the day of my trouble I will call upon You, for You will answer me.* PSALM 86:6–7 NKJV

UNDERSTAND:

- When you run into trouble, whom do you call upon first? A friend? A family member?

....

....

....

....

....

....

- The psalmist states that he will call upon the Lord in his day of trouble. Why? What will the result most certainly be according to today's key verses?

....

....

....

....

....

....

....

APPLY: You know the type of day. Everything goes wrong. Just when you thought you were breaking even financially, your hot-water heater goes out. Or your property taxes go up drastically. Or the school is asking for more money for extra-curricular activities. On top of that, no one in the family can seem to get along. Everyone is bickering. There is eye rolling, and the blame game is nonstop. Tattling and arguing are also abundant. You want to yell out, as the lady in the bubble bath commercial, "Calgon, take me away!"

When you have one of "those" days, whom do you tend to call first? Many women tend to pick up the phone to call a girlfriend, mom, or sister. Next time you are struggling, instead of heading for your cell phone, call on your heavenly Father. God is always there, and He cares. He wants you to turn to Him. He will answer.

_____

_____

_____

_____

_____

_____

_____

_____

_____

_____

_____

PRAY: *Lord, rather than dumping my troubles on my husband or mom, I will choose to call upon Your mighty name. My girlfriends and sisters can only do so much, but You are the sovereign God of the universe. You are big enough to handle even my very worst day. Thank You for hearing my prayers and answering when I am in trouble. Amen.*

Day 2
POWERFUL PRAYER

—— READ MATTHEW 6:5–13; LUKE 11:1–13; JOHN 17 ——

KEY VERSE: *Once Jesus was in a certain place praying. As he finished, one of his disciples came to him and said, "Lord, teach us to pray."* LUKE 11:1 NLT

UNDERSTAND:

• What most impacts you about how Jesus taught others to pray?

....

....

....

....

....

....

....

....

• What most impacts you from Jesus' prayers in John 17?

....

....

....

....

....

....

....

....

....

APPLY: In times of stress, when we feel like we just aren't sure how and what to pray, we can take a deep breath and go straight to the words of Jesus when He said, "This is how you should pray." Sometimes a bullet point list is helpful to follow when our minds feel scattered and unable to focus.

- Begin with praise to the Father.
- Ask for God's kingdom to come and His will to be done.
- Ask God to provide for daily needs without worry for needs of the future.
- Ask for forgiveness of sin and for help in extending forgiveness to others.
- Ask for protection from temptation and deliverance from evil.

We can apply the prayer that Jesus Himself instructed to every situation and need in our lives and the lives of our loved ones for whom we are praying.

PRAY: *Loving Savior, I know I can pray to You about anything and everything, but please also help me keep good perspective and not overcomplicate my prayers, especially during stressful times. Bring me peace with the simplicity yet power of the way You have taught and have shown me how to pray in Your Word. Amen.*

Day 3

YOU ARE KNOWN
AND UNDERSTOOD

———— **READ PSALM 139** ————

KEY VERSES: *For you created my inmost being; you knit me together in my mother's womb. I praise you because I am fearfully and wonderfully made; your works are wonderful, I know that full well.* PSALM 139:13–14 NIV

UNDERSTAND:

• Who (aside from God) knows you best?

....

....

....

....

• Think of one thing that makes you unique. Why might your Creator have fashioned you this way?

....

....

....

....

• Is it important to you that you feel understood? Why?

....

....

....

....

....

APPLY: When God created you, He knew you. He didn't need an introduction and time to get to know your quirks and true self. From the moment His artist brush, sculptor hands, and creative mastery formed you, He knew you at the most intimate level. That fact is beautiful and frightening all at once.

On the other hand, we spend so much time creating and wearing masks, conforming to the people and situations around us in order to fit in, to be accepted, to feel normal, that it is a mystery whether we even know ourselves.

Start today by removing your mask. Come before your Creator and loving Father as your true self, the woman He created you to be. Lay your sins, your worries, your regrets, your requests, your heartbreak before Him. He knows you, and He *chooses* to love you, His cherished daughter.

....

....

....

....

....

....

....

....

....

....

....

PRAY: *Who am I, Father? I've put on so many masks over the years that I'm not sure I know my true self. But You accept me (Romans 15:7), call me Your friend (John 15:15), Your beloved child (Romans 8:17), and You set me free from sin (Galatians 5:1). Today I choose to be known. Reveal Your wisdom to me through Your Word. I want to know You more. Amen.*

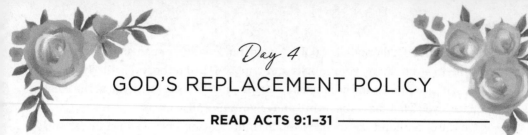

Day 4
GOD'S REPLACEMENT POLICY

──────────── **READ ACTS 9:1–31** ────────────

KEY VERSES: *Immediately, something like scales fell from Saul's eyes, and he could see again. He got up and was baptized, and after taking some food, he regained his strength.* ACTS 9:18–19 NIV

UNDERSTAND:

- Have you ever walked through a season where you felt like you had scales on your eyes and couldn't see clearly? How did you make it through?

....

....

....

....

....

- If you've walked through seasons of rebellion, what finally drew you back to God? Are you motivated more by fear or love?

....

....

....

....

....

....

....

APPLY: Saul was simply walking down the road, minding his own business, when God interrupted his life and brought lasting change. Maybe you've been there too. Maybe you lived your life your own way, according to your own terms, not caring what anyone else thought. Then God ripped the scales from your eyes and gave you brand-new vision to see things as He does. Amazing!

If you've ever experienced a radical transformation like that, then you can surely relate to Saul's journey. Out with the old, in with the new! God has a great replacement policy. He wants to take your old, broken life—the one riddled with worries, cares, and woes—and replace it with a new, whole one. He wants to point you in the right direction and win your heart. What an amazing and loving God He is.

PRAY: *Lord, thank You for Your transformative power! I'm so grateful You've intervened in my life and given me a second chance. I choose to live my life for You, Father. Amen.*

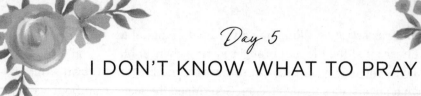

Day 5

I DON'T KNOW WHAT TO PRAY

──────── READ ROMANS 8:22–28 ────────

KEY VERSE: *We do not know what we ought to pray for, but the Spirit himself intercedes for us through wordless groans.* ROMANS 8:26 NIV

UNDERSTAND:

• What does the phrase "wordless groans" say to you? Is it a good description of how you feel when you don't know how or what to pray? Why or why not?

....

....

....

....

....

• Notice that this Bible passage uses the same word—*groan*—to describe both the Holy Spirit's intercession and the state of all creation as it waits for the birth of something new. What do you think this implies?

....

....

....

....

....

....

APPLY: In childbirth, a woman moves past the ability to talk in coherent words. The process of delivery is so intense that every morsel of her being—mental, emotional, and physical—is completely focused on this amazing act that breaks her open in order to bring new life into the world.

In this passage of Paul's letter to the Romans, he compared our current state of reality to that intense process of birthing a baby. We cannot control our circumstances, any more than a woman can control childbirth. With that in mind, we don't *need* to know what to pray. After all, we can't tell God what needs to happen, and He doesn't need us to tell Him. Instead, we can simply surrender to the Spirit. God is with us in this process. He feels the same pain we do, and He will pray through us, birthing His Spirit into our hearts and the world around us.

PRAY: *Loving Lord of life, I don't know how or what to pray—so I ask that You pray through me. I surrender myself to Your Spirit. Be born in me. Amen.*

Day 6

MIND CONTROL

READ ROMANS 8:1-8

KEY VERSE: *So letting your sinful nature control your mind leads to death. But letting the Spirit control your mind leads to life and peace.* ROMANS 8:6 NLT

UNDERSTAND:

• How do you know your sinful nature is rearing its head for control of your mind?

....

....

....

....

• How do you know the Holy Spirit is controlling your mind?

....

....

....

....

• How could your day be different if you allowed the Spirit full control?

....

....

....

....

....

....

APPLY: For most of us, our minds are in overdrive even before our feet hit the floor in the morning. Our brains are so jam-packed with schedules and responsibilities and to-do lists that we barely have time to think about anything outside of what must be done—now.

But even with an overloaded mind, there are still negative feelings or harsh criticisms or resentful feelings or spite or even lustful fantasies that barge in. These thought patterns are all evidence that our sinful nature is in control, and Romans 8 tells us that leads to death when left unchecked.

But that's not the end! Life and peace are there for each of us when we let the Holy Spirit control our minds. How? Right now, first thing this morning, surrender your mind to God's perfect will. Ask for His guidance. And continue to give your mind over to the Spirit throughout the day. He is faithful to supply life-giving thoughts, grounded in the love of God.

....

....

....

....

....

....

....

....

....

....

....

PRAY: *God, I'm done giving my sinful nature control of my mind. Today I choose to surrender my thoughts and feelings to Your will. I invite the Holy Spirit to take the helm of my mind. I know with You in control, I will live a peaceful life filled with Your promises. Amen.*

Day 7

LIVE FOR TODAY

--- **READ GENESIS 19:15–26** ---

KEY VERSE: *But Lot's wife looked back, and she became a pillar of salt.* Genesis 19:26 NIV

UNDERSTAND:

- Like Lot's wife, you've probably been tempted to look back a time or two. Think of a particular time when God instructed you to move forward, but you felt tempted to glance back over your shoulder.

....

....

....

....

....

....

- What's the most precarious situation God has delivered you from? Aren't you glad you don't have to go back to that?

....

....

....

....

....

....

....

APPLY: My goodness, Lot went through a *lot*. When it came time for him to leave Sodom and Gomorrah, God gave him specific instructions. He was not to look back. No gazing at the past. Unfortunately, his wife disobeyed God's commands and turned back for one last glance. She paid the ultimate price with her life.

Maybe you've been there. Maybe you've camped out in a place of unbelief and surrounded yourself with people who encouraged you to live the wrong way. You've done your time in Sodom and Gomorrah. But now you have regrets. You want out. God has a way of pulling you out of such places and seasons. When He does, you can count on Him to say, *"Don't look back." "Don't let the past define you." "Live for today."*

Take heart! There are better days ahead. Just keep looking forward and putting one foot in front of the other. And, whatever you do, don't be tempted to glance back over your shoulder.

PRAY: *Lord, I'm so glad my days of sin and rebellion are behind me. Thank You for delivering me! I'm so grateful for a happy road ahead. With Your help, I won't look back. Amen.*

Day 8

ARE YOU ARGUMENTATIVE
OR PEACEFUL?

READ PROVERBS 27

KEY VERSES: *A continual dripping on a very rainy day and a contentious woman are alike; whoever restrains her restrains the wind, and grasps oil with his right hand.* PROVERBS 27:15–16 NKJV

UNDERSTAND:

• Would your husband (or others close to you) describe you as peaceful or argumentative?

....

....

....

....

....

• Is it easy to restrain the wind or grasp oil with one's hand? Consider the meaning of these verses. Is it even possible to do so? How does this impact your attitude about being quarrelsome?

....

....

....

....

....

....

APPLY: Proverbs gives advice for having a God-centered life. The key verses today point us toward understanding the seriousness of the contentious wife. The New Century Version uses the word *quarreling* in place of *contentious*.

What is the first thing you say to your husband each morning? The last thing you discuss at night? Are you affirming him for a hard day's work or pestering him about the chores that remain undone? Do you greet him with a hug or kiss? Or with a list of complaints?

Take note of this proverb's warning. No man wants to make his home with a contentious woman. Trying to change this trait in a woman is like attempting to hold back the wind or hold oil in one's bare hand. Next time you start to pick a fight, hold your tongue. Find a way to praise your husband instead. See what a difference this makes in your marriage.

....

....

....

....

....

....

....

....

....

....

....

PRAY: *Lord, I have not meant to be argumentative, but I do find myself dwelling on the negative lately. Help me to focus on my husband's strengths and be a wife who is supportive and loving. Look deep into my heart, and help me to root out any contentiousness that lives there. Amen.*

Day 9
BE YOURSELF

---- **READ MATTHEW 6:5–13** ----

KEY VERSES: *"When you pray, do not be as those who pretend to be someone they are not. They love to stand and pray in the places of worship or in the streets so people can see them. . . . When you pray, go into a room by yourself. After you have shut the door, pray to your Father Who is in secret. Then your Father Who sees in secret will reward you."* MATTHEW 6:5–6 NLV

UNDERSTAND:

- Why might someone be tempted to try to sound more spiritual than they really are?

....

....

....

....

....

....

- Do you use different words when you pray in public than when you pray silently? Why or why not?

....

....

....

....

....

APPLY: God doesn't require eloquent speech, complete sentences, or even coherent thoughts in prayer. He wants to hear from your authentic self, speaking intimately and from your heart.

If you get the opportunity to pray aloud in public, be sure that your prayer motives are pure. God doesn't want a show, and He doesn't want you to pretend to be someone you aren't. In these instances, others—especially children—may look to you as an example of how to pray, and the best example you can set is one of a pure heart with a singular desire to connect with your heavenly Father.

Practice being authentic in prayer behind closed doors, and that authenticity will flow into other areas. Be yourself—perfectly loved and forgiven by God.

PRAY: *Father, I come before You this morning with no motive other than to be in Your presence. I am not pretending to be better than I am. I admit that I have no answers. I realize that I can't do life today without You. I need You, God. Please be near, and never leave me. Amen.*

IN THE MIDDLE OF EVERY STORM

— **READ MATTHEW 8:23-27; MARK 4:35-41; LUKE 8:22-25** —

KEY VERSE: *When Jesus woke up, he rebuked the wind and said to the waves, "Silence! Be still!" Suddenly the wind stopped, and there was a great calm.* MARK 4:39 NLT

UNDERSTAND:

• Do you see any differences in the accounts of Jesus calming the storm in these three different Gospels?

....

....

....

....

....

....

• What storm are you needing Jesus to calm right now in your life or the life of a loved one?

....

....

....

....

....

....

APPLY: "Don't You care that we're going to drown?" the disciples asked. We feel that frustrating question too when we're in the middle of our own storms, right? We question how God can stay quiet—*Is He sleeping on the job?* we might wonder—and not intervene exactly when we think He needs to. *Don't You care about me, Jesus?* we desperately wonder and cry too. But when the disciples asked their question, it included a false statement. They were sure they were going to drown, and that was not true. Jesus knew they wouldn't. How often do we cry out to Jesus like He doesn't care, because we're positive we know what the awful outcome will be if He doesn't come to our rescue right away? But it's a false positive. When we stop, think, and humble ourselves, we remember we surely don't know it all. Only God does. And He is perfect in all His thoughts and ways—which are far, far higher than ours (see Psalm 145; Isaiah 55:8–9). Never forget that no matter what the storm is, Jesus will calm it, one way or another, in His perfect timing.

PRAY: *Dear Jesus, please forgive me when I think I know more or better than You do. Please forgive me when I accuse You of not caring. That is so unfair since You love me so much that You literally died to save me. I choose to trust that You are always working out what is best for me, even when I don't understand. Help me to patiently trust You and Your perfect ways in the middle of every storm! Amen.*

Day 11

I CAN'T SLEEP

--- **READ PROVERBS 3:21–26** ---

KEY VERSE: *When you lie down, you will not be afraid; when you lie down, your sleep will be sweet.* PROVERBS 3:24 NASB

UNDERSTAND:

• What keeps you awake at night? Is it fear and anxiety—or something else?

....

....

....

....

....

....

....

• How does wisdom apply to insomnia, as this passage of scripture suggests? Could it be the sleeping aid you need?

....

....

....

....

....

....

....

....

APPLY: The Bible speaks of "wisdom" as though she were a person, making clear that wisdom is something far more than mere knowledge or intelligence. Some Bible scholars have even suggested that wisdom may be one of the roles Jesus took in the Old Testament. In any case, wisdom implies the deep sense of knowing that comes only from an intimate connection with God. In this scripture passage, the author of the book of Proverbs advises us to actively pursue wisdom, to keep it constantly with us like a piece of jewelry we wear around our necks. This constant soul connection with God will make us come alive spiritually—and it is the best antidote for sleepless nights. It will allow us to relax, confident that God has everything under control.

PRAY: *Lord of infinite wisdom, I want to follow only You. When sleep escapes me, may I still rest in Your presence. Fill my nighttime hours with the assurance of Your love. Amen.*

Day 12
GIVING

─── READ MALACHI 3 ───

KEY VERSE: *"Bring the whole tithe into the storehouse, that there may be food in my house. Test me in this," says the* LORD *Almighty, "and see if I will not throw open the floodgates of heaven and pour out so much blessing that there will not be room enough to store it."* MALACHI 3:10 NIV

UNDERSTAND:

• What is God's promise here in relation to tithing?

....
....
....
....
....
....

• Do you currently give 10 percent of all that you earn to the Lord? If not, do these verses motivate you to begin giving regularly to the work of the Lord?

....
....
....
....
....
....

APPLY: What is the first check you write after payday? Whether it's the beginning of each month or at the end of each two weeks, you probably have a regular day that you receive payment for your work. One of the greatest habits a Christian can form is that of giving back to the Lord. After all, everything we have comes from Him in the first place!

1 Corinthians 16:2 points out that believers should give regularly, individually, and in proportion with our income. Many believers give 10 percent. Others start with this and increase their giving. The exact amount that you give to the Lord is personal, between you and God. What matters is that you give not out of duty but cheerfully (see 2 Corinthians 9:6–7). The Bible promises that those who give generously are, in turn, blessed. This is a promise you can take to the bank!

PRAY: *Lord, I am so blessed to have the opportunity to give back to Your kingdom work. Allow me always to see giving and tithing as a blessing and never as a burden. In Jesus' name I pray. Amen.*

Day 13
REPAY THE RIGHT WAY

— READ 1 PETER 3:8-22 —

KEY VERSES: *Keep your conscience clear. Then if people speak against you, they will be ashamed when they see what a good life you live because you belong to Christ. Remember, it is better to suffer for doing good, if that is what God wants, than to suffer for doing wrong!* 1 PETER 3:16–17 NLT

UNDERSTAND:

• In what ways do you search for peace and work to maintain it?

....

....

....

....

....

....

• How does suffering for what is right draw you into closer relationship with Jesus? Have you experienced this?

....

....

....

....

....

....

....

....

APPLY: If you've ever been insulted or spoken against unfairly, you know the instant urge to retaliate. It's in our sinful human nature to want to pay someone back for the hurtful thing they said. If you find yourself struggling with those frustrating feelings tonight—wanting to get revenge yet knowing you shouldn't, yet *really* wanting to anyway—let this scripture in 1 Peter 3 help settle your heart and mind. It certainly is a struggle to maintain self-control, especially in a situation where you are clearly in the right and the other party is clearly in the wrong. So maybe you need to put verse 9 (NLT) on repeat in your mind: "Don't repay evil for evil. Don't retaliate with insults when people insult you. Instead, pay them back with a blessing. That is what God has called you to do, and he will grant you his blessing." As difficult as it is sometimes, choose to obey this scripture. It doesn't mean you are a doormat anyone can walk all over; it means you are a faithful child of God, and you choose to believe His promises. He is perfectly just and good, and we humans are not. Let Him handle the one who has wronged you, and let Him bless you as you choose to obey.

PRAY: *Heavenly Father, I am angry tonight, but I give this awful situation over to You. Please take away my anger and replace it with Your peace. Please help me to trust with patience that You will handle the situation in which I have been wronged. Show me how You want me to repay mistreatment with a blessing, and please shower me in return with Your blessing for being obedient. Thank You! Amen.*

Day 14
CHOOSE TO BE FREE

--- **READ JOHN 8:31–47** ---

KEY VERSE: *"So if the Son sets you free, you will be free indeed."* JOHN 8:36 NIV

UNDERSTAND:

- In what ways does the world tell us we can find freedom? How are these flawed?

....

....

....

....

....

....

....

- What is keeping you from experiencing the complete freedom that Jesus offers?

....

....

....

....

....

....

....

....

APPLY: Under Old Testament law, there existed a way to be right with God, but even the most righteous could not follow every rule. The way to freedom was shackled with unachievable requirements.

Without Jesus, sin had a death grip on each of us. Our own selfish desires and destructive habits and thought patterns kept us oppressed, fearful, and clinging to our own filth because, we thought, at least it was our filth, and we were comfortable in it, even if that meant we were a slave to it.

But that false sense of comfort was and still is a lie from Satan, and the life-giving truth of Jesus is the only way to break free of the death grip of sin. "Now a slave has no permanent place in the family, but a son belongs to it forever," Jesus said in John 8:35 (NIV). You are a beloved child of God, dear to Him and an important part of His family.

Today, Jesus has set you free. Grasp on to the truth of your worth, your value, the preciousness of your salvation, and be free!

_____

_____

_____

_____

_____

_____

_____

_____

_____

_____

PRAY: *Jesus, fill me with Your truth today so that I may live in real freedom. I admit that I too often return to my own filth and selfish desires, and sometimes I start to feel sin's death grip try to take hold again. Forgive me. I am here, standing in the love of our Father as Your sister and friend. Amen.*

Day 15

THE HEM OF HIS GARMENT

—————— **READ MATTHEW 9:18–34** ——————

KEY VERSES: *Just then a woman who had been subject to bleeding for twelve years came up behind him and touched the edge of his cloak. She said to herself, "If I only touch his cloak, I will be healed."* MATTHEW 9:20–21 NIV

UNDERSTAND:

• Have you ever been through a particularly hard health battle, one you were afraid would never end? How did it affect your faith? Were you anxious?

....

....

....

....

....

• When you think of the woman pushing her way through the crowd of people to get to Jesus, what images come to mind? Have you ever pushed through a situation to get to the Lord?

....

....

....

....

....

....

....

....

APPLY: Twelve years. She waited twelve long years for her miracle. Years of being ostracized and an outcast. Years of painful, embarrassing bleeding. Twelve years of not being welcome at social events or get-togethers.

And then, in a moment of desperation, she came up with a plan: Push through the crowd. Grab the hem of Jesus' garment. Pray for a miracle. With desperation leading the way, she did just that, and eventually she landed at Jesus' feet, arm outstretched as she grabbed hold of the fabric on His cloak.

Can you relate to this woman? Have you ever been so desperate to see God move in your life that you would press through any circumstance, risk ridicule or jeering, just to get to Him? God honors that sort of desperation. He longs to see His kids healed and whole, their anxieties a thing of the past. So go on! What's holding you back? Press through the crowd and stretch your arm in His direction. God's got big things planned for you!

PRAY: *Father, thank You for the many times You've answered my prayers of desperation. I know You will never cast me aside, Lord. What a good, loving Father You are. Amen.*

Day 16

I'M TIRED OF BEING SICK

READ PROVERBS 3:8–12

KEY VERSE: *Your body will glow with health, your very bones will vibrate with life!* Proverbs 3:8 msg

UNDERSTAND:

• The Bible connects physical health with spiritual commitment. Have you experienced this in your life?

....

....

....

• This passage promises physical blessings, including good health—but it also implies that God's followers have learning opportunities whenever they face trials and other challenges. Has God taught you anything through your illness?

....

....

....

• Have you honored God by giving everything to Him, including your sickness?

....

....

....

....

APPLY: When we're sick, we don't feel very shiny. Instead, we feel dull, lifeless. Our limbs feel heavy and weak. Our emotions are weighed down by our bodies' condition, and discouragement and depression often set in.

But again and again throughout the Bible, God promises to bless those who give everything to Him. Whether it's our money, our children, or our health, however, surrender is the necessary first step. God can't bless our lives until they're truly His.

God may not heal our physical illness as quickly as we wish He would. In some cases, we may never experience physical healing. But God *always* wants to bless us. He wants us to glow with spiritual health. He wants the deepest structure of our souls to vibrate in tune with the Spirit's life.

PRAY: *Dearest Lord, I am so weary of being sick. I don't know how I can be of any use to You when I've been ill so long. I want so much to be well. But for today, I'll take the first step and give You my illness. I put my body in Your hands, trusting You to bless me in whatever ways I need most. Amen.*

Day 17
YOUR FATHER SEES

READ MATTHEW 6

KEY VERSES: *"But when you do a charitable deed, do not let your left hand know what your right hand is doing, that your charitable deed may be in secret; and your Father who sees in secret will Himself reward you openly."* MATTHEW 6:3–4 NKJV

UNDERSTAND:

• What are some charitable deeds that you have done recently or thought about doing?

....

....

....

....

....

....

....

• Why do you think it is important to God that believers do these deeds in secret?

....

....

....

....

....

....

....

APPLY: Have you ever received an anonymous gift? Perhaps it was something small like a candy bar you found on your desk or in your mailbox at the office with no note attached. Maybe it was a larger gift such as a debt that was paid off by an unknown hero. How did it make you feel?

God wants His children to give generously. His favorite type of giver is a cheerful one (see 2 Corinthians 9:7). And He sees when we go about giving in a quiet manner. God doesn't want us to get the glory for our gift. Instead, through our quiet or anonymous giving, He receives the glory!

Give God all the glory today. Perform a random act of kindness and smile as you walk away, knowing that you are not looking for man's praise but a reward that comes only from your Father in heaven.

_____

_____

_____

_____

_____

_____

_____

_____

_____

_____

_____

_____

PRAY: *Lord, help me to be one who performs charitable deeds not for the glory of man but in order to bring You glory. I will seek not the reward of those around me but the reward that comes only from You. Amen.*

Day 18

PRAISE BE TO GOD

READ PSALMS 66–67

KEY VERSES: *"All the earth bows down to you; they sing praise to you, they sing the praises of your name." Come and see what God has done, his awesome deeds for mankind!* PSALM 66:4–5 NIV

UNDERSTAND:

- How has God tested and refined you like silver?

....

....

....

....

....

....

- Whom have you shared with lately about the good things God is doing in your life?

....

....

....

....

....

....

....

APPLY: When you head to bed after an awesome day full of goodness and blessing, praise God and thank Him! Let Psalms 66 and 67 inspire your words of gratitude. The anonymous writer of these psalms was clearly celebrating answered prayer. And don't miss a huge key to that, answered in prayer in Psalm 66:18–20 (NIV): "If I had cherished sin in my heart, the Lord would not have listened; but God has surely listened and has heard my prayer. Praise be to God, who has not rejected my prayer or withheld his love from me!" As you celebrate blessings and answered prayer, think back to what sin you have avoided or recently confessed. Remember that God loves to listen to and reward those who faithfully obey Him, but He will turn His ear away from and withhold answers and blessing from those who cherish sin.

PRAY: *Heavenly Father, thank You for the many precious ways that You have listened to me and blessed me! Please always be so gracious to me, and shine Your face on me. Help me to never cherish sin but rather confess it to You. I will praise You and help proclaim You and Your goodness to all people! Amen.*

Day 19

DAILY PURITY

—— READ 1 JOHN 1:5–10 ——

KEY VERSE: *If we confess our sins, he is faithful and just and will forgive us our sins and purify us from all unrighteousness.* 1 John 1:9 NIV

UNDERSTAND:

• Why is it important that God offers us forgiveness time and time again?

....

....

....

....

• Are you ever tempted to deny that you've sinned at all? What is the result?

....

....

....

....

• How does forgiveness feel on a heart level?

....

....

....

....

APPLY: We Christians talk a lot about forgiveness and rightfully so. God's forgiveness and grace are essential to our faith and salvation. But God's forgiveness is a bigger concept than simply pardoning our sin. The forgiveness available to us through the blood of Jesus Christ purifies us just as if we had never sinned in the first place, leaving us holy, righteous, and blameless in the sight of God.

God's perfect forgiveness offers us purity. It makes us without blemish and whole. Because of that, we can stand confident before the King of kings and Lord of lords. These are the things we stand to gain when we humble ourselves and confess our sins to God. Confession leads to transformation as we grow to be more like Christ. There's no other way to start again, to join Him in the light of His goodness.

Start today in confession. Admit where you've failed. God is listening, and He will purify you again.

....

....

....

....

....

....

....

....

....

....

....

PRAY: *Father, I come before You this morning seeking Your forgiveness. I messed up. . .again. My sin creates a divide between You and me, and I can't bear it. Although I feel unworthy to ask You to do it again, please purify my heart. Cover me in Your grace and make me righteous before You. Amen.*

Day 20

IT'S A CHOICE

──────── **READ LUKE 10:25-37** ────────

KEY VERSES: *"Which of these three do you think was a neighbor to the man who fell into the hands of robbers?" The expert in the law replied, "The one who had mercy on him." Jesus told him, "Go and do likewise."* LUKE 10:36–37 NIV

UNDERSTAND:

• When you read the story of the Good Samaritan, which character do you most relate to—the one in need, the one passing by, or the one stopping to offer help?

....

....

....

....

....

....

• Think of a time when a Good Samaritan intervened in your life. How did the actions of this person change the outcome of your situation?

....

....

....

....

....

....

....

APPLY: Likely you've known this story from childhood—the tale of the Good Samaritan caring for the man in need on the side of the road. Maybe you've skimmed over the story, convinced it has nothing to do with your current reality.

Then you pass by a coworker in her cubicle. She's crying because she's in an abusive marriage and doesn't know what to do.

Or you drive by a man on the street corner, begging for food. He's exhausted. Overheated. Completely defeated by life.

Or maybe you receive a call from a friend riddled with anxiety because her child has wandered away from the Lord.

The truth is life gives us many opportunities to play the role of Good Samaritan. Whether you're working at the church's food pantry, volunteering to coach at the neighborhood Little League, or letting a friend cry on your shoulder, you've got what it takes to minister to others. And God is very, very proud of the work you are doing.

PRAY: *Lord, I don't often feel like I'm doing enough to help others. Show me ways to touch those who are hurting. May I, like the Good Samaritan, really make a difference in someone's life today. Amen.*

Day 21
I FEEL BETRAYED

———— **READ PSALM 41:9–13** ————

KEY VERSE: *Even my close friend, someone I trusted, one who shared my bread, has turned against me.* Psalm 41:9 NIV

UNDERSTAND:

- Verse 12 (NIV) of this passage says, "Because of my integrity you uphold me." How might you demonstrate integrity in your own situation?

....

....

....

....

....

- When hurt and bitterness overcome you, can you make a conscious effort to turn to God?

....

....

....

....

....

....

....

APPLY: There are few things that hurt more in life than being betrayed by someone we love, whether it's a friend, family member, or spouse. Of course, all of us let each other down now and then; we're human and fallible. But betrayal goes deeper. It's a denial of the relationship we thought was so secure. It's like taking a step on what we took for granted was solid ground, only to find ourselves falling into a chasm. It may make us doubt ourselves and our own worth. The emotional anguish may make us sink into depression.

When the psalmist experienced this, he took his pain to God. Instead of begging his betrayer to change back into the person he thought he could count on, he asked God to be the one to restore his sense of balance and security. He affirmed God's love for himself and praised God.

PRAY: *Lord, help me to have integrity even in the midst of this pain. Thank You that Your love will never fail me. You will never betray me. I praise You! Amen.*

Day 22
DO NOT JUDGE

— **READ MATTHEW 7** —

KEY VERSES: *"Why do you look at the speck that is in your brother's eye, but do not notice the log that is in your own eye? Or how can you say to your brother, 'Let me take the speck out of your eye,' and behold, the log is in your own eye? You hypocrite, first take the log out of your own eye, and then you will see clearly to take the speck out of your brother's eye."* MATTHEW 7:3–5 NASB

UNDERSTAND:

• Are you ever tempted to judge someone before you know the person?

....

....

....

....

....

• Why is this dangerous?

....

....

....

....

....

....

....

....

APPLY: Sometimes a child will tattle on another child in order to make themselves look better. This is not just a childish act. Unfortunately, we as adults often put others down in order to build ourselves up. It's easier to focus on another's fault than on our own.

Have you ever made the mistake of passing judgment on someone and later realized that you were wrong? Isn't it easy to look at the divorced woman and wonder what she did to ruin her marriage? Have you ever judged parents at the grocery store or in a restaurant for letting their children run wild?

God is love, and He wants us to love one another. We are not to gossip or slander or pass judgment on one another. That is not God's way. The next time you are tempted to judge someone else, consider this: *What challenges might that person have faced that you have been spared?* It will change the way you see others.

....

....

....

....

....

....

....

....

....

....

....

PRAY: *God, help me to see people as You do. Help me to see their hurts and wounds and not just their actions. So often, I am quick to judge before I know the whole story. Give me grace and compassion and a loving heart that I might honor You in the way I view others. Show me where I can be an agent of Your love today. Amen.*

Day 23
PERFECT HARMONY

── **READ COLOSSIANS 3:1-17** ──

KEY VERSES: *Put on then, as God's chosen ones, holy and beloved, compassionate hearts, kindness, humility, meekness, and patience, bearing with one another and, if one has a complaint against another, forgiving each other; as the Lord has forgiven you, so you also must forgive. And above all these put on love, which binds everything together in perfect harmony. And let the peace of Christ rule in your hearts.* COLOSSIANS 3:12–15 ESV

UNDERSTAND:

• Does the Word of Christ dwell in you richly?

....

....

....

• What is an example of setting your mind on things above instead of things of earth?

....

....

....

....

• What does it mean to do everything in the name of Jesus?

....

....

....

....

APPLY: Our days can be full of conflicts—little ones and big ones, with family members or friends, coworkers or managers, strangers at the store or in traffic. On a really bad day, maybe you've had conflict with all of them. Sometimes we handle conflicts well, and sometimes we don't. As you reflect on your day, you might smile with satisfaction over how you controlled your tongue in one setting but cringe at how you overreacted in another. Or you might still be holding on to lots of anger and frustration. Whatever the case, give it to God, and remember that His grace covers you. Ask Him to reveal your sin and show you where you need to forgive and to seek forgiveness. Let Him help you communicate well. Don't run from all conflict or difficult conversations tomorrow, but as you face them, remember that you are one of God's chosen. You can demonstrate a compassionate heart, kindness, meekness, and patience. You can give grace and forgiveness to others because you know how much grace and forgiveness God gives to you. Let His love bind everything together, and let His peace rule in your heart.

PRAY: *Heavenly Father, please focus my mind on heavenly things, not the things of earth. Help me to rid my life of sin and fill it up with all the good things of You. I am one of Your chosen. I want to represent Your love and peace to others in everything I do. Amen.*

Day 24

ALL THINGS

───── **READ ROMANS 8:18-30** ─────

KEY VERSE: *We know that God makes all things work together for the good of those who love Him and are chosen to be a part of His plan.* ROMANS 8:28 NLV

UNDERSTAND:

• How does Romans 8:28 give you hope?

....

....

....

....

• Do you trust that God has good in store for you? Why or why not?

....

....

....

....

• What are you hopefully waiting for that you do not have now (see Romans 8:24)?

....

....

....

....

....

APPLY: Romans 8:28 ranks high on the list of verses that Christians commit to memory. You may have learned it as a song when you were a child or written it on an index card to remember the hope it carries: no matter what, God makes *all things* work together for the good of His children.

Not some things. Not just the easy things. Not just the good things. All things. The hard things. The heartbreaking things. The frustrating things. The moments when it seems like nothing good can come, God is working it for our good.

The unspoken part of Romans 8:28 is that we're often waiting while He is working. And waiting is hard. But waiting with the promise of this verse brings hope. What are you hoping for today? Ask God to reveal His work to you as you wait. He is faithful to deliver on His promises in His time.

....

....

....

....

....

....

....

....

....

....

....

....

PRAY: *Good, good Father, thank You for the hope of Your promise that You're working all things together for my good. When I don't understand what You are doing, it's hard for me to wait, but still I hope. And I know my hope in You is never in vain. Give me patience to wait on Your timing and Your plan. Amen.*

Day 25

THE BURNING BUSH

——————— **READ EXODUS 3:1-17** ———————

KEY VERSE: *"Do not come any closer," God said. "Take off your sandals, for the place where you are standing is holy ground."* EXODUS 3:5 NIV

UNDERSTAND:

- Think of a time when you truly felt like you were in God's presence. What did it feel like?

....

....

....

....

....

....

- Picture yourself in Moses' sandals. What might he have thought as the Lord spoke to him through the burning bush?

....

....

....

....

....

....

....

APPLY: When you're walking through a stressful season and you're looking for the perfect place to calm your nerves, the very safest (and most peaceful) place is the presence of God. When you cross over the invisible line into the holy of holies, everything else disappears. Worries cease. Cares flee. Troubles vanish. All the things that have kept your stomach in knots have to go in His presence.

What's troubling you today? Can you, like Moses, stand in front of the burning bush and let go of the things that have held you in their grasp? Can you toss them into His fiery presence and see them consumed? God longs for you to live in peace, and your first step toward finding peace is getting into God's presence.

What's holding you back? Take off those sandals and run into His holy presence today.

....

....

....

....

....

....

....

....

....

....

....

....

PRAY: *Lord, today I choose to spend quality time with You. I let go of my fears, my troubles, my anxieties. I place my hand in Yours and cross—feet bare—into Your holy presence. Thank You for what You're doing in my life, Lord. Amen.*

Day 26

I'M JEALOUS

READ 1 CORINTHIANS 3:1–9

KEY VERSE: *You are still worldly. For since there is jealousy and quarreling among you, are you not worldly? Are you not acting like mere humans?* 1 CORINTHIANS 3:3 NIV

UNDERSTAND:

• When Paul said he gave the people of Corinth milk rather than solid food, what do you think he meant?

• What makes you jealous? How might your jealousy be changed if you could see yourself as a coworker in God's service?

• Paul referred to various factions in the Corinthian church. Do you think jealousy plays any role in today's divided political arena?

APPLY: Jealousy is a painful thing to feel. Usually, it springs from our own feelings of inadequacy or insecurity. We are jealous of others' appearance, talents, power, or popularity, feeling that whatever others possess will overshadow and diminish what we have. Or we may be jealous of the attention a friend or spouse shows to another individual. In both cases, we feel we will lose something that's vitally important to us, whether that's our own self-regard or the love of another person.

These are natural, human feelings. But Paul tells us in this passage of scripture that we are called to rise above the human perspective and instead see things from the Spirit's perspective. When we do so, we'll be able to see that in God we have everything we need. We are safe, secure, and valued. In His eyes, we are all equals, all called to work for the same goals, despite our individual ideas and perspectives. Together, in the words of the New International Version, we are "God's field, God's building" (verse 9 NIV).

....

....

....

....

....

....

....

....

....

....

PRAY: *God of love, help me to focus on You so that there's no room in my life for jealousy. Wean me from the spiritual milk I've needed, so that I can begin to eat Your solid food. Amen.*

Day 27

I'M EXHAUSTED

READ ISAIAH 40:28–31

KEY VERSE: *Those who trust in the Lord will find new strength. They will soar high on wings like eagles. They will run and not grow weary. They will walk and not faint.* Isaiah 40:31 NLT

UNDERSTAND:

• Do you ever feel guilty for being tired? These verses make it clear that exhaustion is a normal part of human life.

....

....

....

....

....

....

....

• Have you ever considered that if we had the energy to do everything we want, we might forget to turn to God? Our weakness reminds us that we need Him.

....

....

....

....

....

....

....

APPLY: Life can be exhausting. Whether we're parents coping with the demands of young children, busy professionals with schedules crammed with meetings, or retired folk with to-do lists as long as our arms, we all sometimes feel as though we just don't have the energy to go on.

And yet we have to. Although we can take steps to simplify our lives, letting go of what's unnecessary, some tasks are unavoidable. Children and elderly parents need care. Our jobs have demands that are simply part of the work we've been hired to do. Meals need to be prepared, houses cleaned, lawns tended, and errands run. Life doesn't stop because we're tired!

Humans have experienced weariness since the beginning of time. And over the long centuries, God has promised us His strength. *"Trust Me,"* He says. *"Let Me do the heavy lifting. I am the source of all your energy. Let Me give you what you need to face your life today."*

....

....

....

....

....

....

....

....

....

....

PRAY: *God of strength and love, thank You for caring so much about me. You know how tired I feel. You understand—and You want to help. So today I'll lean on You. I want to soar on Your wings. Amen.*

Day 28
THE WATER'S EDGE

—————— **READ PSALM 23** ——————

KEY VERSES: *He makes me lie down in green pastures, he leads me beside quiet waters, he refreshes my soul. He guides me along the right paths for his name's sake.* PSALM 23:2–3 NIV

UNDERSTAND:

- Have you ever walked through a season where the Lord specifically instructed you to rest, to lie in green pastures beside still waters?

....

....

....

....

....

....

- What's the hardest thing about resting for you?

....

....

....

....

....

....

....

APPLY: *He leads me beside still waters.* How many times have you quoted those words? But have you ever paused to consider their meaning? When God leads us beside still waters, He's drawing us away from the cares and anxieties of life, far from the busyness, the harried schedule, the pressures of the day. At the water's edge, things are calm, still. The only things moving are the wind whispering through the trees and the gentle waters of the brook below.

He leads me beside still waters. . .so that I can rest my mind. Stop my crazy thoughts from tumbling through my brain. Quiet my heart.

He leads me beside still waters. . .so that my soul can be restored, my joy replenished, my hope resurrected.

He leads me beside still waters so that anxieties will cease.

Today, allow the Lord to take you by the hand and lead you beside still waters. You'll find all you need and more.

PRAY: *Father, thank You for drawing me away from the chaos and the pain to a peaceful place with You. I willingly follow You to the still waters, that I might find peace. Amen.*

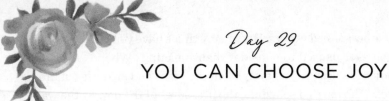

Day 29
YOU CAN CHOOSE JOY

──────── **READ PSALM 118** ────────

KEY VERSE: *This is the day the L*ORD *has made. We will rejoice and be glad in it.*
PSALM 118:24 NLT

UNDERSTAND:

• What are some of the difficulties written about in Psalm 118?

....

....

....

....

• Why do you think the psalmist still chooses to praise God?

....

....

....

....

• How can you rejoice in today even if you are going through a hard season?

....

....

....

....

APPLY: Psalm 118 starts and ends in the same way: "Give thanks to the Lord, for he is good! His faithful love endures forever" (verses 1, 29 NLT). This statement of praise and appreciation for God bookends a chapter filled with great challenges and great victories. Through hostility and attacks from enemies, the psalm writer continues to come back to the fact that God is the rescuer, that He hears and answers prayer, that He puts purpose and joy in each day.

What if you started and ended your day in joyful appreciation for what God is doing? "Thank You, Lord, for being so good to me. Your faithful love endures forever!" This morning, set the stage for rejoicing in today, and tonight, before you lay your head on the pillow, thank Him again. Rejoice and be glad in today, knowing that God is working all things together for your good (see Romans 8:28)!

PRAY: *God, today I am choosing joy. Not because everything is perfect and not because I feel overly happy. I'm choosing to rejoice in today because it is the day You made. And I know it is good because You are good. Thank You for loving me today and every day. Thank You for giving me a reason to rejoice! Amen.*

Day 30

ANSWERS IN
UNASSUMING WAYS

──────── **READ 2 KINGS 5** ────────

KEY VERSES: *Now Naaman was commander of the army of the king of Aram. He was a great man in the sight of his master and highly regarded, because through him the LORD had given victory to Aram. He was a valiant soldier, but he had leprosy. Now bands of raiders from Aram had gone out and had taken captive a young girl from Israel, and she served Naaman's wife. She said to her mistress, "If only my master would see the prophet who is in Samaria! He would cure him of his leprosy." Naaman went to his master and told him what the girl from Israel had said. "By all means, go," the king of Aram replied.* 2 KINGS 5:1–5 NIV

UNDERSTAND:

• Has God ever spoken to or led you in a totally unexpected, unassuming way?

....

....

....

....

• Who are the children in your life? How do they speak into your life and encourage you?

....

....

....

....

....

....

APPLY: Sometimes when we're praying for great needs, we hope for bold and impressive provision and guidance from God. Yet He often speaks to us and leads us in the most unassuming ways. This was the case for Naaman, who was a valiant army commander, highly respected by his master, the king of Aram. Yet he was obviously a humble man too and was willing to listen to a mere servant girl from Israel who had been taken captive and given to Naaman's wife. The young girl's advice—to go to Elisha, the prophet of the God of Israel, for healing from leprosy—was solid. Naaman was soon healed, and he gave God all the glory. We too should be humble like Naaman when we seek answers from God. Never be unwilling to listen to even the meekest, most modest among us if they are pointing us to more faith and dependence on God and His perfect Word.

....

....

....

....

....

....

....

....

....

....

....

PRAY: *Heavenly Father, I want to listen for You and sense Your direction and provision through any kind of circumstance or any person, whether impressive or modest. Please always keep me humble and teachable. Amen.*

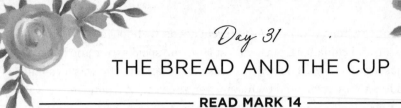

Day 31

THE BREAD AND THE CUP

——— **READ MARK 14** ———

KEY VERSE: *While they were eating, He took some bread, and after a blessing He broke it, and gave it to them, and said, "Take it; this is My body."* MARK 14:22 NASB

UNDERSTAND:

• What does the bread symbolize when we take communion, or the Lord's Supper? The wine?

....

....

....

....

....

....

• How do the disciples disappoint Jesus in the garden? Do you relate more to Jesus or to the disciples in the scenario?

....

....

....

....

....

....

....

....

APPLY: There is something special about taking communion, or the Lord's Supper. It is an ordinance of the Church that comes to us directly from Jesus' command to do this in remembrance of Him. When you take the bread and the cup, do you stop to really ponder their significance?

The bread represents Jesus' body, broken for us on the cross. The cup, or the wine, symbolizes His blood, shed for the forgiveness of sins. The Old Testament law required the spilling of blood. Christ fulfilled that. He was the unblemished Lamb of God, without sin, and it is only through Him that we can stand before a holy God, blameless and righteous.

He died once, for all. It was an amazing sacrifice, and the ordinance of communion should be taken seriously and scripturally.

PRAY: *Help me, Lord, to honor Your memory by taking communion with reverence and respect. Thank You for Your death on the cross that provided a way for me to come before a holy God. Thank You that through You, I am found righteous and pure. Amen.*

Day 32
FREE IN CHRIST

— **READ JOHN 8** —

KEY VERSES: *Jesus replied, "Very truly I tell you, everyone who sins is a slave to sin. Now a slave has no permanent place in the family, but a son belongs to it forever. So if the Son sets you free, you will be free indeed."* JOHN 8:34–36 NIV

UNDERSTAND:

- How is a sinner freed from sin?

....

....

....

....

....

....

....

....

- What does it look like for you as a believer to be "free indeed" in today's society?

....

....

....

....

....

....

....

....

APPLY: Jesus' death on the cross paid the wages of our sin. He set us free when we placed our trust in Him to do so. There is no other way by which anyone can be saved except through Him.

We are set free from the sins of our past, and we are set free from sin that easily entangles us. Living in a society that is filled with temptation to sin is not easy, but as a believer, you have the power to overcome temptation through Christ.

Thank your heavenly Father that you are no longer a slave to sin. Because of Jesus' death for you, you are completely free. You will never again be shackled by a lifestyle of sin, but instead, you will turn in repentance when you begin to take your eyes off Him and He will lead you back to His side. You are saved from sin, and yes, you are free indeed.

PRAY: *Thank You, Jesus, for saving me from my sin. Thank You that because of my faith in You as Savior, I can be free indeed! Amen.*

A HARVEST OF RIGHTEOUSNESS AND PEACE

---------- **READ HEBREWS 12** ----------

KEY VERSE: *No discipline seems pleasant at the time, but painful. Later on, however, it produces a harvest of righteousness and peace for those who have been trained by it.* HEBREWS 12:11 NIV

UNDERSTAND:

• How has discipline produced a good harvest in your life?

....

....

....

....

....

• What does it mean that "God is a consuming fire" (Hebrews 12:29 NIV)?

....

....

....

....

....

....

....

APPLY: The word *discipline* doesn't always bring peaceful thoughts to mind. We might think of angry arguments and punishments of the growing-up years and other kinds of consequences during rebellious times in our lives. But Hebrews 12 shows us how we *can* view discipline with peace—by realizing the hardship we endure is the discipline from God that is good for us in a loving, fatherly way. If we let Him, He strengthens us and proves our faith this way—just like good parents shouldn't always rescue their children from every hard thing. Rather, they let them experience difficulty and consequences so that they can develop strength and confidence in their own capabilities, plus learn from their mistakes. Once we have grown up, we appreciate the discipline good parents gave us as we develop into mature adults who contribute well to the world around us. Likewise, once we have reached the other side of a particular hardship, we can see how God used it in our lives to develop us, plus produce "a harvest of righteousness and peace" that contributes to His kingdom.

PRAY: *Heavenly Father, please help me to focus on hardship in a positive way as good discipline from You. Teach me, strengthen me, and develop me in the midst of it, and give me peace that You are working it all for good. Amen.*

Day 34

GOD HEARS YOU

──────── **READ 1 JOHN 5:13–20** ────────

KEY VERSES: *This is the confidence we have in approaching God: that if we ask anything according to his will, he hears us. And if we know that he hears us—whatever we ask—we know that we have what we asked of him.* 1 John 5:14–15 NIV

UNDERSTAND:

• Are you confident that God hears your prayers? Why or why not?

....

....

....

....

....

....

• How can you know your prayers are in line with God's will?

....

....

....

....

....

....

....

APPLY: From an early age, children are taught that praying is thanking God and asking Him for things that they need or want to happen. If we're not careful, we can incorrectly think of God as a heavenly vending machine that will dole out the goods if we say the right words and push the right buttons.

But prayer is *not* about pushing our agenda and hoping God will be on board with it. Prayer is approaching our loving Father with a heart that sincerely wants to be in line with His. When we pray this way, the things we ask of Him will fit into His good and perfect will for our lives and His creation as a whole. And *that's* when He hears us and we will receive what we have asked for.

What is God's will? Ask Him to show you. Seek Him in His Word. Talk to friends who are strong in their faith, and see what God is doing in their lives. He's listening. He hears you.

....

....

....

....

....

....

....

....

....

....

....

....

PRAY: *Father, I am confident in my prayers to You. Give me Your wisdom to approach You with requests that You will hear and grant. I long to be in the center of Your good and perfect plan, God. Amen.*

Day 35

THE SHELTER OF
THE MOST HIGH

─────────── **READ PSALM 91** ───────────

KEY VERSE: *Whoever dwells in the shelter of the Most High will rest in the shadow of the Almighty.* PSALM 91:1 NIV

UNDERSTAND:

• Have you walked through a season where you needed God's protection and shelter? How did He take care of you?

....

....

....

....

....

....

....

• Have you ever had to shelter others under your wings?

....

....

....

....

....

....

....

APPLY: If you've ever had to run for cover during a rainstorm, you know that anything will do—an awning, a car, a shopping center, even a tent. Whatever serves to hold back the rain works just fine for you.

Shelters don't just keep out the rain; they provide a psychological covering as well. When you've got something over your head, you feel safer. That's how God wants you to feel when you run to Him with your troubles. When you hide under the shadow of His wings (as a baby chick would hide under its mother's wings), He's got you covered. He's like a papa bear, daring anyone to mess with His cub.

Here's an interesting fact: God wants to keep you covered at all times. But let's face it. . .we have a way of tucking ourselves under other, counterfeit shelters. Maybe it's time to do an assessment, to make sure you've got the right covering. Whatever you're facing, God wants to protect you as you go through it.

PRAY: *Thank You for the reminder that You're my protector, Lord! I'll do my best not to run to the counterfeit shelters when I've got the real deal. Amen.*

MY KIDS ARE
DRIVING ME CRAZY

─────── **READ EPHESIANS 4:1–6** ───────

KEY VERSES: *Walk in a manner worthy of the calling with which you have been called, with all humility and gentleness, with patience, showing tolerance for one another in love.* EPHESIANS 4:1–2 NASB

UNDERSTAND:

• Have you ever considered that it takes humility to be a parent? How might a lack of humility be contributing to your frustration with your children?

....

....

....

• Do you ever think of your children as fellow members of Christ's body, sharing with you in the Spirit's life? How might your attitudes change if you were to keep this idea at the forefront of your consciousness?

....

....

....

• Why do you think Paul reminded his readers that he was in prison as he wrote these words? Does your life as a parent ever feel like a prison you wish you could escape?

....

....

....

....

APPLY: Being a parent is hard work. In fact, it's one of the most (if not *the* most) challenging, frustrating, crazy-making jobs we'll ever face. Children's demands on our time and attention are relentless. As parents, we'd like to feel we're in control. We may think that's what it means to be a good parent, exercising discipline over our children, and so we're frustrated and upset when our children seem uncontrollable. Of course, it *is* our job to teach our children, using loving discipline to shape them into responsible adults—but we can't reason with them the way we would with another adult. We can't tell our newborn to stop waking us up in the middle of the night. . .or our toddler to stop asking a million questions a day. . . or our teenager to stop being so emotional.

All we can do is follow Paul's advice: be humble, patient, tolerant, diligent— and do our best to be as good a parent to our children as God is to us.

PRAY: *Divine Parent, when my children drive me crazy, remind me that they share with me in Your love and life. Use me to demonstrate to them Your loving care. Amen.*

HAVE YOU BEEN WITH JESUS?

—— **READ ACTS 4** ——

KEY VERSE: *Now when they saw the boldness of Peter and John, and perceived that they were uneducated and untrained men, they marveled. And they realized that they had been with Jesus.* ACTS 4:13 NKJV

UNDERSTAND:

• Do others know that you have been with Jesus?

....

....

....

....

....

• How do they know, or why are they unsure?

....

....

....

....

....

....

....

....

APPLY: Peter and John had been with Jesus. It was evident. They were warned not to speak of Him, but they said this was not possible. They knew Jesus, and they could not be quieted.

These were blue-collar fishermen called as disciples of Christ. And yet they boldly preached and healed in the name of Christ.

When people examine your life, do they know you are a Christian? Do you stand out as a Christ follower? Do you find ways to bring Jesus into everyday conversations? Or are you more like the teenager who wants her dad to drop her off a block from school so that no one will know she is associated with him?

Consider these things. Dwell upon them. Pray about them. Make changes as needed. You want to be a woman who is known for having "been with Jesus."

PRAY: *Lord Jesus, I will live boldly for You. I want to be known as one who walks with You. Examine my heart, Jesus. Point out to me areas where change needs to occur. I am not ashamed of You. I want to be bold like Peter and John. I want to be known as a Christian even if it is not popular in some circles. Amen.*

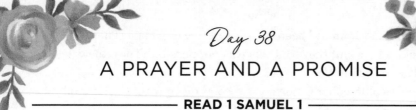

A PRAYER AND A PROMISE

—————————— **READ 1 SAMUEL 1** ——————————

KEY VERSES: *Hannah was in deep anguish, crying bitterly as she prayed to the Lord. And she made this vow: "O Lord of Heaven's Armies, if you will look upon my sorrow and answer my prayer and give me a son, then I will give him back to you. He will be yours for his entire lifetime, and as a sign that he has been dedicated to the Lord, his hair will never be cut."* 1 SAMUEL 1:10–11 NLT

UNDERSTAND:

• What was Eli's first response as he observed Hannah praying? Have you ever experienced something like that? How did that make you feel?

....

....

....

....

....

• How do you think Hannah must have felt as she followed through on her promise and took Samuel to the temple to live at such a young age? What does that say about her and her faith?

....

....

....

....

....

....

APPLY: Hannah knew what it felt like to think maybe God had forgotten or didn't care about her. Can you relate? Maybe you too are desperately praying for children right now, and God has not answered that desire. Or maybe you've been asking God to answer other requests to no avail. Whatever the case, don't give up. Let Hannah's story inspire you and give you peace tonight. She continued to pray for a son, and she showed her love and devotion to God by promising that if He agreed, she would let that son live at the temple to serve God his whole life. When God finally answered and blessed her with Samuel, Hannah followed through on her promise and was rewarded even more for her faithfulness. And Samuel grew to be a great prophet for God. He was a blessing to all the people of Israel because of Hannah's faithful prayer and promise.

PRAY: *Heavenly Father, please hear my requests and desires. Please help them to match Your perfect will for me. I promise to use my blessings to give back to You! Please help me to always keep that promise. Amen.*

Day 39

YOU ARE RESILIENT

—————— **READ ZEPHANIAH 3:14–20** ——————

KEY VERSES: *"Do not fear, Zion; do not let your hands hang limp. The Lord your God is with you, the Mighty Warrior who saves. He will take great delight in you; in his love he will no longer rebuke you, but will rejoice over you with singing."* Zephaniah 3:16–17 NIV

UNDERSTAND:

• What challenge are you facing today that has your hands hanging limp?

....

....

....

....

• What makes you feel strong?

....

....

....

....

• How does it change your perspective when you realize that God, the Mighty Warrior who saves, is with you?

....

....

....

....

....

APPLY: Each single day brings its own challenges, but life often hurls difficult seasons at us. For days, weeks, months, or years, challenging times can leave us weary, afraid, and may even threaten to defeat us.

What are you facing today?

Take courage, for you are the daughter of the mighty Lord. Be confident in the fact that you are a resilient woman of God—not because of your own strength but because God, the King and Mighty Warrior who saves, is with you. He will not make fun of you for struggling in times of distress—He wants to love you, protect you, and fight with you through it. He takes delight in you and rejoices over you with singing! He is your rescuer and the reason you can overcome any challenge you face.

Praise Him for past victories and stand strong in Him today.

....

....

....

....

....

....

....

....

....

....

....

PRAY: *Defender God, thank You for saving me. I praise You for the strength You instill in me. Today I will lift my head and raise my hands in Your victory even in the midst of my struggles. I delight in You, Father. Your ways are good and perfect, so please lead me today. Amen.*

Day 40

HE ANSWERED ME

—————— **READ GENESIS 21:1–21** ——————

KEY VERSES: *Now the Lord was gracious to Sarah as he had said, and the Lord did for Sarah what he had promised. Sarah became pregnant and bore a son to Abraham in his old age, at the very time God had promised him.* Genesis 21:1–2 NIV

UNDERSTAND:

• During anxious seasons, it's easy to give up. Have you ever had to persevere like Abraham and Sarah? What was the outcome of your perseverance?

....

....

....

....

....

....

• God moved in a miraculous way in Sarah's life. Have you ever experienced a miracle in your own life?

....

....

....

....

....

....

....

APPLY: Abraham and Sarah were elderly when their son, Isaac, was born. No wonder Sarah laughed when she learned she was having a child. Not many women in their golden years give birth to babies!

Isaac was the long-awaited promise, the child they'd always longed for. His arrival was the culmination of many years of hoping, praying, and believing despite the odds.

Maybe you've been waiting a long time for something—a spouse, a child, a new job, a home. You've pleaded with God, and it all seems to be in vain. You're nearly ready to give up. Circumstances have almost convinced you it's never going to happen.

Today, let your faith be invigorated again. Read through Abraham and Sarah's story, and allow your heart to dream once more. God is a dream giver and a dream fulfiller. Allow Him to see this miracle all the way through.

....

....

....

....

....

....

....

....

....

....

....

PRAY: *Father, thank You for the reminder that the dreams You've laid on my heart are God breathed and will be God fulfilled. I remove my hands and choose to trust You today, Lord. Amen.*

Day 41

MY SPOUSE IS DRIVING ME CRAZY

——————— **READ 1 CORINTHIANS 13:4–7** ———————

KEY VERSE: *Love is patient, love is kind.* 1 Corinthians 13:4 nasb

UNDERSTAND:

- It's easy to blame our spouse for our negative reactions. If you look at the last time you were upset with your spouse, though, can you see the role that your own selfishness played? How might you have been seeking your own way?

....

....

....

....

....

- What do you think verse 5 (nasb) means when it says that love does not "take into account a wrong suffered"? What "wrongs" committed by your spouse have you added up in an "account"?

....

....

....

....

....

....

APPLY: The people we love the most also have the ability to upset us the most. They get on our nerves. Their little habits bug us. They hurt our feelings. Day after day, week after week, we tend to add up their offenses, keeping score, using them to justify our own hurtful actions. If our spouse did such and such, then surely we have the right to do *this* or *that*!

Luckily for us, that's not the way God treats us. He shows us what real love looks like—patient, kind, unselfish, enduring. He doesn't keep track of everything we've done wrong and hold each thing against us. Instead, He rejoices in all we do that's true and beautiful.

How might our marriages change if we were to make a conscious effort to love our spouses the way God loves us?

....

....

....

....

....

....

....

....

....

....

....

....

PRAY: *Today, Lord of love, bring to my attention all the things my spouse does that are good, truthful, and loving. Help me to be more patient with the actions that annoy or hurt me. Give me the strength to be kind. Amen.*

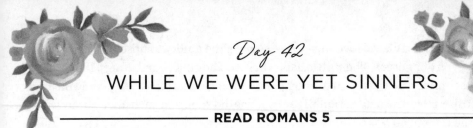

Day 42
WHILE WE WERE YET SINNERS

─────── **READ ROMANS 5** ───────

KEY VERSE: *But God showed his great love for us by sending Christ to die for us while we were still sinners.* ROMANS 5:8 NLT

UNDERSTAND:

• What state were you in when Christ died for you?

....

....

....

....

....

....

....

• Do you ever feel like you need to clean up your act before you can talk to God? Is this accurate?

....

....

....

....

....

....

....

....

APPLY: Christ died for us while we were yet sinners. In other words, He did not wait for us to straighten up and clean up and fess up and do better. We couldn't. We were incapable of living any other way until we met Him. We could not be "better enough" to come before a holy God. We were full of sin and we were in a heap of trouble. We needed salvation. And Jesus rescued us.

Remember this the next time you feel too guilty to talk to Jesus, too dirty to come into His presence, or too ashamed to pray. Jesus Christ went to the cross and took on all your sin. He bore the weight of the sin of the entire world. He carried His cross to Calvary. He willingly died while we were yet sinners. There was no other way. It was God's plan from the beginning to redeem His people from sin.

PRAY: *Thank You, Jesus. Thank You from the bottom of my heart for dying for me while I was still neck deep in sin. You did not wait for me to clean up my act. You cleaned it up. You who had never sinned took on my sin. You paid a debt You did not owe. I am eternally grateful. Amen.*

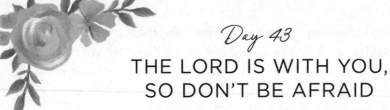

Day 43

THE LORD IS WITH YOU,
SO DON'T BE AFRAID

───── **READ NUMBERS 13:1–14:12** ─────

KEY VERSES: *"If the LORD is pleased with us, he will bring us safely into that land and give it to us. It is a rich land flowing with milk and honey. Do not rebel against the LORD, and don't be afraid of the people of the land. They are only helpless prey to us! They have no protection, but the LORD is with us! Don't be afraid of them!"* NUMBERS 14:8–9 NLT

UNDERSTAND:

• Do you ever struggle with complaining to God about your circumstances or what He has asked you to do? How does the account of the twelve spies in Canaan help you correct that?

....

....

....

....

• Have you experienced a time when you listened to fear rather than let God make you confident and brave? Or do you celebrate a time when you were tempted to give in to fear but were motivated by God's promises instead? What did you learn?

....

....

....

....

....

APPLY: Obeying God's direction, Moses sent out men to explore the land of Canaan because God had said to Moses that He was one day soon going to give it to His people, the Israelites. So Joshua, Caleb, and ten other men went to spy on the land of Canaan for forty days. When they returned, they reported that the land was wonderful, flowing with milk and honey and all kinds of bounty. However, the people of Canaan were very powerful, and the cities were well protected. Joshua and Caleb weren't intimidated though. They were confident that with God's help they could still take over Canaan. But the ten other spies adamantly opposed because of their fear. The ten spread fear so well among the Israelites that they rebelled and complained against Moses and Aaron. God grew angry with the Israelites because they listened to fear rather than listening to the courage and faith of Joshua and Caleb. So He punished the majority of the people but blessed Joshua and Caleb.

PRAY: *Heavenly Father, like Joshua and Caleb, I know You are with me, and I don't need to be afraid of what might seem too hard for me to handle. I have Your power and strength with me at all times. I want to choose faith over fear, no matter what I am facing. Please embolden and bless me according to Your will. Amen.*

Day 44
YOU CAN BE CONTENT

— **READ PHILIPPIANS 4:10-20** —

KEY VERSES: *I know how to live on almost nothing or with everything. I have learned the secret of living in every situation, whether it is with a full stomach or empty, with plenty or little. For I can do everything through Christ, who gives me strength.* PHILIPPIANS 4:12–13 NLT

UNDERSTAND:

• In what areas of your life are you most content? Why?

....

....

....

....

....

....

• In what areas of your life are you most discontented? Why?

....

....

....

....

....

....

....

APPLY: Contentment is one of those virtues that the world almost entirely dismisses. Why should anyone be content when there's always more to be had? More wealth, more power, more status, better toys, bigger houses, newer technology, latest trends. But all that striving leaves us exhausted, frustrated, and discontent in heart and mind.

So, what's the best way to practice contentment? Start with an attitude of thankfulness. When you take stock in the ways God provides for you, when you praise Him for all He's done, your heart will learn the secret to living satisfied and grateful in any situation. God will give you the strength and the untold peace that can only be found in Him.

Contentment doesn't come naturally to many of us, so start this morning by being intentional in thanking God. When you focus on His goodness, the world's shouted messages of "More, more, more!" will become nothing but background noise.

PRAY: *God, I admit that I struggle with being content. My selfishness always seems to compare my situation with someone who has a little bit more. Forgive me for being ungrateful for all You provide. Teach me to be content in any situation, and if ends aren't meeting, give me the faith to trust that You will provide. Because I know You will. Amen.*

Day 45
A SOUND MIND

READ LUKE 4:1-13

KEY VERSE: *When the devil had ended every temptation, he departed from him until an opportune time.* LUKE 4:13 ESV

UNDERSTAND:

- Think of a time when the enemy reared his head against you. Did you fall for his lies?

....

....

....

....

....

....

- When you're tempted to give in to the enemy's tactics, what can you do to turn things around?

....

....

....

....

....

....

....

APPLY: If you read the opening lines of this story, you'll learn a lot: Jesus was full of the Holy Spirit and led by the Holy Spirit into the wilderness. When you submit yourself to the Spirit of God, when you say, "I'll let You be the one to lead and guide me," then you're always in a safe place.

Like Jesus, we will go through seasons of temptation. The enemy will do everything in his power to veer us off in the wrong direction. We might even wonder why or how we got to a place of confusion.

But when we're full of the Spirit of God, when we're completely and wholly submitted to the process of learning all we can learn, we have to trust that God is still in control, even when we're in the middle of the wilderness.

Where are you today? Feeling a little lost? Wondering how you got there? Instead of questioning the Lord or letting anxieties get the best of you, ask the Spirit of God to fill you to the top. He will guide you exactly where you need to go.

PRAY: *I know that the safest place to be, Lord, is where Your Spirit guides me. Fill me today, I pray, and lead me where You will. I will gladly follow. Amen.*

Day 46

MY FEELINGS ARE HURT

──────── **READ EPHESIANS 6:10–18** ────────

KEY VERSES: *Be strong in the Lord and in his mighty power. Put on the full armor of God.* EPHESIANS 6:10–11 NIV

UNDERSTAND:

- When your feelings are hurt, do you ever consider that there may be something going on behind the scenes in the spiritual realm? How might the devil use your hurt feelings to further the forces of evil in the world?

....

....

....

....

....

....

- Do you think of the person who hurt you as an enemy? Can you see that your struggle is not with that individual but rather with a larger, spiritual reality?

....

....

....

....

....

....

....

APPLY: The people we care about have the power to hurt us—and whether they intend to or not, sooner or later, inevitably, they injure our feelings (as we do theirs!). We can allow the hurt to drive us apart, turning loved ones into enemies. That's not what God wants, though, and if we allow it to happen, then we have allowed the devil to win. God's purpose for our lives is peace and harmony with others; He wants us to learn to walk more and more steadily in His love.

And so when our feelings are hurt, we need to protect our hearts with God's shining armor of love rather than the devil's rusty shield of bitterness and anger. It's not easy. That's why this scripture reminds us to stay alert and pray for one another (verse 18). God's Word and Spirit will be the protection we need.

PRAY: *Lord, You know the hurt I'm feeling. But I ask You to make me strong in Your power. Put Your belt of truth around my waist, shield my heart with Your breastplate of righteousness, remind me to wear Your shoes of peace, and help me to cling tight to Your shield of faith. Amen.*

Day 47

YOU ARE LOVED

──── READ ROMANS 8:1-39 ────

KEY VERSES: *But in all these things we overwhelmingly conquer through Him who loved us. For I am convinced that neither death, nor life, nor angels, nor principalities, nor things present, nor things to come, nor powers, nor height, nor depth, nor any other created thing, will be able to separate us from the love of God, which is in Christ Jesus our Lord.* ROMANS 8:37–39 NASB

UNDERSTAND:

• What can separate the Christian from God's love?

....

....

....

....

....

....

• What does it mean that you are more than a conqueror in all things through Christ?

....

....

....

....

....

....

APPLY: Unconditionally—that is how God loves His children. These verses in Romans provide the Christian with a great deal of peace. Even death is not able to separate you from God's love. Why is this? You will not truly experience death. You have eternal life. To be absent in your current body is to be in the presence of the Lord. So even the moment that you take your final breath on this earth you will not be separated from God!

As you go about your day, remember that God's love surrounds you. He has declared you to be more than a conqueror through Jesus. In other words, in all things—trials, tests, hardships, and even your deepest loss or disappointment—you have the power to overcome.

You are an overcomer, and you are deeply loved. Claim the scripture and walk with your head held high as a daughter of the King.

PRAY: *Heavenly Father, Your Word is so rich and full of assurances. Help me to claim them! Thank You for loving me unconditionally and making me more than a conqueror over all things. In Jesus' powerful name I pray. Amen.*

Day 48
SIMPLIFY

━━━━━━━━━ **READ MATTHEW 25:31–46** ━━━━━━━━━

KEY VERSE: *"The King will reply, 'Truly I tell you, whatever you did for one of the least of these brothers and sisters of mine, you did for me.'"* Matthew 25:40 NIV

UNDERSTAND:

- What areas of life or relationships cause you the most concern about whether you are doing a good job or doing enough?

....

....

....

....

....

....

- How has your relationship with Jesus grown as you care for others in need?

....

....

....

....

....

....

....

....

APPLY: As women, we so often worry about whether or not we are doing enough, doing the right things, and doing them well—in our marriages, our parenting, our friendships, our homes, our jobs, our ministry, and so on. Sometimes we need to simplify and stop trying so hard. We need to ask God to help us focus on the good things He planned for us to do when He created us. We should ask Him to show us the relationships He wants us to invest in the most, starting with Him. And this scripture in Matthew should remind us that the very best job anyone can have is to serve our King by serving others. We are always doing the right thing if we are doing even the simplest act of kindness for someone in need. There is such peace and contentment when we realize how rewarding it is to care for others as if caring for Jesus Himself—because truly we are.

....

....

....

....

....

....

....

....

....

....

....

....

PRAY: *Loving Savior, please remind me how my service and care for others in need is truly service and care for You. With every good thing I do to help someone else, I grow closer to You. Thank You for such wonderful purpose in my life. Please help me to simplify my life and focus on the good things You have planned for me to do. Amen.*

Day 49

A FRESH START

---------------- **READ LAMENTATIONS 3:22-33** ----------------

KEY VERSES: *Because of the L*ORD*'s great love we are not consumed, for his compassions never fail. They are new every morning; great is your faithfulness.*
LAMENTATIONS 3:22–23 NIV

UNDERSTAND:

• What comfort do you take knowing that God's compassion doesn't run out?

....

....

....

....

• Why do you think morning is a good time to seek God's forgiveness?

....

....

....

....

• Who in your life needs to receive daily mercy from you (whether they ask for it or not)?

....

....

....

....

....

APPLY: Yesterday is done, and you messed it up again. You snapped at your kids and husband. You told that little fib at work. Through a lens of green, you saw the neighbors' new SUV and slammed the door of your junky vehicle a little harder than necessary. You told yourself you'll never be good enough, so why even try?

Yesterday felt like a train wreck, but this morning is a new day, and your Father God is here. He's saying, "Let's start again."

The truth is that God's forgiveness is available to us any hour of the day. He is faithful to show mercy whenever we ask Him for help. But time spent with our Father in the morning will result in a clear focus, renewed hope, and a greater understanding of our worth in Christ. It sets the day into motion in the best way possible.

....

....

....

....

....

....

....

....

....

....

PRAY: *Merciful Father, this morning I seek Your refreshing forgiveness. I had every intention of perfection yesterday, but I messed up again. I'm ashamed of my sin, but I'm choosing to look up to You and admit I need Your kind compassion every day. I dedicate this new day to You, God. And I will live it as Your imperfect child who is perfectly loved by You. Amen.*

Day 50
HOPE IN THE PIT

—— **READ GENESIS 37** ——

KEY VERSES: *They said to one another, "Here comes this dreamer. Come now, let us kill him and throw him into one of the pits. Then we will say that a fierce animal has devoured him, and we will see what will become of his dreams."* GENESIS 37:19–20 ESV

UNDERSTAND:

• Joseph was thrown into the pit by his own brothers. Have you ever been betrayed by someone you trusted? How did you overcome?

....

....

....

....

....

....

• Even in the pit, Joseph never gave up. Maybe you've walked a mile in Joseph's shoes. How do you keep your head up even when circumstances seem to be against you?

....

....

....

....

....

....

APPLY: Some would argue that young Joseph had it coming. All that bragging about being the favored child didn't exactly put him in good standing with his brothers, after all. Those dreams of his were a source of contention among the siblings.

But imagine finding yourself at the bottom of a pit, bruised, dirty, and hurting, while those you thought you could trust jeered at you from above. The feelings of betrayal must have been overwhelming. Perhaps Joseph even wondered if those dreams of his had been from God or were the result of something bad he'd eaten.

Maybe you've been there. You've faced betrayal from someone you trusted—a spouse, a parent, a child, a sibling, a friend. You're staring up, up, up from the bottom of a pit, your heart broken into a thousand pieces as your dreams seemingly come to an end.

Just remember, Joseph's story didn't end in the pit. God redeemed the situation and turned everything around. He'll do the very same for you. So don't give up. The Lord has big plans for you, and they're just around the corner.

PRAY: *Father, I feel so betrayed. Those who claimed to care about me turned their backs on me when I least suspected. Like Joseph, I feel as if I'm in a pit. Rescue me, I pray. Give me hope, comfort, and deliverance. Amen.*

Day 51

I WISH SOMEONE
UNDERSTOOD ME

—— **READ PSALM 139:1–2** ——

KEY VERSE: *I'm an open book to you; even from a distance, you know what I'm thinking.* PSALM 139:2 MSG

UNDERSTAND:

• Why do you think others are unable to understand you? Is the fault theirs or yours—or no one's? Can you forgive them for their lack of understanding?

....

....

....

....

....

• Are you comfortable knowing that God knows your most private thoughts even when He seems distant from you? Does His understanding comfort you—or scare you? Why?

....

....

....

....

....

....

....

APPLY: All of us have moments when we feel as though no one in the entire world understands us. It's a lonely feeling! We all need the sense that at least one other person understands our thoughts and feelings. That understanding would make us feel we're not strange or bad or unacceptable in some way. Without it, we feel as though there might be something wrong with us. We feel sad, rejected, alone.

In reality, if we had the courage to share our hearts with others, we'd probably find that they can understand more than we think they might. But until we have the confidence we need to reveal our true selves, we can allow God's understanding to heal our wounded hearts. Even if we think He is far away, even when we reject Him, He understands what we're going through. He is the Friend who will never fail us. He's on our side.

PRAY: *My God, I thank You that You understand me even when no one else seems to. I open my heart to You. I don't want to hold back any part of myself from You. Teach me to rely more and more on Your friendship. Amen.*

Day 52

A CREATIVE CREATOR

READ GENESIS 1

KEY VERSE: *God saw all that he had made, and it was very good. And there was evening, and there was morning—the sixth day.* GENESIS 1:31 NIV

UNDERSTAND:

- Consider the intricate details seen in nature. The petals of a flower that are arranged in a set pattern. The perfect curve of a nautilus shell. The instincts of a lion. Think of three examples of your own.

....

....

....

....

....

....

- If the world came about after a "big bang," as some scientists say, how could the detail seen in nature be explained?

....

....

....

....

....

....

APPLY: The book of Genesis begins with the words "In the beginning God created..." If God was already creating *in the beginning*, then that means He was not Himself created, but rather, He is the great Creator of all things.

God separated day from night. He made the stars, moon, and sun. He created the many varieties of trees and flowers, each one intricate in its design! God made all of the animals—the unique hippo and giraffe, the enormous elephant and whale, the majestic lion.... God is a creative Creator!

God's greatest creations were made in His image. Men, women, and children are special to God. We bear some of His traits. We are His masterpieces.

Remember to notice the details of God's glorious creation as you go about your day. Take care of the earth. It was designed by your Father. Respect all other people. They, like you, bear the image of God.

PRAY: *Heavenly Father, You have made all things. You are the Creator who sustains life. You knit me together in my mother's womb. May I treat with great respect all of Your creation, even that which others may devalue. In Jesus' name I pray. Amen.*

Day 53

FAITHFUL FRIENDSHIP

──── READ RUTH 1 ────

KEY VERSES: *Ruth replied, "Don't ask me to leave you and turn back. Wherever you go, I will go; wherever you live, I will live. Your people will be my people, and your God will be my God. Wherever you die, I will die, and there I will be buried. May the LORD punish me severely if I allow anything but death to separate us!"* RUTH 1:16–17 NLT

UNDERSTAND:

• Orpah was conflicted at first, but then she decided to leave Naomi. What motivated Ruth's fierce loyalty to Naomi instead of choosing to go with Orpah?

....

....

....

....

• Have you ever felt as low as Naomi as described in Ruth 1:20–21? How did God lift you up?

....

....

....

....

....

....

APPLY: Every woman needs such a loyal woman in her life as Ruth was to Naomi. If you have that kind of faithful friend or relative, praise God for her and make sure she knows how grateful you are for her. Nurture that relationship. If you have more than one woman in your life like that, you are extremely blessed! And if you need a faithful friend, pray for God to help you make the connection. He knows and cares that you need good friendship, and He will help you find it. His Word says, "Two people are better off than one, for they can help each other succeed. If one person falls, the other can reach out and help. But someone who falls alone is in real trouble. Likewise, two people lying close together can keep each other warm. But how can one be warm alone? A person standing alone can be attacked and defeated, but two can stand back-to-back and conquer. Three are even better, for a triple-braided cord is not easily broken" (Ecclesiastes 4:9–12 NLT).

PRAY: *Heavenly Father, thank You for the gift of loyal friendship. Please bless my friends, and help us grow in our relationships with each other and with You! Amen.*

Day 54
THE BEST GIFT

---- **READ EPHESIANS 2:1–10** ----

KEY VERSE: *For by His loving-favor you have been saved from the punishment of sin through faith. It is not by anything you have done. It is a gift of God.* EPHESIANS 2:8 NLV

UNDERSTAND:

- When you understand that your salvation isn't based on how good you are or your achievements or work in God's kingdom, how does that change your perception of God?

....

....

....

....

....

....

- God made a way for your salvation long before you accepted His gift. What does that tell you about His will and plans for your life?

....

....

....

....

....

....

APPLY: Hard work is valuable. Diligence and a can-do attitude to finish a job right are admirable. Achievement and giving your best no matter what are important and can lead to personal satisfaction and rewarding results. But all these things rely on self, and if we could earn grace based on a points system, we'd compare our grace with the grace others have earned. We'd become our own saviors instead of relying on the saving work that Jesus did when He died on the cross.

God's good plan for our salvation is that He offers it freely to everyone who accepts His gift. Well before we learned such a gift was available to us, He designed and executed that perfect gift through Jesus.

Your salvation is God's good work. Praise Him today for His best gift!

PRAY: *Life-giving God, I am absolutely thankful for Your gift of salvation. It's a gift that seems too good to be true, yet Your promises never fail, and I have full confidence that I am saved by Your grace. Help me to lead others to accept Your gift, Father. Give me the words and actions that show Your loving-kindness to everyone around me. Amen.*

Day 55

A TREK THROUGH THE DESERT

———— READ JOSHUA 1 ————

KEY VERSES: *"Moses my servant is dead. Now then, you and all these people, get ready to cross the Jordan River into the land I am about to give to them—to the Israelites. I will give you every place where you set your foot, as I promised Moses."* JOSHUA 1:2–3 NIV

UNDERSTAND:

- We don't always reach the promised land in a hurry. Think of a time when you had to wait on your miracle.

....

....

....

....

....

....

- What have you learned as you've trekked through the desert?

....

....

....

....

....

....

....

....

APPLY: The Israelites wandered in the desert for forty long years. A journey that should have taken them weeks took far longer. It was riddled with complications, rebellion, frustration, and so on.

Maybe you feel a bit like you're trekking through the desert right now. Your promised land isn't far off. You've got it in your sights. But there are times when you wonder if you'll ever pass over the river and actually enter. The process just seems too hard, the anxieties too great.

Maybe you're a couple of college courses away from your degree, but nothing is going right. Or perhaps your income is just a bit too low to get that house you're dreaming of. Maybe you're inches away from getting that job promotion you deserve and wondering if it will ever come through. You're right at the brink of your miracle, but it seems to be eluding you.

Don't give up! You will cross over the Jordan in God's time. And when you do, you can celebrate in style. Until then, don't continue to trek through the heat and sand. Stop and bask in God's promise. He will see you through.

PRAY: *Lord, sometimes I feel like I won't make it to the promised land. I'm tempted to give up. Thank You for the reminder that You're with me, even in the desert. Increase my faith today, I pray. Amen.*

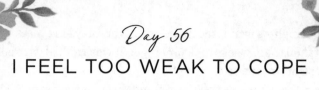

Day 56

I FEEL TOO WEAK TO COPE

──────── **READ NEHEMIAH 8:9–12** ────────

KEY VERSE: *"Don't be dejected and sad, for the joy of the LORD is your strength!"*
NEHEMIAH 8:10 NLT

UNDERSTAND:

• Have you ever felt that God is asking too much of you? That you're not strong enough to live up to His expectations?

....

....

....

....

• What part do your emotions play in your sense of weakness?

....

....

....

....

• How can you create a small celebration today so that you can experience God's joy? Nehemiah suggested indulging in special foods and drinks—and also sharing gifts of food with others. Is there someone you could invite to share a meal with you? If so, notice what happens to your feelings of weakness.

....

....

....

....

....

APPLY: How funny—when God's people heard His words for them, they started to cry! And yet don't we often respond in a similar way to God's voice? We feel we are too weak to cope with the demands He has placed on us. "We're only human," we whine. "He can't expect us to actually live *all the time* in the way the Bible describes!"

God doesn't want to make us cry! His very nature is one of love and joy, and He wants us to experience both. He's not concerned with whether we're weak or strong in our own abilities and resources; He just wants us to listen to His words . . .and then celebrate!

As this passage of scripture indicates, celebrations are not meant to be private affairs. They're occasions to share with others. Doing so just might lift our sense of weakness, replacing it with the joy of our Lord.

....

....

....

....

....

....

....

....

....

....

....

....

....

PRAY: *God of joy, take my sense of depression and helplessness and replace it with Your strength. Turn me outward, toward others. Help my life be a celebration of Your love. Amen.*

Day 57

FEAR GOD ABOVE MAN

— **READ EXODUS 1** —

KEY VERSE: *But the nurses feared God, so they did not do as the king told them; they let all the boy babies live.* EXODUS 1:17 NCV

UNDERSTAND:

• When is it right to disobey civil leaders?

_____

_____

_____

_____

_____

_____

_____

• What did God do for the two midwives of Exodus 1 because they feared Him?

_____

_____

_____

_____

_____

_____

_____

APPLY: Shiphrah and Puah. They are not names mentioned at the average family's dinner table! Have you heard of them? As we read Exodus 1, we find that these two midwives are the heroines of the story! They were told to kill the Israelites' baby boys as soon as they were born. They feared God more than they feared the possibility of being caught disobeying the law of the land. They knew that God created and valued the life of each baby—Egyptian or Israelite. They had a holy reverence for life. After all, their job was to help women deliver their babies.

God does not want us to disobey the leaders of our government; however, there are times when this is the right choice. Pray that you would be as wise as Shiphrah and Puah to know the difference between times when you should submit to authority and times when you should not. As a believer, if something goes against God, you are not to do it even if your leader calls you to.

....

....

....

....

....

....

....

....

....

....

....

PRAY: *Lord, thank You for the boldness of the two midwives who knew what the king ordered was wrong. They chose life! Thank You for the opportunities I have to do what is right even when it may be hard or frightening. May I be as bold as Shiphrah and Puah if following You becomes as dangerous for me as it was for them. Amen.*

Day 58

GOD IS ALWAYS THE SAME

– READ PSALM 102; MALACHI 3:6; HEBREWS 13:8; JAMES 1:17 —

KEY VERSES: *You made the earth in the beginning. You made the heavens with Your hands. They will be destroyed but You will always live. They will all become old as clothing becomes old. You will change them like a coat. And they will be changed, but You are always the same. Your years will never end.* PSALM 102:25–27 NLV

UNDERSTAND:

• What are the ways you enjoy change, and what are the things you wish would always stay the same?

....

....

....

....

• What changes cause you the most stress?

....

....

....

....

• In addition to Psalm 102, how do the scriptures in Malachi 3:6, Hebrews 13:8, and James 1:17 give you peace, knowing that God is unchanging?

....

....

....

....

APPLY: Life is always changing. Some of us thrive on that and some of us don't. We all have some things we would love to change and other things we wish would always stay the same. No matter what changes we experience in our circumstances, relationships, and the world around us, it's so good to know that God is our one true constant. He is steady and strong and eternally true, and we can put all our faith in Him. We can build our lives on Him. We can trust that He is the perfect Creator with perfect plans, and He is sovereign over all places and times forever. That truth should fill us with a steady, strong peace that prevails throughout our lives.

PRAY: *Heavenly Father, thank You for being the same yesterday, today, and forever. I need Your steady, unchanging presence and love every moment of my life. I need to remember that You always have been and always will be, and Your perfect plans for all of creation will prevail no matter what. Amen.*

Day 59

YOU ARE CONFIDENT IN HOPE

—————— **READ EPHESIANS 1:15–23** ——————

KEY VERSE: *I pray that your hearts will be flooded with light so that you can understand the confident hope he has given to those he called—his holy people who are his rich and glorious inheritance.* EPHESIANS 1:18 NLT

UNDERSTAND:

• How does knowing that God calls you His child give you confident hope?

....

....

....

....

• What does it mean that you are God's rich and glorious inheritance?

....

....

....

....

....

• Where do you need God's power to be evident in your life today?

....

....

....

....

....

APPLY: Where light shines brightly, you can be confident in your next step. You don't fear unseen obstacles or holes to fall into. You can see your surroundings as they are and not wonder what's really out there. That kind of bright light is what Paul is praying illuminates the hearts of the believers in Ephesus—light that leads them to greater understanding, spiritual wisdom, and confident hope in today, tomorrow, and forever.

The hope we have through God's grace is not a mystical, vague feeling that everything will be okay. Our confident hope is a complete, steadfast understanding that we will be victorious through God. This certainty comes to us through the Holy Spirit who works in us.

Just as the sun rises this morning, ask God to flood your heart with His light. He will give you confident hope as you face today's challenges. You've got this because God's got this.

PRAY: *Jesus, You are the Light of the world. Shine on me today. Holy Spirit, You are my Helper. Move in my heart today. God, You are my Mighty Defender. Walk ahead of me today and be victorious over the struggles and frustrations and roadblocks that inevitably come my way. Amen.*

Day 60
GOOD FRUIT

──── READ GALATIANS 5:13-26 ────

KEY VERSES: *But the fruit of the Spirit is love, joy, peace, forbearance, kindness, goodness, faithfulness, gentleness and self-control. Against such things there is no law.* GALATIANS 5:22–23 NIV

UNDERSTAND:

• Are there any fruits lacking in your life? How can you remedy that?

....

....

....

....

....

....

....

• When you're anxious or upset, which fruits are most beneficial to you and why?

....

....

....

....

....

....

....

....

APPLY: Have you ever wondered why the various fruits of the Spirit are called "fruit" in the first place? Perhaps it's because a fruit is something sweet that is produced when the vine is healthy. If you have a healthy orange tree, you'll yield a healthy crop of oranges. If your grapevine is robust, there will be juicy grapes attached.

The same is true in your life. If you stay close to your Creator, rooted and grounded in Him, your spiritual life will be healthy and robust. You'll begin to produce fruit for all to enjoy—love, joy, peace, forbearance, kindness, goodness, faithfulness, gentleness, and self-control. You won't have to summon these up; they will come as a natural result of spending time with your Savior.

So prepare yourself for a fruity future! Brace yourself for days filled with love for others, joy even in the midst of sorrow, unexplainable peace even when things are going wrong, patience with even the most annoying customer at work, and gentleness with your kiddos. God can do all this and more when you stick close to Him.

PRAY: *Father, thank You for the reminder that I can see good results when I stick close to You. I want to bear fruit in my life so that I can be a good witness to others. Help me, I pray. Amen.*

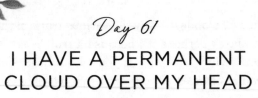

Day 61

I HAVE A PERMANENT CLOUD OVER MY HEAD

— READ PSALM 30 —

KEY VERSE: *You have turned my mourning into joyful dancing. You have taken away my clothes of mourning and clothed me with joy.* PSALM 30:11 NLT

UNDERSTAND:

• Why is there a cloud over your head? What shape does it take? What brought it there?

....

....

....

• If you remember that clouds bring rain and rain brings new growth, can you bear more patiently with this cloud?

....

....

....

• If this cloud has been over your head for a very long time, with no sign of either moving or letting down its rain, you may need to seek professional help. Talk to your doctor, your minister, or a counselor. God can use these individuals to restore you to a happier, healthier frame of mind.

....

....

....

....

APPLY: Depression can cast a cloud of gloom over our entire life. It can make it hard to see (or think) clearly. We feel as though God has abandoned us. We may think He is angry with us.

In reality, however, God has not gone anywhere, and nothing can change His love for us. He longs to lift us up above the clouds. He hears our cries, and He is already taking action to help us. Weeping may endure through the long, dark night—but a new joy will come with the rising of the sun (verse 5).

....

....

....

....

....

....

....

....

....

....

....

....

PRAY: *Hear me, Lord, and have mercy on me. Help me, Lord. Turn my mourning into joyful dancing. Take away my clothes of mourning and clothe me with joy, that I might sing praises to You and not be silent any longer. I will exalt You, Lord, for You rescued me. I cried to You for help, and You restored my health. You brought me up from the grave. You kept me from falling into the pit of death. I will give thanks to You forever! Amen. (See verses 10–12, 1–3 NLT.)*

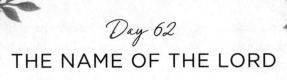

Day 62

THE NAME OF THE LORD

READ EXODUS 20:1–21

KEY VERSE: *"You shall not take the name of the L*ORD *your God in vain, for the L*ORD *will not hold him guiltless who takes His name in vain."* EXODUS 20:7 NKJV

UNDERSTAND:

• Do you take the Lord's name in vain? Why or why not?

....

....

....

....

....

....

....

• Are there ways that people take the Lord's name in vain without actually speaking His name?

....

....

....

....

....

....

....

....

APPLY: It has become common in our culture to take God's name in vain. "Oh my. . ." followed by the Lord's name is a phrase that rolls off the tongues of our society's young children. Why? Because they hear it everywhere. The phrase is sprinkled into every movie and TV show. It is an exclamation spoken by adults all around them, often even their parents and teachers. And so they assume it must be okay. But is it?

God gave Moses Ten Commandments for the people to follow. This was God's law. One of the Ten Commandments states clearly that we are not to take the Lord's name in vain.

Are you taking this command seriously? Are you honoring the name of your God? Do you use it when you are speaking to Him or sharing with others about His great glory? Or do you use it as a slang word, defaming your God each time it is spoken?

PRAY: *Lord, I love You and I will follow Your command to honor Your name, never mindlessly using it in vain. Please help me always to fear and respect You as the sovereign God of the universe. In this casual society, help me not to come before You casually but with the utmost respect. In Jesus' name I pray. Amen.*

Day 63

YOU DO YOU

──── READ 1 CORINTHIANS 12 ────

KEY VERSES: *God works in different ways, but it is the same God who does the work in all of us. A spiritual gift is given to each of us so we can help each other.*
1 Corinthians 12:6–7 NLT

UNDERSTAND:

• How has God shown you what your gifts, talents, and abilities are?

....
....
....
....

• Do you sometimes wish you had more or different gifts instead?

....
....
....
....

• How are you using your gifts to strengthen the body of believers and serve God and others?

....
....
....
....

APPLY: Too often, we compare ourselves to others and wish we could be like them. If you find yourself doing that, let 1 Corinthians 12 refresh you. You have been given the specific gifts, talents, and personality you have on purpose by God through His Holy Spirit. He has plans and purposes that are unique for you. You are not supposed to be exactly like anyone else because God wants you to do you. By incredible design, God will work what His plans are for you in coordination with what His plans are for others to create unity, love, and care among believers. When the Church does this as God intends, it is the best way to display the great love He has for us and help others want to become believers as well.

PRAY: *Heavenly Father, please remind me that my gifts are unique. I want to use what You have given me enthusiastically for You, doing my special part in the body of believers. Help me not to compare or become dissatisfied or envious. I am grateful to serve You and demonstrate Your love. Amen.*

Day 64

PRACTICE SECRET BLESSINGS

READ MATTHEW 6:1-4

KEY VERSES: *"But when you give to the needy, do not let your left hand know what your right hand is doing, so that your giving may be in secret. Then your Father, who sees what is done in secret, will reward you."* MATTHEW 6:3-4 NIV

UNDERSTAND:

• Have you ever received a blessing in secret? How was it different than if you'd known who was behind the giving?

....

....

....

....

• Aside from God's promise of rewarding your secret generosity, why is giving in secret appealing?

....

....

....

....

• How can you meet a need in secret today?

....

....

....

....

....

APPLY: Pleasant surprises are one of life's greatest gifts. Whether you're on the giving or receiving end, a generous surprise that fills a need can buoy a spirit, turn a bad day into the best one, and even be a turning point in someone's life.

But God, in His wisdom, knows that when we give publicly—in a way that proclaims our goodness and generosity—it has a way of puffing up our pride. It feels good to be appreciated after all! If we're not careful, we're setting ourselves up to be praised above the one who is the giver of all good things.

That's why He asks us to give in secret. Give anonymously. Give with a thankful heart, hopeful that the recipient directs all gratitude to the Great Provider as well. Even though others don't see you, He sees you, and that's what's important.

PRAY: *Generous God, thank You for the ability to give to others—to meet real needs in Your name. Show me opportunities to give in secret, and keep my motives pure so that I'm not seeking praise or glory for myself. Everything I have is from You, Father. I am so blessed. Amen.*

Day 65
THE GREATEST OF THESE IS LOVE

--- **READ 1 CORINTHIANS 13** ---

KEY VERSE: *So these three things continue forever: faith, hope, and love. And the greatest of these is love.* 1 Corinthians 13:13 NCV

UNDERSTAND:

- Why do you suppose God went to the trouble to let us know that love is greater than any other trait we might have?

....

....

....

....

....

- When God says that faith, hope, and love continue forever, what does He mean?

....

....

....

....

....

....

APPLY: Perhaps there is no chapter in the Bible quoted more often than the Love Chapter. You hear 1 Corinthians 13 most often at weddings. Love is the greatest of all the gifts. We read that, nod, and say, "Sure. I get it." But do we?

If love supersedes all, then we have to share it, even when we don't feel like it. When the neighbor's dog digs a hole under the fence. . .again. When the woman in the parking lot rams into your car. When the clerk at the supermarket double-charges you for something but doesn't want to make it right.

Love has to show up in every relationship, every encounter, every disagreement, every bump in the road. When you offer it to others, you're truly offering them the greatest gift.

Is love leading the way in your life today?

_____

_____

_____

_____

_____

_____

_____

_____

_____

_____

_____

PRAY: *Lord, thank You for the reminder that love needs to lead the way. So often, I let my emotions get the best of me. I struggle to show love. When I don't feel it, Father, will You please love through me? Only then can I be a true reflection of You. Amen.*

Day 66

I'M EMBARRASSED

─── **READ 2 TIMOTHY 2:14–19** ───

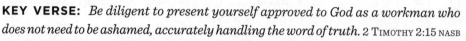

KEY VERSE: *Be diligent to present yourself approved to God as a workman who does not need to be ashamed, accurately handling the word of truth.* 2 TIMOTHY 2:15 NASB

UNDERSTAND:

• What causes your embarrassment? Is it pride? The fear of looking foolish to others? Something else?

....

....

....

....

....

• Do you think God is embarrassed on your behalf? If not, does that help you feel less embarrassed? Why or why not?

....

....

....

....

....

....

APPLY: Embarrassment is an unpleasant feeling that makes us wish we could crawl into a hole and disappear. The original meaning of the word had to do with something that bars our way, that impedes us, blocks us, or hinders us from moving forward. When we consider embarrassment in that light, we can see that it's an emotion that can easily hold us back from serving God.

These verses tell us the sort of actions that *should* embarrass us: silly arguments over semantics, empty chatter that does nothing to build up others or ourselves, and lies and deceptions. Our words have power to build or destroy, and this passage of scripture reminds us to use them carefully.

Any other embarrassment we might feel about looking silly in others' eyes is a false sense of shame. God couldn't care less! If we are diligent to please Him and do His work, why should we care what others think of us?

PRAYER: *Help me, God, to care less about what others think of me—and more about what You think. Remind me to use my words with care, in Your service. Amen.*

Day 67

TEACHABLE MOMENTS

READ DEUTERONOMY 6

KEY VERSES: *"And these words which I command you today shall be in your heart. You shall teach them diligently to your children, and shall talk of them when you sit in your house, when you walk by the way, when you lie down, and when you rise up."*
DEUTERONOMY 6:6–7 NKJV

UNDERSTAND:

• When were the Israelites commanded to speak of the Lord's words and to whom were they to teach these words diligently?

....

....

....

....

....

....

• When do you grasp teachable moments with your children?

....

....

....

....

....

....

....

....

APPLY: There are so many teachable moments packed into every day. The challenge is to lay hold of them and not let them pass by untapped. While the command here in Deuteronomy was for Israelite parents of that day, we know it is true for us today as well.

Had Deuteronomy been written today, perhaps this verse would read: *Teach them to your children diligently. Talk of them when you sit in your car driving back and forth to school and extracurricular activities. Teach them when you are going through the drive-through and waiting in line at the grocery store. . . .* You get the idea. Times have changed, but the Word of God remains the same yesterday, today, and tomorrow.

Grasp those teachable moments as you are walking and talking with your children. They need to know the Word of God, and they will only know it if you teach them.

....

....

....

....

....

....

....

....

....

....

PRAY: *Lord, I get so busy. I am guilty of putting a phone or tablet in my kids' hands far too often just to occupy them so I can find my sanity again. Please help me to use the teachable moments You give me each day with these children. Time passes so quickly, and I want them to know, love, and honor Your Word. Amen.*

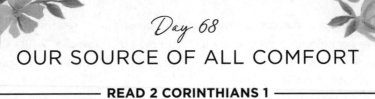

Day 68
OUR SOURCE OF ALL COMFORT

———— **READ 2 CORINTHIANS 1** ————

KEY VERSES: *All praise to God, the Father of our Lord Jesus Christ. God is our merciful Father and the source of all comfort. He comforts us in all our troubles so that we can comfort others. When they are troubled, we will be able to give them the same comfort God has given us.* 2 CORINTHIANS 1:3–4 NLT

UNDERSTAND:

• Have you ever felt crushed and overwhelmed beyond your ability to endure (verse 8)? How did God rescue you and comfort you?

....

....

....

....

....

....

• Can you say with confidence and a clear conscience that you have lived with a God-given holiness and sincerity in all your dealings (verse 12)?

....

....

....

....

....

....

....

APPLY: When you're all tucked in for the night, thank God for that cozy feeling, because it's a gift from Him. Yes, it might also come from your favorite soft pajamas and your pillows positioned just right, but ultimately even those are from God. The apostle Paul calls God the source of all comfort. Every bit of goodness you receive that eases your distress or weariness in any way is given by God to encourage, strengthen, and refresh you. And it doesn't stop with you. God calls you to share that comfort with others—maybe even with gifts like pj's and pillows but most importantly with the encouragement and peace that God filled you with at just the right time. Maybe your comfort came through a scripture God brought to mind on a really bad day or a straight-to-your-heart sermon on the radio when you were stuck in traffic. Maybe it came through a worship song repeated throughout your week or a friend who brought you coffee and cried and prayed with you. God shares His comfort in a zillion ways, both big and small. As you receive it, praise Him with gratitude and then spread it around generously.

PRAY: *Heavenly Father, I think back on this day and see the many ways You provided comfort to me when I needed it. Help me to always be aware those are blessings from You and to be filled with gratitude for how You care for the details of my life. Thank You for providing the dear people and the precious gifts that encourage, refresh, and comfort me. Help me to generously pass them on. Amen.*

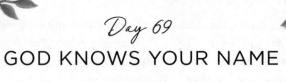

Day 69

GOD KNOWS YOUR NAME

READ ISAIAH 43:1-13

KEY VERSE: *"Do not be afraid, for I have ransomed you. I have called you by name; you are mine."* ISAIAH 43:1 NLT

UNDERSTAND:

- What does the fact that God calls each of us by name tell you about Him?

....

....

....

....

- How does God demonstrate to you that you are precious to Him?

....

....

....

....

- Whom can you encourage today by reminding them that God knows their name?

....

....

....

....

APPLY: As small children, we instinctually give names to the possessions and people dearest to us. From a name for a beloved toy or a pet to a loving nickname for a sibling or a grandparent, putting our own label on something seems to say "I've claimed you. You are mine."

God does the same for us, His cherished children. He doesn't merely group us all together and love us as a mass of humanity. No, our Father God calls us *each* by name. He promises to be with *each* of us when we are going through difficulties. He has ransomed *each* of us and claimed *each* of us as His prized possession.

Our Creator knew us before He formed us. Before our parents imagined our names, He knew us and claimed us. Listen for His voice as He whispers your name today, and know that your identity is in Him.

....

....

....

....

....

....

....

....

....

....

....

PRAY: *God, when I read Isaiah 43, I am overwhelmed by Your kindness to me. You tell me I am precious to You and You love me. You remind me again and again that You are with me no matter what and that I have nothing to fear. Forgive me when I forget these truths. Write them on my heart so I will always find my security in You. Amen.*

Day 70
THE WAIT IS ON

—— READ ACTS 1 ——

KEY VERSES: *Once when he was eating with them, he told them not to leave Jerusalem. He said, "Wait here to receive the promise from the Father which I told you about. John baptized people with water, but in a few days you will be baptized with the Holy Spirit."* ACTS 1:4–5 NCV

UNDERSTAND:

- Jesus instructed His followers to wait on the promise of the Holy Spirit. Has God ever asked you to wait on a particular promise? Are you good at waiting?

....

....

....

....

....

- The disciples were "in one accord" on the day of Pentecost. What is the importance of being in one accord with fellow believers as you wait on God to move in a miraculous way?

....

....

....

....

....

....

....

APPLY: *Wait.* Oh, how we hate that word. In this modern age, everything is instant, from popcorn to fast food to social media posts. Even our cars come with buttons to turn them on before we get inside. We don't want to wait on a thing.

Need that check deposited in the bank quickly? Do a mobile deposit. Need to sign a document to buy a home? E-sign it. Need a recommendation for a plumber? You'll find one online in seconds. Pretty much anything you need is at your fingertips.

Because we've gotten used to the notion that things should be instant, we forget that God often calls us to wait. Like the disciples in Jerusalem, we have to tarry. It's not just a matter of physically waiting. We must change our thinking. Instead of demanding instant gratification from God, we should praise Him during the waiting period.

What are you waiting on right now? Do you have a sense of urgency? If so, relax. Let those anxieties go. God's got this. The wait will be behind you soon. In the meantime, be found faithful.

PRAY: *Lord, I'm sorry for my impatience! I've been demanding with You in the past, but those days are behind me now. I want to be found faithful in the waiting, Father. Help me, I pray. Amen.*

Day 71

I CAN'T CONTROL
MY THOUGHTS

READ ROMANS 8:5–14

KEY VERSE: *Those who are dominated by the sinful nature think about sinful things, but those who are controlled by the Holy Spirit think about things that please the Spirit.* ROMANS 8:5 NLT

UNDERSTAND:

• What sort of thoughts plague you most? Worries? Sexual thoughts? Resentment, jealousy, or envy? Something else? Identifying the thoughts that are disturbing your relationship with God can be the first step toward letting God take them from you.

....

....

....

....

• What role do you think selfishness plays in your unruly thoughts? Are you truly willing to give them up? Or does some part of you actually enjoy them? Are you secretly holding on to them, reluctant to let them go?

....

....

....

....

....

APPLY: Thoughts can be destructive. We may think that so long as we don't act on our interior thoughts, they will hurt no one. These verses remind us, however, that when we let selfishness and sinfulness control our minds, we are heading down a road that leads toward inner and outer death. God's Spirit of love leads in the opposite direction, toward life and peace (verse 6).

Selfishness does not acknowledge God's right to our lives. It is hostile to His purpose for our lives (verse 7). It seems as though it will bring us the things we want most, but in reality, it takes from us everything that our hearts truly need—the love and companionship of God and others.

We need to pay attention to our thoughts. When we see that they are leading us away from God, we can consciously turn them around. If we clean out all the garbage from our minds, the Spirit will have room to dwell there.

PRAY: *Spirit of God who raised Jesus from the dead, live in me, I pray. Destroy all that is sinful and selfish in me. May my every thought lead me closer to You. Amen.*

Day 72
A VOW KEPT

READ 1 SAMUEL 1

KEY VERSES: *"For this child I prayed, and the LORD has granted me my petition which I asked of Him. Therefore I also have lent him to the LORD; as long as he lives he shall be lent to the LORD." So they worshiped the LORD there.* 1 SAMUEL 1:27–28 NKJV

UNDERSTAND:

- For what had Hannah prayed? What shows us in these verses that she had prayed fervently and over an extended period of time?

....

....

....

....

....

- What was her vow to the Lord, which she fulfilled when Samuel was born?

....

....

....

....

....

....

....

APPLY: Hannah prayed to the Lord for a child. She didn't just pray now and then. No, she wept and prayed earnestly and often. She prayed so fervently in the presence of Eli that the priest thought she was drunk.

When Samuel was born, Hannah kept the vow that she had made. As soon as he was weaned, Hannah took him to Eli. She dedicated and gave Samuel to the Lord.

After God had granted Hannah's desire for a child, she could have forgotten her promise. Don't you imagine she longed to keep her beloved son with her and watch him grow? This is a story of earnest prayer that availed much and a vow kept.

For what do you long? Do you pray earnestly for it? Is the prayer for something that can bring glory to God? Examine your own heart as you read the story of Hannah.

PRAY: *Heavenly Father, You know my deepest longings and desires. Mold my heart and mind so that I will think like You and desire only that which will bring You glory. Like Hannah did, help me to honor You with all the good gifts You bestow upon my life. Amen.*

Day 73

EVEN THOUGH THE SHIP
WILL GO DOWN

──────── **READ ACTS 27:18–28:2** ────────

KEY VERSES: *"But take courage! None of you will lose your lives, even though the ship will go down. For last night an angel of the God to whom I belong and whom I serve stood beside me, and he said, 'Don't be afraid, Paul. . . . God in his goodness has granted safety to everyone sailing with you.'"* Acts 27:22–24 NLT

UNDERSTAND:

• What stresses in life make you feel like your ship is going down? Have you experienced a total shipwreck? How did you see God rescue and provide?

....

....

....

....

....

• How has God brought you the most peace and encouragement to keep you moving forward after a big failure in life?

....

....

....

....

....

....

....

APPLY: Paul was a prisoner on a ship in a horrible storm, and his words to the crew and other passengers were somewhat comforting but very unsettling too. We might wonder, *Why didn't God just stop the storm? Why let them shipwreck at all?* But we must remember that God has never promised to always protect us from shipwrecks—literal or figurative. Yet even in the midst of them, He can save our earthly lives. And what He does promise is heavenly life forever when we trust in Jesus as our one and only Savior. Just as God promised, eventually Paul and everyone on board the ship were safe. And we see how God provided for their needs through the good people of the island they landed on. This account helps give us peace when we feel our own ships are going down. Even when they do, God will always provide the people and resources we need to survive and then lead us on a new course according to His will.

PRAY: *Heavenly Father, I don't always understand why we have to endure "shipwrecks" in our lives. But I know You rescue according to Your will and ultimately save and give forever life to everyone who believes in Your Son. Thank You for always providing for my needs and bringing me aid in every hard situation. Amen.*

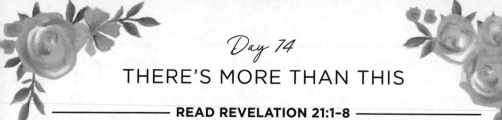

Day 74

THERE'S MORE THAN THIS

──────── **READ REVELATION 21:1–8** ────────

KEY VERSE: *"He will wipe away every tear from their eyes, and death shall be no more, neither shall there be mourning, nor crying, nor pain anymore, for the former things have passed away."* REVELATION 21:4 ESV

UNDERSTAND:

• How does knowing there is something more after this life help you face today?

....

....

....

....

• What is one way you imagine heaven might be like?

....

....

....

....

• How might your relationship with God be different when you are fully present with Him in eternity?

....

....

....

....

....

APPLY: This old earth is broken and full of sadness. Stresses pile up and frustrations mount. Loss leaves us reeling, and pain is inevitable. In seasons when it feels like Murphy's Law reigns, we begin to wonder if the hurting will ever stop.

Revelation 21:4 is an encouraging Bible promise that we can cling to during the darkest times. Eternity for Christians includes a new heaven, a new earth, and a new reality that we simply cannot comprehend. No tears. No death or mourning or crying or pain.

Even better—God will make His home with us. He will dwell among us, closer than a next-door neighbor. We will have unbridled access to Him and all His goodness and mercy and love and abundance.

No one can say for certain what heaven will be like, but imagine what amazing things lie in store. And praise God for them.

PRAY: *Heavenly Father, I am so thankful for the confidence I have in an eternity with You. I can't fathom the wonders that Your creative hand has in store for the new heaven and the new earth, and I can't wait to see Your masterful work! I long for that renewal personally too. Make me new today; change me to be more like You. Amen.*

Day 75

A BETTER CHOICE

READ GENESIS 3

KEY VERSE: *When the woman saw that the tree was good for food, and that it was pleasant to the eyes, and a tree to be desired to make one wise, she took of the fruit thereof, and did eat, and gave also unto her husband with her; and he did eat.* GENESIS 3:6 KJV

UNDERSTAND:

• Eve saw that the tree was good for food, so she took the fruit. . .even though God had told her not to. She let something that looked good outweigh God's best. Have you ever done that?

....

....

....

....

....

• When we deliberately choose to disobey, what are the consequences?

....

....

....

....

....

....

....

APPLY: Life is filled with choices. We make dozens of them a day. Will we get out of bed when the alarm goes off? What shoes will we wear today? What clothes? Should we eat breakfast or skip it? Do we drop off the kids at school or make them ride the bus? Do we start the slow cooker before leaving for work or pick up fast food on the way home this evening?

These are just a few of the choices we make.

Of course, there are bigger choices too: Who will we marry? How many children should we have? Where will we live?

The biggest choice we'll ever make, though, is far more important than any of these: Will we give our heart to Jesus Christ and make Him Lord of our life?

Following God is the best choice we could ever make. And listening to His voice as we move forward from day to day is critical for our survival. Eve wanted to walk in relationship with God in the garden, but she wanted to have it her way too. She made a poor choice, one that had devastating consequences for mankind. May we learn from her mistake so we're not destined to repeat it.

PRAY: *Father, I want to make good choices! I long to have a solid relationship with You, so I'll listen for Your still, small voice. Give me clear instructions so that I can follow hard and fast after You, Lord. Amen.*

Day 76
I'M NOT SURE GOD IS LISTENING

—— **READ ISAIAH 58:1–59:2** ——

KEY VERSE: *Listen! The Lord's arm is not too weak to save you, nor is his ear too deaf to hear you call.* Isaiah 59:1 NLT

UNDERSTAND:

• When you read these verses, what strikes you?

....

....

....

• Can you see what came between God and His people?

....

....

....

• How can you apply this to your own life? Are you truly seeking God—or are you merely going through the motions?

....

....

....

....

• What does God expect of His people, according to these verses?

....

....

....

....

APPLY: God's people felt that He wasn't hearing them. They believed they were living the way He wanted—going to church, praying, following all the rules—and yet they were allowing injustice to dwell in their midst.

God's message to them was loud and clear: *"I'm not the one who has gone deaf! I don't care how many times you go to church. What I really want is for you to free those who are wrongly imprisoned. Lighten the burden of those who work for you. Let the oppressed go free, and remove the chains that bind people. Share your food with the hungry, and give shelter to the homeless. Give clothes to those who need them, and do not hide from relatives who need your help. That's what I want from you!"*

PRAY: *God, thank You that You always hear my prayers. Teach me to hear You better. Show me how I can serve You in real and practical ways, reaching out to those who need my help. Amen.*

Day 77
CONFIDENCE IN GOD

──────── **READ 1 SAMUEL 17** ────────

KEY VERSE: *And David said, "The Lord who delivered me from the paw of the lion and from the paw of the bear, He will deliver me from the hand of this Philistine." And Saul said to David, "Go, and may the Lord be with you."* 1 Samuel 17:37 NASB

UNDERSTAND:

• What gave David the confidence to fight Goliath, the Philistine giant?

....

....

....

....

....

....

• What experiences have you had that give you confidence to face an unknown future with a known God?

....

....

....

....

....

....

....

APPLY: As a shepherd, David was to watch over the sheep. This job entailed fighting off wild animals that intended to kill the sheep. David had become skilled at his work. God had protected him. He had not died from a bear or lion attack, and for a shepherd, these were very real possibilities.

What David had faced in his past enabled him to face a new challenge with confidence. But notice this: It was not David's confidence in himself or in his own strength or ability that led him to fight the giant. It was his trust in the Lord.

"The LORD who delivered me" was the one David bragged on, not himself.

Look back in your life. Where has God protected or delivered you? God will use each of your experiences to prepare you for the next. Be prepared for a greater challenge that lies ahead.

PRAY: *Lord, thank You for the times You have protected me and provided a way of escape. You have built up in me a confidence that next time and the time after that You will remain faithful. You will show up. Help me to trust in Your strength as You continue to use me and to put challenges in my path. Amen.*

Day 78

PLEASANT AND PEACEFUL

─────── **READ PHILIPPIANS 2** ───────

KEY VERSES: *God is helping you obey Him. God is doing what He wants done in you. Be glad you can do the things you should be doing. Do all things without arguing and talking about how you wish you did not have to do them. In that way, you can prove yourselves to be without blame. You are God's children and no one can talk against you, even in a sin-loving and sin-sick world. You are to shine as lights among the sinful people of this world.* PHILIPPIANS 2:13–15 NLV

UNDERSTAND:

• How does imitating Christ in His humility help fill you with peace?

....

....

....

....

....

• How does keeping a positive attitude, without grumbling or complaining, help fill you with peace?

....

....

....

....

....

....

APPLY: Yikes, it's terribly hard to do *all* things without ever arguing or complaining, isn't it? But that's what this scripture encourages us to do. It's something with which we all need a lot of help from God. But if we can keep positive with our words as we obey God and follow the plans He has for us, we shine as extrabright lights in the dark and sinful world around us. Hopefully, people who do not trust Jesus as their Savior will want to know more about God's love because they will see our lights shining in our pleasant and peaceful attitudes, no matter the situation.

PRAY: *Heavenly Father, please help me to be extraordinary light in the darkness of sin around me in this world. I want to shine so brightly that others want to know Jesus as their Savior too. Amen.*

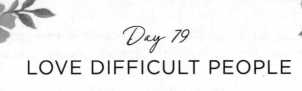

Day 79

LOVE DIFFICULT PEOPLE

—— **READ LUKE 6:27–35** ——

KEY VERSES: *"I say to you who hear Me, love those who work against you. Do good to those who hate you. Respect and give thanks for those who try to bring bad to you. Pray for those who make it very hard for you."* LUKE 6:27–28 NLV

UNDERSTAND:

• Who is the most difficult person in your life, and what makes them such a challenge?

....

....

....

....

• How, practically, can you do something good and show respect for this person today?

....

....

....

....

• How could your perspective change if you make it a priority to pray for this person?

....

....

....

....

....

APPLY: Most of us are conflict avoiders. Apart from those rare few who are wired to enjoy a good combative exchange, we intentionally structure our lives to be harmonious in whatever ways we can.

But there's always that person who is just so difficult. Maybe it's a coworker who seems to sabotage your efforts. Maybe it's an in-law who has never warmed to your presence in the family. Maybe it's someone who struggles socially, and it comes across as disrespect, creating awkward situations. Maybe it's simply someone who doesn't like you, and they make no qualms about it.

Jesus says love them anyway. Do good to them. Respect them and pray for them. This might be one of Jesus' most challenging commands, yet He demonstrated it over and over in His ministry on earth. With His help, you can do it.

PRAY: *This is a hard one, God. I receive no respect, so everything inside me wants to disrespect in return. And love them? Do good to them? I can't do this on my own, Father. Inhabit this relationship. Give me Your eyes to see them the way You see them. That's the only way I will be able to love. Amen.*

Day 80

IN SPITE OF

READ JOB 1

KEY VERSE: *In all this Job did not sin or blame God.* Job 1:22 NLV

UNDERSTAND:

- Have you ever wanted to point the finger at God, to blame Him for the bad things happening in your life?

....

....

....

....

....

....

- Where is God when things are falling apart?

....

....

....

....

....

....

....

....

APPLY: In spite of everything, Job did not sin or blame God. Let those words sink in for a moment. In spite of pain. Sickness. Death. Loss. Destruction.

Us? We're so quick to blame. When a meal isn't right, we blame the cook or waitress. When our team doesn't win, we blame the umpire or referee. When we show up late for an event, we're loaded with excuses for how others slowed us down.

Pointing the finger is a natural defense, but maybe it's time to adopt Job's attitude. Even when he lost everything, he didn't point the finger at God. He could have. (Let's face it, most of us would.) He could have pointed to heaven and shouted, "Why are You doing this to me? What did I ever do to You?"

The truth is, even in the hardest of times, God wants us to keep our eyes fixed on Him and our hope elevated. So toss those anxieties out the window. Stop blaming. Keep your eyes on the one who plans to deliver you; then watch as He works all things together for your good.

PRAY: *I needed that reminder today, Lord! I'm so quick to point the finger. Today I choose to adopt Job's stance and remind myself that, in spite of everything, You are still good. Amen.*

Day 81

I CAN'T FORGIVE WHAT THEY DID TO ME

READ MATTHEW 6:9–14

KEY VERSE: *If ye forgive men their trespasses, your heavenly Father will also forgive you.* MATTHEW 6:14 KJV

UNDERSTAND:

• What offenses that you've experienced from others seem unforgivable? Why?

....

....

....

....

....

....

....

• Does the reminder that you need God's forgiveness give you a better sense of perspective about the things others have done that hurt you? Why or why not?

....

....

....

....

....

....

....

APPLY: When Jesus taught His followers how to pray, He included the line "forgive us our debts, as we forgive our debtors" (verse 12 KJV), and then, after saying amen, He reinforced that message by repeating how important forgiveness is to the kingdom of heaven. When He links God's forgiveness of our sins to our ability to forgive others, it may sound as though God will punish us for our hard hearts—but hard, scientific research has found that people who are unable to forgive hurt themselves, physically and emotionally. Jesus knew that the spiritual effects are just as detrimental.

Forgiving others doesn't mean that what the other person did to hurt us doesn't matter or that it was okay for them to do what they did. Forgiveness *does* mean being willing to let go of whatever happened and move on. It allows us to move into a place of greater freedom, a place where God has space to bless us.

PRAY: *Jesus, help me to live as You did when You were on earth. Help me to forgive those who have hurt me. I want to be part of Your kingdom. Amen.*

Day 82

SIMPLE ACTS OF KINDNESS

--- **READ 2 KINGS 4** ---

KEY VERSES: *The woman said to her husband, "I know that this is a holy man of God who passes by our house all the time. Let's make a small room on the roof and put a bed in the room for him. We can put a table, a chair, and a lampstand there. Then when he comes by, he can stay there."* 2 KINGS 4:9–10 NCV

UNDERSTAND:

• Have you gone out of your way to show hospitality to someone?

....

....

....

....

....

....

• Has someone ever been particularly kind to you? How did it make you feel?

....

....

....

....

....

....

....

....

APPLY: The Shunammite woman saw a need and wanted to meet it. She recognized that Elisha was a holy man of God. She proposed to her husband that rather than just feeding him a meal each time he passed their way, they should provide a room for him in their home. Isn't it kind how she planned the details? She decided that a table, chair, and lampstand in addition to the bed would go into the small room on the roof for Elisha.

This simple act of kindness and hospitality was not done for a reward. The woman did not ask for anything in return. But, amazingly, she was granted a son because of her gesture.

When you see a need that you are able to meet, meet it. The most basic act of kindness can make all the difference in someone's life. And God sees your good deeds. If not in this life, you will find your reward in heaven. The Lord is pleased when we serve and love one another.

....

....

....

....

....

....

....

....

....

....

PRAY: *Lord, all of my resources come straight from Your hand. Nothing that I own—my home, my car, even the food in my pantry—belongs to me. It is all on loan from You. Please show me opportunities to use my resources to meet the needs of those around me. Make me hospitable and kind like the Shunammite woman. In Christ's name I pray. Amen.*

Day 83
THE VINE AND THE BRANCHES

—————————— **READ JOHN 15** ——————————

KEY VERSES: *"I am the true grapevine, and my Father is the gardener. He cuts off every branch of mine that doesn't produce fruit, and he prunes the branches that do bear fruit so they will produce even more. You have already been pruned and purified by the message I have given you. Remain in me, and I will remain in you. For a branch cannot produce fruit if it is severed from the vine, and you cannot be fruitful unless you remain in me. Yes, I am the vine; you are the branches. Those who remain in me, and I in them, will produce much fruit. For apart from me you can do nothing."* JOHN 15:1–5 NLT

UNDERSTAND:

• What good fruit are you producing in your life right now?

....

....

....

....

....

• What ways can you improve on staying connected to Jesus, the vine?

....

....

....

....

....

....

APPLY: Jesus described Himself as a vine and God the Father as the gardener. We are the branches. The fruits we grow on our branches are the good things we do for God that He has planned for us—the work He created us for, serving and giving to others, sharing God's love, and helping others to know Jesus as Savior. And we can't produce any good fruit unless we stay connected to Jesus, the vine. If you are feeling worn out and unproductive and like you're spinning your wheels at times, there might be an easy answer: you might need to check your connection to Jesus. Humbly ask the loving gardener to show you any problems and nourish you back to nearness with Jesus. God can make you thrive again with lots of good fruit growing on you!

....

....

....

....

....

....

....

....

....

....

....

....

....

....

....

PRAY: *Heavenly Father, please nourish me in my connection to Jesus, the vine. Help me to stay connected and grow the good fruit You want me to. Amen.*

YOU DON'T HAVE TO UNDERSTAND EVERYTHING

READ ISAIAH 55:6-13

KEY VERSES: *"For My thoughts are not your thoughts, and My ways are not your ways," says the Lord. "For as the heavens are higher than the earth, so are My ways higher than your ways, and My thoughts than your thoughts."* Isaiah 55:8–9 NLV

UNDERSTAND:

• How do you feel when you don't understand something?

....

....

....

....

• How does it change when you don't understand, but you do trust the person who is in control of the situation?

....

....

....

....

• Can you trust God even when you don't understand what He's thinking or doing? Why or why not?

....

....

....

....

APPLY: If we can't be in control, it at least helps when we understand why something is happening. But God doesn't promise us understanding. In fact, there are some things about God we simply *cannot* grasp this side of heaven.

God says in scripture that His ways are "far beyond anything you could imagine" (Isaiah 55:8 NLT). That doesn't mean that He won't give us insight into what He's doing, but the fact remains that sometimes His plans may seem confusing and downright undecipherable to our human minds.

Rather than letting this scripture frustrate you, take comfort and encouragement in knowing that you don't have to understand everything. You don't have to have everything under control and figured out! God's ways are the *best* ways, and He will never leave you. He is working a perfect plan in you and around you.

PRAY: *Lord God, sometimes Your ways are a complete mystery to me. I don't understand what You're doing, and I realize—yet again—that I'm not in control. But the truth is I am thankful Your ways and plans are better, more holy, and absolutely perfect. So even when I don't understand, lead on. Amen.*

Day 85

USHERED IN!

——— **READ JOHN 4:1-26** ———

KEY VERSE: *The Samaritan woman said to him, "You are a Jew and I am a Samaritan woman. How can you ask me for a drink?" (For Jews do not associate with Samaritans.)* JOHN 4:9 NIV

UNDERSTAND:

• Jesus spoke with such compassion and love to the woman at the well. Do you ever marvel at His ability to speak with such love to you, even when you're caught in sin?

....

....

....

....

....

....

• What was the living water that Jesus spoke of in this chapter?

....

....

....

....

....

....

....

....

APPLY: The woman at the well didn't set off to have a one-on-one encounter with the Savior of the world. She was just going about her daily routine, gathering water at the well. When the stranger struck up a conversation with her, she couldn't help but be drawn in. He was, after all, a Jew. She was a Samaritan and an outcast at that. The idea that He would speak to her at all was mesmerizing.

And all those things He said! He seemed to know everything about her. To top it off, He spoke with such compassion, such love, that she found herself completely at ease.

Have you ever felt like that woman—outcast, set apart from the crowd? Have you wondered if Jesus would welcome you into a conversation? Maybe you've judged yourself harshly and convinced yourself that you don't fit in with other Christians.

Think again. God welcomes all. If Jesus took the time to speak with such love and affection to this woman, then surely He will usher you into His presence as well.

PRAY: *Father, I feel like I don't fit in at times. Thank You for including me, for putting me at ease and welcoming me in that loving, tender way. I'm so grateful, Lord. Amen.*

Day 86

MY HOPE IS GONE

———————— **READ ZECHARIAH 9:9–12** ————————

KEY VERSE: *Return to your fortress, you prisoners of hope; even now I announce that I will restore twice as much to you.* ZECHARIAH 9:12 NIV

UNDERSTAND:

• When you feel hopeless, in what way are you a "prisoner of hope"? What might freedom mean for you?

....

....

....

....

....

....

• What do you think the fortress is that's referred to in the key verse? Can you think of "fortresses" in your own life where you might be able to return for safety?

....

....

....

....

....

....

APPLY: Sometimes life looks pretty hopeless. Whether we're facing a personal problem or considering the state of our world, the situation gives us little cause for hope. As hard as we try, we just can't see any solutions.

When that happens, we often become afraid to hope any longer. Because we've had our hopes dashed so often, hope becomes something painful. It seems like a prison, a trap that holds us back from facing reality rather than something positive that gives us courage.

But the kind of hope the Bible talks about isn't merely wishing that things will turn out the way we want them to. Instead, it's a confident expectation that no matter how bad things look, God is behind the scenes working out something better than anything we could ever come up with on our own. The result may not be what we wished would happen—but ultimately, God tells us, it will be twice as good!

PRAY: *God of hope, show me Your fortress where I will be safe during this time when it's so hard to hold on to hope. I'll stop looking for my own solutions and instead will wait for You to act. My hope is only in You. Amen.*

Day 87
WAITING WELL

---------------- **READ PSALMS 130–132** ----------------

KEY VERSE: *I wait for the LORD, my whole being waits, and in his word I put my hope.* PSALM 130:5 NIV

UNDERSTAND:

• Have you ever had to wait a long time for something? How did it feel?

....

....

....

....

....

....

....

• What do you think it looks like to put your hope in God's Word as you wait?

....

....

....

....

....

....

....

....

APPLY: Many times in life we are called upon to wait. We wait in lines at movie theaters and grocery stores. We wait for Christmas and birthdays. As humans, we certainly know about waiting. What kind of a waiter are you? Do you grumble or lose faith? Or do you patiently put your trust in God?

The psalmist says that his whole being waits for the Lord. When we rest before God with every part of our being, He meets us right there where we are. Seek to rest mentally, emotionally, physically, and spiritually before God. He is your Abba Father, your Daddy. He has your best interest at heart, and He is never early or late but always right on time.

Wait upon the Lord, and claim the promises He has given you in His Word. He has not forgotten you. He will never leave you. He is your Good Shepherd. He will see you through, and the waiting will be worth it in the end.

PRAY: *Lord, as I wait, please help me to know that Your timing is always right for me. You always have my best interest at heart. In the waiting, help me to claim Your promises and to trust in Your Word. Amen.*

Day 88

THE ONE WHO LIVES IN YOU

---- **READ 1 JOHN 4** ----

KEY VERSE: *My children, you are a part of God's family. You have stood against these false preachers and had power over them. You had power over them because the One Who lives in you is stronger than the one who is in the world.* 1 John 4:4 NLV

UNDERSTAND:

• What does this passage say is the test for knowing what is truly from the Spirit of God?

....

....

....

....

....

....

• How do verses 16–18 speak comfort to any anxieties in your life right now?

....

....

....

....

....

....

....

APPLY: "The One Who lives in you is stronger than the one who is in the world"—that last part of 1 John 4:4 is such a short and simple yet powerful scripture to memorize and repeat when you need strength and courage in any situation. Our enemy the devil is the one stirring up all kinds of evil in this world. And you will be under attack from him sometimes, in all sorts of different ways—through stressful times for your family, through painful times of loss, through illness, and so on. But no matter how strong the enemy and his evil seem against you and your loved ones, he is never stronger than the power of God in you through the Holy Spirit. Don't ever forget that. Call on Him to help you be strong, calm, and patient and to help you see how He is working and taking care of you through it all.

....

....

....

....

....

....

....

....

....

....

....

....

PRAY: *Heavenly Father, deep down I know You are always stronger than any evil attack against me, any hard thing I'm going through. But I do forget that truth sometimes, and I'm sorry. Please remind me, fill me with Your power and peace, and do the fighting for me. Amen.*

Day 89

YOU CAN LIVE WITHOUT FEAR

—————— **READ ISAIAH 41:8-14** ——————

KEY VERSES: *"For I have chosen you and will not throw you away. Don't be afraid, for I am with you. Don't be discouraged, for I am your God. I will strengthen you and help you. I will hold you up with my victorious right hand."* Isaiah 41:9–10 NLT

UNDERSTAND:

- Have you ever considered the fact that God will not throw you away? How does that fact make you feel?

....

....

....

....

....

....

- How can knowing God is with you make you less fearful? Less discouraged?

....

....

....

....

....

....

....

APPLY: Fear is something like a strain of influenza. Just when we think we've figured out the proper vaccine to safeguard ourselves, the virus changes, and the flu rears its ugly head once again. And just when we think we've overcome our fear, some new worry or anxiety pops up, and anxious thoughts return, sometimes leaving us down for the count.

The only true cure for fear is unconditional trust in God. Faith that He will keep His promises all throughout scripture. He has chosen you. He will not throw you away. He is with you. He is your God who will strengthen you and help you. He will hold you up.

Do you believe Him? When your fears threaten to take over again, remember His faithfulness in keeping these promises in the past. He has never failed you yet, and He will not start now.

PRAY: *Almighty God, no matter what I face, I know You are with me. You chose me for a reason, and I know You have a perfect plan for me safe inside Your will. Be near me, Father, especially when I am feeling unsure of the way. Hold me up when I can't stand on my own, and usher me into Your victorious presence forevermore. Amen.*

Day 90
REBORN!

───────── **READ JOHN 3:1–21** ─────────

KEY VERSE: *"You should not be surprised at my saying, 'You must be born again.'"*
JOHN 3:7 NIV

UNDERSTAND:

- It's impossible to remember your own physical birth, but do you have a memory of the day you gave your heart to the Lord? What was that day like?

....

....

....

....

....

....

....

- When you explain the salvation process to others, do you share from your own journey? What do you say?

....

....

....

....

....

....

....

APPLY: Countless Bible stories tell tales of men and women who messed up and wanted to start over. Thank goodness God is in the do-over business. He loves to offer second chances.

There's one do-over that outshines every other, and it's found in one little word: *salvation.* When we accept Jesus Christ as Lord and Savior, when we step into relationship with Him, we are reborn.

Think about that prefix "re-" for a moment. It means "again." When we accept Jesus, we're born. . .again. We get a do-over. A big one! Gone are the mistakes of the past. Washed away are our sins. Gone are the worries about who we used to be. In place of all these things, a clean slate. What an amazing gift from our Father, God!

PRAY: *Thank You, Lord, for offering me new life in You. I've been born again, Father! My heart now belongs to You. I can hardly wait to get started on this journey together. Amen.*

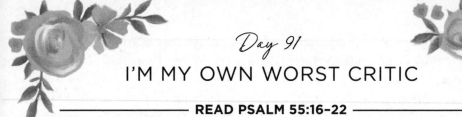

I'M MY OWN WORST CRITIC

—————— **READ PSALM 55:16–22** ——————

KEY VERSE: *As for me, I will call upon God; and the L*ORD *shall save me.* PSALM 55:16 KJV

UNDERSTAND:

- This psalm speaks of an exterior battle—but often the fiercest battles are waged within our hearts. In what ways do you attack your own self?

....

....

....

....

....

....

....

- What do you hate most about yourself? Can you give it to God, believing that He can truly sustain you (verse 22)?

....

....

....

....

....

....

....

....

APPLY: Self-criticism is like a sharp sword that attacks our inner strength. It destroys the peace God wants us to experience. It can even make us believe that God has broken His promises to us. Self-criticism may seem like modesty or humility—but it's actually a demonic attack on all God has given us.

We need to treat those inner voices that tell us we're unworthy with the discipline they deserve. Sometimes, though, our strength is too weak to stand up to the whispers that slide like oil into our minds. When that happens, we need to turn immediately to God and call for help. He has the strength to carry us through this inner battle. His love will hold us firm.

PRAY: *Dear Lord, I'm calling on You for help. The enemy I face is inside my own heart, and I don't know how to fight it. Save me! Amen.*

Day 92
NEVER ALONE

READ REVELATION 3

KEY VERSE: *"Here I am! I stand at the door and knock. If anyone hears my voice and opens the door, I will come in and eat with that person, and they with me."*
REVELATION 3:20 NIV

UNDERSTAND:

- If you are a believer in Christ, are you ever truly alone?

....
....
....
....
....
....
....

- Why do you think Jesus refers to eating with the person who allows Him into their heart?

....
....
....
....
....
....
....
....

APPLY: If you have Christ as your Savior, you are never truly alone. On your darkest day and in your loneliest hour, He stands ready to eat with you. Why would He use these words? One might wonder if it's because eating a meal together is an intimate act. We typically eat our meals as a family or with close friends, not strangers. We talk as we eat. It's a time to slow down and spend time with loved ones. It's a shared experience.

Even if there is no one else, there will always be Christ. He is your Savior and Redeemer, your Friend, your Prince of Peace, and King of Glory. He is always there for you. You are never truly alone.

Christ not only saves you, but He promises to be with you always, never leaving or forsaking you. He comes in and makes His home with you. You are His beloved, and He longs to fellowship with you.

PRAY: *Lord Jesus, thank You for coming into my heart. Thank You that I am never really alone because I have You. May I always recognize the great gift of my fellowship with You. Amen.*

Day 93

THE HEROES WHO HAVE GONE BEFORE US

READ HEBREWS 11

KEY VERSE: *They were longing for a better country—a heavenly one. Therefore God is not ashamed to be called their God, for he has prepared a city for them.* HEBREWS 11:16 NIV

UNDERSTAND:

• Which of the faith heroes described in Hebrews 11 do you relate to the most?

_____

_____

_____

_____

_____

_____

• Do you feel like a foreigner and nomad here on earth? Why is that important?

_____

_____

_____

_____

_____

_____

APPLY: We have to admit, sometimes we do get weary of keeping the faith. We wonder why God isn't answering a specific prayer or creating the breakthrough we think we need or proving Himself exactly like we want Him to. We sometimes have doubt and need to be honest about it. In those times, Hebrews 11 is such a powerful chapter to read to revitalize you. It defines what our faith is—being sure of what we hope for and certain of what we do not see—and gives us an incredible overview of so many heroes who've gone before us holding to their faith. This reminds us and inspires us to keep on believing and being obedient to God, like they did, even when we can't see all of His plans or the final result. If you are ever tempted to give up the faith, open your Bible to Hebrews 11. Read and reenergize. Think of how you'd like your name to be remembered among your family and friends and generations as one who never gave up on God. Though we cannot see all that He is doing right now, we absolutely will one day soon.

....

....

....

....

....

....

....

....

....

....

PRAY: *Heavenly Father, please strengthen my faith in You as I remember the heroes of old who never gave up on You. Thank You for their examples in Your Word. Please remind me every day that I am looking to and living for a place far, far better than this world—the heavenly home where You make all things right and good. Amen.*

HE IS NEAR TO THE BROKENHEARTED

---- **READ PSALM 34** ----

KEY VERSES: *The Lord is near to the brokenhearted and saves the crushed in spirit. Many are the afflictions of the righteous, but the Lord delivers him out of them all.* Psalm 34:18–19 esv

UNDERSTAND:

- Do you feel the presence of God more during times of joy or times of sorrow? Why?

....

....

....

....

....

....

- Think about a time when you called out to God with a crushed spirit. How did He respond?

....

....

....

....

....

....

APPLY: God's Word doesn't promise a life of unbridled bliss for God's children. On the contrary, Jesus tells us in John 16:33 (NLT), "Here on earth you will have many trials and sorrows."

But God is near, and during life's toughest situations, He will rescue us from despair. His path will guide us through and give us the strength to overcome anything. Maybe you've seen friends or family go through impossible things like this and come out the other side stronger in their faith.

Yes, God will walk with us, carrying us when necessary, through life's many trials and sorrows. But the best news of all is what Jesus said in John 16, right after telling us to expect difficult times. "But take heart," He says in the second half of verse 33 (NLT), "because I have overcome the world." Christ wins. We are victorious in Him.

PRAY: *Lord of all my days, thank You for always being near. I love to celebrate with You when things are going well, but I am also deeply grateful that You come even closer when I am brokenhearted, grieving, and crushed in spirit. You are faithful to bring me through and are so patient with me when I am struggling. I don't deserve such kindness, but I am so thankful for it! Amen.*

Day 95

HERE AM I. . .SEND ME

━━━━━━━━━━ **READ ISAIAH 6:1-8** ━━━━━━━━━━

KEY VERSE: *Then I heard the voice of the Lord, saying, "Whom shall I send, and who will go for Us?" Then I said, "Here am I. Send me!"* ISAIAH 6:8 NASB

UNDERSTAND:

• Can you remember a time in your life when the Lord specifically called you to go someplace out of your comfort zone? Did you hide in fear or respond, like Isaiah, "Here am I. Send me!"?

....

....

....

....

....

....

• When was the last time you felt the Lord nudge you to do something difficult or unusual?

....

....

....

....

....

....

....

APPLY: Isaiah found himself in an amazing position, didn't he? When the Lord asked the question "Whom shall I send, and who will go for Us?" Isaiah was faced with a choice—to stay or to go. With no hesitation, he responded, "Here am I. Send me!"

If you've ever spent time in God's presence, really drawing close to Him, perhaps you've had those little nudges. Maybe you've heard God whisper to your heart, *"Go here,"* or *"Do this"* or *"Do that."* When the almighty author of the universe speaks, how do you respond? Ideally, like Isaiah!

If God reveals something to you during your quiet time with Him, don't be afraid. Simply raise your hand and say, "I'm here, Lord. I hear You, and I'm willing to go." But don't be surprised where He sends you once you've said it! Your journey is about to get really interesting!

PRAY: *Lord, here am I. Send me. Send me to my friends that I might be a witness. Send me to my coworkers that I might show compassion. Send me wherever You choose that I might shine brightly for You. Amen.*

Day 96

I LACK SELF-CONFIDENCE

───── **READ 2 CORINTHIANS 10:12–18** ─────

KEY VERSES: *We do not dare to classify or compare ourselves with some who commend themselves. When they measure themselves by themselves and compare themselves with themselves, they are not wise. We, however, will not boast beyond proper limits, but will confine our boasting to the sphere of service God himself has assigned to us.* 2 CORINTHIANS 10:12–13 NIV

UNDERSTAND:

• How much of your lack of confidence comes from comparing yourself to others?

....

....

....

....

• Do you feel guilty or embarrassed to identify your own unique abilities? Why?

....

....

....

....

• What attitude do you think God wants you to take toward the skills and talents He has given you?

....

....

....

....

APPLY: Self-confidence is a necessary aspect of being a healthy, productive human being. Without it, we will be afraid to do the work God has called us to do. And yet often, especially as Christians, we are afraid to lay claim to our own strength. We confuse self-confidence with egotistical pride.

In this passage of scripture, written by Paul to the church at Corinth, the apostle makes it clear that there's an enormous difference between selfish, prideful boasting and the humble acknowledgment of skills God has given us to use in His service. To pretend that we have not each been given unique abilities would be like a carpenter who was given a hammer but refused—out of a sense of modesty —to put it to use. God wants us to pick up our abilities and use them confidently to build His kingdom.

....

....

....

....

....

....

....

....

....

....

....

....

PRAY: *Thank You, God of grace, that You have given me the skills that I possess. Don't let my lack of self-confidence prevent me from seeing clearly what You have given me, so that I can offer it back in service to You. Amen.*

Day 97

THAT YOU MAY *KNOW*

---------- **READ 1 JOHN 5** ----------

KEY VERSE: *These things I have written to you who believe in the name of the Son of God, that you may know that you have eternal life, and that you may continue to believe in the name of the Son of God.* 1 John 5:13 NKJV

UNDERSTAND:

• Do you ever doubt your salvation?

....

....

....

....

....

....

• Ephesians 2:8–9 states that we are saved by grace through faith. How does 1 John 5:13 confirm this?

....

....

....

....

....

....

....

APPLY: There is no way to predict whether you will be diagnosed with a life-altering disease. We can't know for sure if our houses will flood or if we will lose our jobs. Many things are unknowns.

There is one thing you can be assured of if you have trusted in Jesus Christ as your Savior: the fact that you have eternal life in heaven with God.

1 John 5:13 says that we may *know* that we have eternal life. It does not say that we can *hope* or *dream* or *imagine*. It says that we may *know*. This means that you don't ever have to wonder again or doubt that you will truly spend eternity in heaven. It is not about how good you are or aren't. It is a free gift that came to you at the time of your salvation. God doesn't take that gift back!

The next time Satan tempts you to doubt this fact, read 1 John 5:13 again, and tell Satan to stay away from you. God wants you to be assured of where you are going!

PRAY: *Father, thank You that I don't have to wonder where I will spend eternity. You want me to rest assured in Your promise that I will be with You. Help me to cling to this promise so that I do not waste valuable time worrying. All of that worry is unnecessary! In Jesus' name I pray. Amen.*

PEACE IN OUR TROUBLES

---------- **READ ROMANS 5** ----------

KEY VERSES: *We are glad for our troubles also. We know that troubles help us learn not to give up. When we have learned not to give up, it shows we have stood the test. When we have stood the test, it gives us hope. Hope never makes us ashamed because the love of God has come into our hearts through the Holy Spirit Who was given to us.* ROMANS 5:3–5 NLV

UNDERSTAND:

• What is a trouble you have gone through that you look back and are thankful for because of the way it strengthened you and your hope for the future?

....

....

....

....

....

• Who in your life needs to hear the message of salvation and hope in Romans 5? How can you share it with them?

....

....

....

....

....

....

APPLY: Nothing is stress-free in life. Even a perfectly planned, all-expenses-paid vacation in paradise will have moments of anxiety, at least here and there. We don't need to go asking for trouble, for sure, because it will gladly come our way uninvited. But rather than constantly trying to avoid and prevent it in our lives, we need to realistically expect it and proactively decide what to do with it. Romans 5 helps us think of trouble in a healthy, positive way. We can learn to be glad about it by remembering that it helps us learn not to give up and strengthens our hope that things will be better in the future. When our hope is in the right place—in God who has saved us through His Son and has given us His Holy Spirit now and eternal, perfect life in heaven for the future—we will never be ashamed or defeated. Just as God sent His Son to save us at just the right time, He will always deliver us out of any trouble at just the right time.

PRAY: *Heavenly Father, help me not to run away from trouble but rather face it with the right perspective. You use stress and problems to help me learn to depend on You and to not give up. You have saved me through Your Son, and You are my ultimate hope and peace, dear Father. I trust You and praise You! Amen.*

Day 99

RELY ON HIM

KEY VERSES: *Don't count on your warhorse to give you victory—for all its strength, it cannot save you. But the* LORD *watches over those who fear him, those who rely on his unfailing love.* PSALM 33:17–18 NLT

UNDERSTAND:

- Have you ever put your faith in someone or something that left you disappointed? What did you learn from that experience?

....

....

....

....

....

....

- How do you know you can trust God to take care of you?

....

....

....

....

....

....

....

....

APPLY: Scripture uses the beautiful Shepherd/sheep analogy to describe our relationship with God. Passages like Psalm 23 can fill us with peace and security to know that He takes care of us no matter what.

But just like sheep, we sometimes make dumb choices about whom or what to trust. Ever been burned by the latest self-help craze? Has a friend or family member let you down? Maybe someone betrayed a trust after you shared something deeply personal. Quick fixes and three steps to a brand-new you can leave us feeling defeated, empty, and hopeless.

But our Good Shepherd is there, always seeking us, calling us back to Him. His love is unfailing, and His saving grace is absolute. Trust in Him to guide you, to protect you, to make your path clear for safe passage to eternity with Him.

PRAY: *Thank You for watching over me, Father. You keep me safe and preserve my life in ways that I won't know this side of heaven. Your strength is what I put my trust in—not my own, not other people's. I am imperfect, and others will let me down whether they mean to or not. Your redeeming love lifts me up and holds me steady even in hard times. Amen.*

Day 100
MANNA

---- **READ EXODUS 16** ----

KEY VERSE: *Then the L*ORD *said to Moses, "I will rain down bread from heaven for you. The people are to go out each day and gather enough for that day. In this way I will test them and see whether they will follow my instructions."* EXODUS 16:4 NIV

UNDERSTAND:

- God is in the "providing" business. The Bible promises that He will take care of His kids. Think of a particular time when God came through for you, pouring down unexpected manna.

....

....

....

....

....

....

- How can you be a manna provider for others in need?

....

....

....

....

....

....

....

APPLY: We often say, "Lord, I don't need much. Just give me what I need, not what I want." Likely, the Israelites prayed that too. "Lord, just a little food will suffice to see us through." Then, manna fell like a feast from the sky. At first the Hebrew children were thrilled to have it. Then, after a while, it wasn't so tasty. They grew tired of it.

What an amazing story this would have been if the Israelites continued to praise and thank God for His provision instead of grumbling. If only they could have seen manna as a blessing instead of drudgery.

Maybe you can relate. What felt like a blessing in the beginning is now part of your everyday humdrum existence. You've forgotten to be thankful. The mortgage gets paid, and you don't remember to thank God. The electric bill is paid, and you let it pass by like it's nothing.

Every day God is blessing you. Don't forget to stop and thank Him for the manna!

....

....

....

....

....

....

....

....

....

....

PRAY: *Lord, thank You for the many times and ways You have provided for me. Show me how to be a blessing to others, I pray. I want to be one who provides manna (refreshment, nourishment) to those You place in my path. Amen.*

Day 101
MY ACHES AND PAINS
MAKE ME MISERABLE

―――――― **READ PROVERBS 17:22–24** ――――――

KEY VERSE: *A cheerful heart is good medicine, but a crushed spirit dries up the bones.* PROVERBS 17:22 NIV

UNDERSTAND:

• Have you ever noticed a connection between your emotions and your physical pain? Certainly, pain can make us emotionally depressed—but do you think a gloomy attitude can make our pain seem more severe? Why or why not?

....

....

....

....

....

• Do you see any connection between verse 22 and the two verses that follow it? What might that connection be?

....

....

....

....

....

....

....

APPLY: We often think of our bodies as being separate from our minds and souls. We look at physical pain as a burden we must shoulder emotionally and spiritually, which in one sense it is. In another sense, as both the Bible and modern science make clear, we cannot divide ourselves into pieces. What is good for our bodies is good for our hearts and souls—and what is bad for our hearts and souls can also damage our bodies. If we are wise and discerning, we'll stop looking here and there for something to take away our misery—and instead take time to search ourselves for a spiritual root to our physical pain.

It's hard to be in a good mood when our bodies are in pain, and not every physical condition can be healed. Choosing to be cheerful rather than complaining, however, could be just the medicine God wants us to take!

PRAY: *God, You know how hard it is to be cheerful when every movement makes me hurt. This pain makes me cross and cranky. Give me the courage to accept Your will for my life, whatever it is. Make me wise enough to choose Your joy, even in the midst of my misery. Amen.*

Day 102
CALLED TO HOLINESS

──────── **READ 1 PETER 2** ────────

KEY VERSE: *People who do not believe are living all around you and might say that you are doing wrong. Live such good lives that they will see the good things you do and will give glory to God on the day when Christ comes again.* 1 PETER 2:12 NCV

UNDERSTAND:

• Why should believers do good deeds? What is the purpose?

....

....

....

....

....

....

• What are you doing that points others to Christ?

....

....

....

....

....

....

....

APPLY: A major way that Christians stand out in the world is by living good lives and doing good things. The choices you make regarding clothing, entertainment, and how you spend your money are noticed by those around you. People know that you are a Christian, and when you live a good life before them, you point them to Christ.

It's hard to argue with good results. When people see your children showing respect to others and making good choices, they will wonder what you are doing differently as a mother. When people notice that you support missions or give of your time to minister to others, they will wonder why.

One of the greatest ways to witness to those around you is by living a godly life before them. When others notice the difference in you, you can point them to Jesus. Our good deeds have one purpose—to bring glory to God.

PRAY: *God, help me to live in such a way that others are drawn to You. I want everything I do and say to reflect the fact that I am a child of the King. Please help me to set a good example and to live above reproach so that others might glorify You, my Father in heaven. Amen.*

Day 103

HONOR AND PRAISE
FOREVER AND EVER

────────── **READ PSALMS 145–146** ──────────

KEY VERSES: *I will honor You every day, and praise Your name forever and ever. The Lord is great and our praise to Him should be great. He is too great for anyone to understand. Families of this time will praise Your works to the families-to-come.* PSALM 145:2–4 NLV

UNDERSTAND:

• Is verse 4 of this passage a goal in your family? Do you strive to praise God and His awesome works and inspire the next generation of your family to do the same?

....

....

....

....

....

• Do you think your praise to God is great? How could it be even greater?

....

....

....

....

....

APPLY: Tonight, let these psalms of praise be as soothing as a bedtime bubble bath. Focus your thoughts on your heavenly Father, and sing and pray the words of Psalms 145–146 to Him. Thank Him for all His mighty acts and kindnesses and for the ways He is slow to anger. Feel His closeness because He is "near to all who call on Him, to all who call on Him in truth" (Psalm 145:18 NLV). Trust that He takes care of you and will destroy the sinful. Do not put your ultimate trust in people who will fail you at times; rather, remember that God alone will never fail you, and your hope in Him is sure. He is your Creator, Provider, Healer, Protector, Deliverer, and your faithful and loving King! If you fill your mind with this kind of truth over and over, there is no room for worry or fear. Let your mind relax in the truth of God's Word, and enjoy sweet rest.

PRAY: *Heavenly Father, You are so great that no one can fully understand it, but I want my praise to You to be great as well. I want my mind and my mouth to be full of constant praise to You and empty of worry and fear. Oh, how I love You, Lord! Amen.*

Day 104

YOU CANNOT LOSE
GOD'S LOVE

──────── **READ PSALM 136** ────────

KEY VERSE: *Give thanks to the God of heaven. His love endures forever.* PSALM 136:26 NIV

UNDERSTAND:

• How does the fact that you cannot lose God's love affect your relationship with Him?

....

....

....

....

• Are you ever guarded in what you say to Him? Why or why not?

....

....

....

....

....

• How is God's love better than any other love?

....

....

....

....

....

APPLY: Psalm 136 repeats the phrase "His love endures forever" twenty-six times. It's as if the writer knows how easily we forget God's faithfulness, so after each statement, he reminds us (and himself), "His love endures forever."

The fact remains, if we are children of the God of heaven, we cannot lose His love. We are His forever—chosen, bought at a price, accepted, forgiven, redeemed, and a full heir to His kingdom.

Yet still we mess up, and doubt creeps in. We're not good enough. Not worthy of being forgiven for the same sin. . .again.

His love endures forever.

We worry and fret; anxious thoughts overtake us as we stumble through life. Forgetting that we've been saved and are protected by a mighty God, we try to fight our battles ourselves, sometimes pushing Him away.

His love endures forever.

You cannot lose His love, friend. Rest in that promise, and thank Him for His steadfastness today.

PRAY: *Unending God, I see Your care for me everywhere. From the beauty of Your creation and the blessings You so generously lavish on me to the people You have placed in my life and the unique talents You have made in me, I feel Your love with every breath I take. Thank You for choosing me. Thank You for loving me always and forever. Amen.*

Day 105

REBUKE THE WAVES

──────── **READ MARK 4:35–41** ────────

KEY VERSE: *He got up and spoke sharp words to the wind. He said to the sea,* "*Be quiet! Be still.*" *At once the wind stopped blowing. There were no more waves.*
MARK 4:39 NLV

UNDERSTAND:

- Life presents unexpected storms sometimes. Think of one that caught you off guard. How did Jesus calm the storm?

....

....

....

....

....

....

- What role can you play as a storm calmer in the lives of others?

....

....

....

....

....

....

....

APPLY: Jesus wasn't bothered by the storm. In fact, He was sound asleep below deck. The disciples, however, were in a panic, convinced they were going down. To still their beating hearts, Jesus rose and spoke a few sharp words to the wind and waves: "Be quiet! Be still." Immediately, the storm ceased.

Likely, you've been through a few storms in your life. The death of a loved one. A tough illness. A bad diagnosis. A job loss. Relationship troubles. Storms have a variety of faces. But they often throw us into a state of panic, much like the disciples found themselves in that night.

We have to remember that Jesus is in the boat with us. No matter what we're walking through, He's right there. And with just a word, He can calm the storm. *"Anxieties, be still!"*

Job situations can turn around. Sick bodies can be mended. Broken relationships can be restored. Lives can be changed in an instant if we just take our hand off the rudder and turn things over to the Lord.

PRAY: *Lord, I'm so glad You're the storm calmer! You've intervened in my life so many times I've lost count. Thank You for staying with me in the boat. I'm so grateful, Lord. Amen.*

Day 106

MY HEART IS POUNDING WITH FEAR

──────── **READ 1 CHRONICLES 28:11–20** ────────

KEY VERSE: *"Be strong and courageous, and do the work. Don't be afraid or discouraged, for the Lord God, my God, is with you. He will not fail you or forsake you."* 1 Chronicles 28:20 nlt

UNDERSTAND:

- Notice the details that are included in this scripture passage regarding the exact specifications for the temple (verses 11–19). Do you think it's just coincidence that these verses were included directly before the key verse? Do you see any connection between such practical directions and the courage that David described in verse 20? Why or why not?

....

....

....

....

- How does fear interfere with your ability to do the work to which God has called you?

....

....

....

....

....

APPLY: Fear makes our hearts pound and our breath come fast. Our stomachs feel sick, and our hands turn cold. These reactions are intended to prepare our bodies to either fight danger or run away from it. In that sense, fear is healthy. It can be our friend.

Often, however, particularly in the modern world, neither fight nor flight is an option. When that's the case, fear is no friend. Instead, it can interfere with our ability to do the work God wants us to do. We may find ourselves confused, getting in even worse trouble as we run back and forth like a frantic rabbit. *If only God would give us precise directions*, we may think to ourselves, *like He gave His people when they were building the temple.*

But He has! His Word, the Bible, contains His directions written in His own hand. It can keep us on course, no matter how scared we are.

....

....

....

....

....

....

....

....

....

....

....

....

PRAY: *Give me the strength and courage I need, God, to be of use to You and Your kingdom. Don't let me be so fearful that I become too discouraged to keep going. Remind me that You are always with me. Amen.*

Day 107

ACCEPTING HELP

READ JAMES 2

KEY VERSES: *A brother or sister in Christ might need clothes or food. If you say to that person, "God be with you! I hope you stay warm and get plenty to eat," but you do not give what that person needs, your words are worth nothing.* JAMES 2:15–16 NCV

UNDERSTAND:

• What is the difference between faith with and without works?

....

....

....

....

....

....

....

• Why do you think James says that faith without works is dead?

....

....

....

....

....

....

....

APPLY: God loves you. All of you. Not just the spiritual parts. He cares about your physical needs as well. The body of Christ should always be about helping one another.

At times you will need help. You may feel tempted to say, "It's okay, thanks anyway, but I've got this." It may be hard for you to accept help. You may feel that you can do it all in your own strength. This may seem strong. It may feel brave. But, in actuality, what you are doing is denying others the opportunity to help you. This denies them a great blessing.

Remember how good it felt last time you extended a helping hand to someone in need? Be sure that you are also allowing God's people to bless you in your own time of need.

....

....

....

....

....

....

....

....

....

....

....

....

PRAY: *Lord, thank You for showing me that faith must involve works. I am saved by grace, but because of Your amazing grace, I am inspired to do good works so that others may come to know You. Help me also to be willing to accept help. In doing so, I allow others to live out their faith as well. In Jesus' name I pray. Amen.*

Day 108
POWERFUL PEP TALK

───── **READ JOSHUA 1** ─────

KEY VERSES: *"Study this Book of Instruction continually. Meditate on it day and night so you will be sure to obey everything written in it. Only then will you prosper and succeed in all you do. This is my command—be strong and courageous! Do not be afraid or discouraged. For the LORD your God is with you wherever you go."* JOSHUA 1:8–9 NLT

UNDERSTAND:

• How is God specifically calling you to be strong and courageous right now?

....

....

....

....

• Are you thriving at meditating on God's Word day and night, or do you need to improve on this?

....

....

....

....

• So far in your life, how has God given you success for your obedience to Him?

....

....

....

....

APPLY: God had called Joshua to be the one who would lead His people into the Promised Land after wandering in the desert for forty years under Moses' leadership. And in Joshua 1, you can read the powerful pep talk God gave to Joshua to help him be the brave new leader. It's not just for Joshua though. This scripture is a powerful pep talk from God to you as well, in whatever situation you find yourself. You have the whole Bible, the complete Word of God, including accounts of the life, teachings, death, and resurrection of Jesus Christ, plus the many books that came after the Gospels to study, memorize, and meditate on. And you have the gift of the Holy Spirit living in you to instruct and guide you as well. So, just as God did for Joshua, let God lead you in the wonderful purposes He has for your life as you follow His Word with strength and confident courage.

....

....

....

....

....

....

....

....

....

....

....

....

PRAY: *Heavenly Father, thank You for guiding me through Your Word. Please help me to focus on it day and night and live a life of obedience to it. I believe that only then will I truly prosper and succeed. Thank You for being with me wherever I go. Amen.*

Day 109
HE PICKS YOU UP

─────────── **READ PSALM 40** ───────────

KEY VERSE: *He lifted me out of the pit of despair, out of the mud and the mire. He set my feet on solid ground and steadied me as I walked along.* PSALM 40:2 NLT

UNDERSTAND:

• How has God lifted you up in the past?

....

....

....

....

....

....

....

• Has God ever used another person to pick you up, set you on solid ground, and steady you as you walked along? How did you realize God was using that person?

....

....

....

....

....

....

....

....

APPLY: Nobody—not even the most self-sufficient among us—can go through life alone. We each have our own struggles, temptations, pitfalls, and burdens that weigh us down and threaten to pull us into what Psalm 40:2 calls a "pit of despair."

Because our Savior, Jesus Christ, stepped out of heaven and lived on earth, He experienced all these same issues. And He is faithful to lift us up out of any muddy pit of sin and shame we may find ourselves in.

There are any number of ways He rescues us. From the encouragement and intervention of a friend or a new sense of hope given to us by the Holy Spirit to a new perspective on a problem or a new purpose and peace that passes understanding —in a matter of a moment, the Father God can set you on solid ground.

If you're in a pit—no matter how deep it is—cry out to God. No hole is your ultimate destination. He will hear you and is faithful to answer. Soon you'll find yourself safely in His arms.

PRAY: *God, thank You for rescuing me. For pulling me out, cleaning me up, and giving me the confidence to walk ahead. Stay with me, and keep me from stumbling or jumping headfirst into another pit of my own making. Amen.*

Day 110

BLESSED ARE THOSE
WHO HAVE NOT SEEN

──────── **READ JOHN 20:19-29** ────────

KEY VERSE: *Jesus said to him, "Have you believed because you have seen me? Blessed are those who have not seen and yet have believed."* JOHN 20:29 ESV

UNDERSTAND:

• Are you one of those "I won't believe it until I see it" types?

....

....

....

....

....

....

....

• Why do you suppose Jesus said that those who have not seen are
  more blessed?

....

....

....

....

....

....

....

APPLY: Near the end of the Gospels, we find a remarkable story about one of the disciples—Thomas. The world knows him as "Doubting Thomas," but Jesus might disagree with that assessment.

Here's the backstory: Jesus had died on the cross just a few days prior. Thomas saw it with his own eyes. He knew that his friend, his mentor, his teacher was gone. There was no disputing that cold, hard fact.

Now the other disciples were talking crazy, saying stuff like "We've seen Him!" Had they lost their minds? Thomas, always the pragmatist, wanted proof. "Unless I see in his hands the mark of the nails, and place my finger into the mark of the nails, and place my hand into his side, I will never believe" (verse 25 ESV).

The Lord made him wait for the proof. Eight days later, Jesus showed up, laying to rest any concerns that Thomas might have had. In an instant, as he touched the wounds in Jesus' hands and side, all doubts disappeared. The doubter became a believer.

PRAY: *Lord, help me in my unbelief. There are so many times I want proof. I want to see things with my own eyes. I know that I will be more blessed if I can learn to trust You, even when I can't see. Help me, I pray. Amen.*

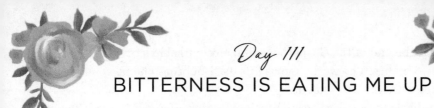

Day 111

BITTERNESS IS EATING ME UP

───── **READ HEBREWS 12:14–25** ─────

KEY VERSE: *See to it that no one falls short of the grace of God and that no bitter root grows up to cause trouble and defile many.* HEBREWS 12:15 NIV

UNDERSTAND:

• What in your life today is leaving a bitter taste in your mouth?

....

....

....

....

....

....

• Notice that verse 17 indicates that sometimes, even though our hearts change, we cannot avoid the consequences of our earlier bitterness. Have you ever experienced this?

....

....

....

....

....

....

....

....

APPLY: Bitterness may start out as anger, hurt, disappointment, frustration, or resentment. It takes root when we refuse to let go of these other emotions, holding them tight until they turn into something cold, hard, and habitual.

No matter how bitterness starts out, this scripture tells us that it can end up causing all sorts of trouble. It can spread from us to others, weakening the body of Christ. It can lead to other forms of brokenness. Worst of all, it will come between our hearts and God's.

"You have no reason to be bitter," God says to us in these verses. *"You're no longer living in the Old Testament world, where I was so often perceived as angry and terrifying. Instead, I've invited you to be a part of the angels' joyful gathering. I've erased the bitter blood Cain spilled when he murdered his brother—and I've sprinkled you with the love of My own Son."*

....

....

....

....

....

....

....

....

....

....

....

....

PRAY: *God of love, I ask that You show me how to pull out any roots of bitterness in my heart. Help me to hear Your voice more clearly so that I can live in Your joy. Amen.*

Day 112

WELCOME THE STRANGER

READ HEBREWS 13

KEY VERSE: *Remember to welcome strangers, because some who have done this have welcomed angels without knowing it.* HEBREWS 13:2 NCV

UNDERSTAND:

• How do you welcome the stranger? What does this look like in your life?

....

....

....

....

....

....

....

• How might someone act differently if they were aware that a stranger was indeed an angel?

....

....

....

....

....

....

....

APPLY: In this day of "stranger danger," it seems unusual to read that we should welcome strangers.

Let's examine what this might look like in your life.

Do you host a community group in the house God has given you? Do you offer missionaries or others in need a room in your home for a short-term or even long-term stay? Do you speak to people when you are in the marketplace and offer a smile? Do you give up the close parking space or the last ice-cold soda so that someone else may enjoy it? Any or all of these could be classified as welcoming the stranger.

You never know when you might be welcoming an angel instead of a mere man. Abraham and Lot are just two men of the Bible who welcomed angels unawares. God rewards those who perform simple acts of kindness. Our heavenly Father says that when we serve even the lowliest among us, we are serving Him (see Matthew 25:40).

PRAY: *Father, may I use my gifts and resources to help others. Make me aware of opportunities to welcome the stranger in my own way. Use me, I pray, in Jesus' precious name. Amen.*

BUILT ON AND ROOTED IN JESUS

—————— **READ MATTHEW 7:24–27; LUKE 6:47–49;** ——————
JEREMIAH 17:7–8; COLOSSIANS 2:6–10

KEY VERSES: *Just as you accepted Christ Jesus as your Lord, you must continue to follow him. Let your roots grow down into him, and let your lives be built on him. Then your faith will grow strong in the truth you were taught, and you will overflow with thankfulness.* COLOSSIANS 2:6–7 NLT

UNDERSTAND:

• How do these four different scripture passages relate?

....

....

....

....

....

....

• In what active ways do you continue to strengthen your foundation and grow your roots deeper into Christ?

....

....

....

....

....

....

APPLY: If we're in the middle of a storm but have a solid structure in which to take refuge, we still have a strong sense of peace. But if we're caught in a tent in the middle of an open field when tornadoes pop up or we're in a shack on the sandy beach of a raging sea, anxiety prevails. And we sure don't build a trustworthy treehouse in a tree without strong roots. So, if it seems anxiety is prevailing too much in our lives, maybe we need to reevaluate and reinspect our shelters and foundations. Have we built on something solid that will last or on things that are weak and temporary? Are there any damages or cracks? Are we continuing to check and repair and strengthen our foundations if needed? Are we nourishing and growing strong roots? Everything of this world is shaky and fleeting, and only what is built strong on and rooted deeply in Jesus Christ and the truth of His Word will endure.

PRAY: *Loving Savior, please help me to constantly keep fortifying my foundation on You and growing my roots deeper into You. Show me the cracks and weaknesses, and help me repair and strengthen them. Please keep my faith strong and unwavering, no matter the storms of life. Amen.*

Day 114

CHALLENGE YOURSELF

READ PHILIPPIANS 3:7–21

KEY VERSES: *I do not say that I have received this or have already become perfect. But I keep going on to make that life my own as Christ Jesus made me His own. . . . My eyes are on the crown. I want to win the race and get the crown of God's call from heaven through Christ Jesus.* PHILIPPIANS 3:12, 14 NLV

UNDERSTAND:

• What are you willing to sacrifice in order to become more like Jesus Christ?

....

....

....

....

....

....

• How can you push yourself in your faith to complete the race where the finish line is heaven?

....

....

....

....

....

....

....

....

APPLY: If anyone should've been satisfied with the state of his faith, it was the apostle Paul. This giant of the early Church experienced a miraculous conversion (see Acts 9), after which he became a world missionary. He wrote nearly half of the New Testament and endured persecution and prosecution for the sake of sharing Jesus Christ. And yet, he knew he still had more growth to do, pressing himself closer to Jesus.

When you accepted Jesus into your life, it wasn't the end of the journey. Whether we've been a Christian for decades or are new to faith, each of us has space to advance toward our ultimate goal of eternal life with the Father, Son, and Holy Spirit in heaven.

What are you doing today to run the race? Sprinting, jogging, or walking, we're each at our own pace. Keep going and do not give up!

PRAY: *God, I am ready for this challenge. This is a race that fills me with joy, and I want to run with excellence. Pick me up when I stumble, and set me on solid footing so I will run again. Amen.*

Day 115

LEAD ME TO THE ROCK

———————————— **READ PSALM 61** ————————————

KEY VERSE: *From the end of the earth I call to you when my heart is faint. Lead me to the rock that is higher than I.* PSALM 61:2 ESV

UNDERSTAND:

- When we are at our weakest, God proves His strength. Think of a time when He did this for you.

....

....

....

....

....

....

- Sometimes we run toward God. Other times we crawl, barely able to gather the strength. Think of a time when you barely made it to the Rock.

....

....

....

....

....

....

....

APPLY: The Bible often refers to Jesus as the Rock. Maybe you've read the story of the wise man who built his house upon the rock. When you build your life—your family, your business, your hopes, your dreams, your hobbies—on Jesus, you will succeed.

Maybe you've been in shifting-sand mode of late. Maybe your business is crumbling or your marriage is in trouble. Maybe you've wandered out from under God's covering, seeking other pleasures. It's not too late to turn around and head back to the Rock. Jesus is right there, waiting.

If your heart is faint today, if you're tired of doing things your way, then run to Jesus. His ways are higher. His thoughts are higher. His plan to redeem you is higher. And remember, when you are at your very weakest, God longs to show you His strength.

So, what's holding you back? Run to the Rock.

PRAY: *Lord, there have been so many times when I've felt weak, unable to keep going. If not for You, my Rock, I would surely have given up by now. Thank You for holding steady, even when everything else in my life feels like shifting sand. I'm so grateful, Lord. Amen.*

Day 116
I'M OVERWHELMED BY MY RESPONSIBILITIES

—— READ 2 CORINTHIANS 1:8–10 ——

KEY VERSES: *We were crushed and overwhelmed beyond our ability to endure, and we thought we would never live through it.... But as a result, we stopped relying on ourselves and learned to rely only on God.* 2 CORINTHIANS 1:8–9 NLT

UNDERSTAND:

- Even the apostle Paul, the great hero of our faith, went through times when he felt life was asking more of him than he could handle.

....

....

....

....

....

- As Paul pointed out, if God can raise the dead to life, He can certainly also handle the demands of our daily lives!

....

....

....

....

....

....

APPLY: Although we may never be called to endure all that the apostle Paul did in his service to God, we all have times when our lives overwhelm us. Our to-do lists just keep getting longer; no matter how hard we try, we can't seem to catch up. We may not think we're going to actually die from the pressure, as Paul did, but we do feel frustrated and hopeless and discouraged. We may blame others for putting these demands on us—or we may blame ourselves for not being able to accomplish more.

But Paul said there's a solution to this problem: stop trying to do so much in our own strength! Day by day, put it all in God's hands. He will accomplish through us what He needs us to do—and whatever remains undone, we can trust Him to handle.

_____

_____

_____

_____

_____

_____

_____

_____

_____

_____

_____

_____

PRAY: *God, You know how busy I am. I'm exhausted from the effort of trying to keep up with everything. I don't know how much longer I can go on like this, so I'm giving it all to You. Accomplish through me whatever needs doing—and I'll leave whatever's still undone in Your hands. Amen.*

Day 117

TEMPTATION

--- **READ GENESIS 3** ---

KEY VERSE: *Now the serpent was more crafty than any of the wild animals the LORD God had made. He said to the woman, "Did God really say, 'You must not eat from any tree in the garden'?"* GENESIS 3:1 NIV

UNDERSTAND:

• Have you ever tried to rationalize a sin that you know you are committing against God?

....

....

....

....

....

....

....

• What will you do the next time Satan tempts you to disobey God?

....

....

....

....

....

....

....

....

APPLY: Satan appears as a serpent in Genesis 3. He tempts the first people, as he tempts believers today, in a sneaky manner.

Adam and Eve had heard God clearly. He had given them free rein in the garden. They could eat of any tree *except* one. He had not restricted them in a harsh way. They had great freedom. They were given one rule, one tree to avoid, one guideline to obey.

Satan was crafty in his approach, wasn't he? He uses this technique with believers today as well. Use caution if you begin to think to yourself: *Does God really have such a guideline for my life? Would He really limit me in this way? Is this really a sin? Is it really so bad?*

God's standards and His rules are for our good. He has drawn boundary lines for us in pleasant places (see Psalm 16:6 NIV). Don't let Satan tempt you to believe otherwise.

PRAY: *God, I am sorry for rationalizing sin. I try to find a way to make sin okay, but sin is never to be swept under the rug. Help me to walk in Your ways and to recognize sin as sin. Please give me strength to withstand temptation. In Jesus' name I pray. Amen.*

Day 118

THE SPIRIT LEADS TO LIFE AND PEACE

———— **READ ROMANS 8:1–17** ————

KEY VERSES: *Those who are dominated by the sinful nature think about sinful things, but those who are controlled by the Holy Spirit think about things that please the Spirit. So letting your sinful nature control your mind leads to death. But letting the Spirit control your mind leads to life and peace.* ROMANS 8:5–6 NLT

UNDERSTAND:

• The only way to know true and lasting peace is to admit your sin nature, accept Jesus Christ as the one and only Savior from sin, and invite the Holy Spirit into your life. Have you done that? Do you have the Spirit of God living in you?

....

....

• When did you accept Jesus Christ as your Savior? What change and growth are evident in your life after doing so?

....

....

....

• What are the active, ongoing ways the Holy Spirit is controlling your mind?

....

....

....

....

APPLY: At the end of good days, maybe you settle down for the night with a satisfied sigh and a heart that feels warm and full and grateful for many blessings. But at the end of bad days, maybe you wearily crawl into your bed with a heavy, aching heart, wishing for a do-over and a different reality, wishing all the sin in the world and especially your own sin were not so real and inescapable. How precious, then, are the words of Romans 8:1–2 (NLT) at the end of those terrible days! "There is no condemnation for those who belong to Christ Jesus. And because you belong to him, the power of the life-giving Spirit has freed you from the power of sin that leads to death." No matter what effects of sin you might be feeling this night, it has no power over you if you have the Spirit of God living in you. Cry out to God in lament. Cry out to God in grief. Cry out to God in confession and repentance. Cry out to God in any or all of the above. Allow Him to show you that "letting the Spirit control your mind leads to life and peace."

PRAY: *Heavenly Father, I praise You for Your Son, Jesus Christ, whom You sent to free me from the law of sin and death. Thank You for such an incredible gift! I trust in Jesus as my Savior, and I give my life and mind to be controlled by Your Holy Spirit. Please lead me in life and peace. Amen.*

Day 119

CHOOSE EXTRAORDINARY

—— READ ROMANS 12 ——

KEY VERSE: *Do not conform to the pattern of this world, but be transformed by the renewing of your mind.* ROMANS 12:2 NIV

UNDERSTAND:

• What is one thing or who is one person you would describe as "extraordinary"? What makes this thing or person extraordinary?

....

....

....

....

....

....

• God created you for an extraordinary purpose. Think of one passion He has put in your heart. How can He use that today for great things?

....

....

....

....

....

....

....

....

APPLY: Wake up; be awesome. Oh, if only it were that easy! But the messages the world shouts keep us feeling inadequate. We're not good enough, beautiful enough, smart enough, thin enough, or rich enough. Soon these messages take root in our hearts, and we're telling ourselves these same lies. Satan knows the ins and outs of that game.

But those lies don't have to be the words you focus on today. This morning, choose to make this day extraordinary by living out God's plan for your life. Romans 12 gives guidance on how to do just that. Refuse to listen to the world's lies, and instead focus on the renewal that God promises. Focus on the talents God has given you, and use them today—for His glory. Intentionally show God's love to those around you today.

Your loving heavenly Father created you for more than a mediocre existence. Choose this day and every day to live an extraordinary life in Christ.

PRAY: *Father, I admit most days I feel more ordinary than extraordinary. But You call me to greatness, not because of what I can achieve but because of Your holiness and Your unending love for me. Each day I aspire to be more like You more extraordinary than the day before. Amen.*

Day 120

HE ALWAYS KNEW YOU

———— READ JEREMIAH 1 ————

KEY VERSE: *"Before I formed you in the womb I knew you, before you were born I set you apart; I appointed you as a prophet to the nations."* JEREMIAH 1:5 NIV

UNDERSTAND:

- If God knew you before you were born, He must have carefully selected the location and year of your birth as well. What if you had been born a hundred years sooner?

....

....

....

....

....

....

- God set you apart to do great things. What does that mean to you? What great things do you hope to accomplish?

....

....

....

....

....

....

APPLY: As you ponder the story of Jeremiah, as you think about how God called him into ministry, think of your own life. Consider the notion that the Creator of the universe knew you before you were born. He was there all along, carefully choosing your parents, your place of birth, even the year you would enter the world.

When you take the time to truly analyze these things, it's easy to see how special you are to God. He cared enough about you, even before birth, to plot out your entrance to the planet. He could have chosen any time, any place, but He knew just when to drop you onto the scene so that you could have the greatest impact for the kingdom of God. Wow!

God is at work, even now. Can you feel the anticipation stirring in your heart? He's got amazing things for you. Sure, there will still be a few bumps and bruises along the way. The road ahead will be filled with twists and turns, but He will guide you (and use you) every step of the way. So, lay down those anxieties and take His hand. He's got this!

PRAY: *Father, thank You for arranging the details of my life. It amazes me to think that You chose my parents, my lineage, my hair color, my personality, and so on. I'm also tickled to think that You chose for me to be born in the very year I was born, and in the very location I was born. Wow, Lord! You've covered it all. Amen.*

Day 121
I FEEL TRAPPED BY
MY SITUATION

———————— **READ PSALM 124** ————————

KEY VERSE: *We escaped like a bird from a hunter's trap. The trap is broken, and we are free!* PSALM 124:7 NLT

UNDERSTAND:

- Feeling trapped is not caused by the modern world's demands; thousands of years ago, the psalmist experienced this same claustrophobic, desperate feeling—which means the answers he found can also apply to us today.

- What circumstances in your life today feel like a trap?

APPLY: Traps come in all shapes and sizes. Our jobs may have become traps, places that eat up our time and energy while giving nothing back to our hearts and minds. An unhealthy relationship may be another sort of trap, one where, in the words of the New Living Translation, we feel as though people want to "[swallow] us alive" (verse 3). A self-destructive habit is still another sort of trap, and illness, depression, and lack of self-confidence are a few others.

Whatever trap has snared you, God can help you to escape. He will not let you be consumed or drowned by your circumstances. He is on your side—and since He is the one who made heaven and earth, He has all the power needed to set you free.

PRAY: *God, I don't see a way out of this situation—but I know You can do the impossible. You made the entire world, so I know You are strong enough to create new circumstances in my life. Amen.*

A TIME FOR EVERYTHING

—— READ ECCLESIASTES 3 ——

KEY VERSE: *To everything there is a season, a time for every purpose under heaven.* ECCLESIASTES 3:1 NKJV

UNDERSTAND:

• Which of the verses in Ecclesiastes 3 have you experienced (e.g., a time to mourn)? Are there any that you have not yet experienced?

....

....

....

....

....

....

• What does it mean that God is sovereign? How is His sovereignty seen in this chapter?

....

....

....

....

....

....

....

APPLY: Have you experienced some of the times mentioned in Ecclesiastes 3?

When a child dies, there is a time to mourn. There is also a time to be silent—simply out of an understanding that there are no words for such a loss. That is the time to be there for the family but not the time to try to fix it with words. The less spoken, the better.

There is a time to rejoice. Have you rejoiced at baptisms, weddings, and other special events? Certainly, these call for celebration.

There are times to weep and times to laugh. Thank God that sorrow comes in waves. Just as the mighty ocean tosses us a strong breaker and we lose our balance, there comes a period of calm when we maintain our footing once again.

Accept the sovereignty of God. Accept the changes that life will throw your way. There is a time for everything.

PRAY: *Heavenly Father, help me to know how to react to change in my life. Guide me as I seek to find the balance between laughter and sorrow, rejoicing and mourning. Life is an adventure. Thank You for being with me in every time and in every season. Amen.*

Day 123

EXPERIENCE GOD'S PEACE

──────── **READ PHILIPPIANS 4** ────────

KEY VERSES: *Don't worry about anything; instead, pray about everything. Tell God what you need, and thank him for all he has done. Then you will experience God's peace, which exceeds anything we can understand. His peace will guard your hearts and minds as you live in Christ Jesus.* PHILIPPIANS 4:6–7 NLT

UNDERSTAND:

• Do you have any disagreements with other women, like Euodia and Syntyche did, in your life right now that you need to resolve and reconcile?

....

....

....

....

....

....

• Do you do well in thinking about things that are true, honorable, right, pure, lovely, admirable, excellent, and worthy of praise? How can you be constantly growing and improving in this (verse 8)?

....

....

....

....

....

....

....

APPLY: God's Word promises that if we pray rather than worry about everything, telling God what we need and thanking Him for what He has done, we will experience God's peace beyond all our understanding. It doesn't say God will instantly fix our problems or immediately give us whatever we ask for, but it promises inexplicable peace, the kind only God can give. Talking to God in prayer with gratitude demonstrates our trust in Him and love for Him. It reminds us of all He has done and is able to do. It fills us with confidence that He has sovereign power over all things, including every detail of our lives. We draw closer in relationship with our Father the more we talk to Him in prayer. The closer we are to the Father, the more we realize we need less of anything else and simply more of focusing on Him, who He is, and all He is able to do, to be in perfect peace.

PRAY: *Heavenly Father, remind me that every problem pales when I focus on You. I thank You for all You have done, and I trust You to provide all that I truly need. Please fill me with Your extraordinary peace. Amen.*

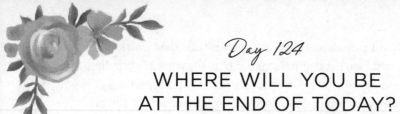

WHERE WILL YOU BE
AT THE END OF TODAY?

───── **READ PHILIPPIANS 3:7–21** ─────

KEY VERSES: *I focus on this one thing: Forgetting the past and looking forward to what lies ahead, I press on to reach the end of the race and receive the heavenly prize for which God, through Christ Jesus, is calling us.* PHILIPPIANS 3:13–14 NLT

UNDERSTAND:

• What can you realistically accomplish today?

....

....

....

....

• What goals are worthwhile to pursue today? Are there others that aren't worth the time?

....

....

....

....

• What do you need to forget to allow you to move forward to the future?

....

....

....

....

APPLY: What's the state of your to-do list? Whether it's a mile long or blessedly under control, life is busy. Stay up late or get up early, we each have only twenty-four hours a day to get everything done.

There are tasks and responsibilities we must attend to, but the apostle Paul, writing to the Philippian church, challenges us to focus on the bigger picture—to make it our priority to know Jesus and experience the mighty power that raised Him from the dead.

How can you come closer to that goal today? You're starting out the day right by spending time in His Word and in prayer. Lean on Him throughout the day, and ask Him to guide your steps, your thoughts, your words, and your actions. Commit to seeking Him every morning, taking a step (or a leap) closer to the glory of your Brother, Jesus.

PRAY: *Jesus, I'm forgetting about my past when I struggled to know my true goals from day to day. Now I'm running toward You. Give me the wisdom to continue in that race while I pursue daily responsibilities. I know when I am doing both, my life can and will glorify You! Amen.*

Day 125

LET PEACE REIGN!

READ MATTHEW 26:17–30

KEY VERSES: *While they were eating, Jesus took bread, and when he had given thanks, he broke it and gave it to his disciples, saying, "Take and eat; this is my body." Then he took a cup, and when he had given thanks, he gave it to them, saying, "Drink from it, all of you. This is my blood of the covenant, which is poured out for many for the forgiveness of sins."* MATTHEW 26:26–28 NIV

UNDERSTAND:

• The disciples didn't have a full understanding of what was coming, but they chose to spend as much time with Jesus as possible. Have you done that in your own life?

_____

_____

_____

_____

_____

• What does the word *communion* mean to you?

_____

_____

_____

_____

_____

_____

APPLY: Have you ever given thought to what must have been going through the hearts and minds of the disciples on the night they broke bread with Jesus? Did they realize that He only had a few more hours with them? Did they understand that He would actually pass away and then rise again?

Surely the disciples had the same attitude that we so often have today—they were hoping for the best but psychologically preparing for the worst. (How many times have you done that?)

Sometimes we have an inkling that something rough is coming; other times we're caught off guard, completely unaware of what's around the bend. We do a lot of things to guard our hearts, to avoid anxiety. But God wants us to know that, even in the darkest valleys, He's still in control. He's still right there, whispering, *"Peace, be still."* So go on. . .drink from the cup. Break the bread. Commune with Him. For only in spending time with Him will true peace be found.

PRAY: *Father, when I take the time to commune with You, to really spend time in Your presence, it makes such a difference in my attitude. Today I choose the peace that comes from being with You, Lord. Amen.*

Day 126

I NEED HUMILITY

READ JAMES 4:6–10

KEY VERSE: *"GOD IS OPPOSED TO THE PROUD, BUT GIVES GRACE TO THE HUMBLE."* JAMES 4:6 NASB

UNDERSTAND:

- What does the word *grace* convey to you?

....

....

....

....

- How do you think pride might act as a wall between you and God?

....

....

....

....

- Notice the effect of pride in your life. What feels good about pride? What aspects of pride have turned hurtful for you?

....

....

....

....

APPLY: There's a healthy kind of pride, a sense of God-given dignity that is the birthright of each of us—but that's not the sort of pride that this scripture is talking about. The word translated as "proud" was a Greek word that meant, literally, to think of oneself as better than others. *Humble,* on the other hand, meant someone willing to take a lower position. HELPS Word-Studies defines scriptural humility as "being God-reliant rather than self-reliant." When we rely on God rather than ourselves, we have humility.

   Selfish, egotistical pride can form a hard shell around our hearts. Sometimes it takes the tears of genuine sorrow to wash it away. Then when we finally come into God's presence, naked, low, with no more pretense, He will lift us up.

PRAY: *God, my proud heart needs Your grace. Wash me with humble tears. I want to come closer to You. Amen.*

Day 127
A CHEERFUL GIVER

── READ 2 CORINTHIANS 9 ──

KEY VERSE: *So let each one give as he purposes in his heart, not grudgingly or of necessity; for God loves a cheerful giver.* 2 CORINTHIANS 9:7 NKJV

UNDERSTAND:

• When you give, do you do so cheerfully or begrudgingly?

_____

_____

_____

_____

_____

_____

• Where do you think your attitude toward giving originated? Does it need any modification or fine-tuning after reading this passage?

_____

_____

_____

_____

_____

_____

_____

APPLY: Have you read the picture book called *The Giving Tree* by Shel Silverstein? It's about a tree that gives and gives to a young boy. As the boy grows, his needs change. The tree willingly gives shade and its branches to the boy. The boy grows old, and the tree has become just a stump, having given tirelessly and completely. The tree meets his final need by providing a place for the old man to sit and rest awhile.

As the reader, it's tempting to grow angry with the boy. But in the end, we see that the tree was happy to give to the boy all his life. It found joy in giving.

Are you like the boy or the tree? Are you a taker? Or are you a giver? When you give, do you give with a joyful attitude? Or do you give so that you might be noticed or praised for your act?

....

....

....

....

....

....

....

....

....

....

....

PRAY: *Heavenly Father, I ask that You reveal to me any change that needs to take place in my heart regarding giving. Whether it is my time, my talents, or my money, I pray that I will give with an open heart and open hands. Make me a cheerful giver, I ask in Jesus' name. Amen.*

GOD FAITHFULLY FORGIVES

──── READ 1 JOHN 1:1–2:14 ────

KEY VERSES: *If we say that we have no sin, we lie to ourselves and the truth is not in us. If we tell Him our sins, He is faithful and we can depend on Him to forgive us of our sins. He will make our lives clean from all sin.* 1 JOHN 1:8–9 NLV

UNDERSTAND:

• How does it feel to hold on to and try to hide sin rather than humbly admit it to God and ask forgiveness and help?

....

....

....

....

....

....

• What does it mean to walk in darkness rather than in light?

....

....

....

....

....

....

....

....

APPLY: It's not fun to humbly admit the sinful things we've done, but we need to tell them to God. To pretend like we don't sin sometimes is ridiculous, because God knows anyway. He sees and knows everything about us, even every single thought we have. So we must take time to confess and ask forgiveness for our sins rather than hide them or act like they're no big deal. Psalm 103:11–12 (NLV) says, "His loving-kindness for those who fear Him is as great as the heavens are high above the earth. He has taken our sins from us as far as the east is from the west." That should fill us with such gratitude and peace. Our heavenly Father loves us so much and never wants to hold our sins against us.

PRAY: *Heavenly Father, I confess_____ to You today, and I ask for Your forgiveness. Thank You for being such a forgiving and good God who gives me endless grace and love! Amen.*

TAKE DELIGHT IN THE LORD

---- **READ PSALM 37:1–9** ----

KEY VERSE: *Take delight in the Lord, and he will give you the desires of your heart.*
PSALM 37:4 NIV

UNDERSTAND:

• What does taking delight in the Lord mean to you?

....

....

....

....

• In what ways do you imagine the Lord delights in you?

....

....

....

....

• Is Psalm 37:4 saying that God will give us *anything* we ask for? Why or why not?

....

....

....

....

....

APPLY: Children are experts in delight. Watch a one-year-old gleefully play with the box her birthday present came wrapped in, and you are witnessing true joy. We can learn much from her today.

Our outlook determines how we interact with the world around us. When we're thankful for and take joy in simple pleasures, disappointments and frustrations become minor bumps in the day rather than catastrophes that derail us. When we count our blessings instead of focusing on what we don't have, we realize how well God provides for us. When we delight in the Lord and praise Him for His goodness and His perfect plan for us, we live safely in the center of His will—the very best place to be.

How is God delighting you today? Spend time this morning looking for ways to be joyful. Whether He's doing big things in your life right now or you simply reflect on His unending faithfulness, live each day as an expert in delight.

....

....

....

....

....

....

....

....

....

....

....

PRAY: *Lord, You fill me with such joy. Today my heart is singing as I delight in You. You are a good, good Father who gives me care, compassion, and kindness every day. Because of You, I have everything I need. Let my heart draw close to Yours, Father. I praise You because of who You are. Amen.*

Day 130
ALIVE!

--- **READ MARK 16** ---

KEY VERSES: *As they entered the tomb, they saw a young man dressed in a white robe sitting on the right side, and they were alarmed. "Don't be alarmed," he said. "You are looking for Jesus the Nazarene, who was crucified. He has risen! He is not here. See the place where they laid him."* MARK 16:5–6 NIV

UNDERSTAND:

- The resurrection of Jesus is one of history's most compelling events. What does it mean to you?

....

....

....

....

....

- Why would the resurrection of Jesus cause alarm?

....

....

....

....

....

....

....

APPLY: If you've ever attended a funeral or visited a grave site, the last thing you expect is for the body to go missing. But that's what happened in this, the most famous death scene ever written. Jesus died on the cross and was buried in the tomb, but on the third day, He sprang back to life.

The entire Gospel story hinges on this one event: the resurrection. If Jesus hadn't risen from the grave, if His death on the cross had ended the story, would we still be celebrating Him today? The resurrection seals the deal! It shows us, His followers, that death has no hold on us. We're meant to live forever with Him. It's also proof positive that Jesus was who He said He was, the Savior of mankind. For only a Savior would rise again with power and authority. And that same authority has been given to us, His kids.

What graveclothes are holding you back today? Speak with authority over your situation, and watch as resurrection power springs you from death to life.

PRAY: *Thank You for the resurrection, Lord! You are exactly who You claimed to be—Messiah and King. Thank You for the authority You've given me. I want to live with resurrection power, no matter what I'm going through. Death has no victory over me. Amen!*

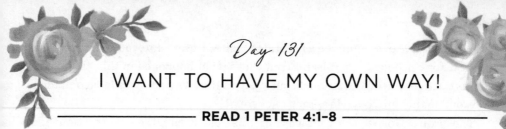

Day 131

I WANT TO HAVE MY OWN WAY!

READ 1 PETER 4:1-8

KEY VERSE: *Since Jesus went through everything you're going through and more, learn to think like him. Think of your sufferings as a weaning from that old sinful habit of always expecting to get your own way.* 1 PETER 4:1 MSG

UNDERSTAND:

• In what areas of your life is it hardest for you to give up your own way?

....

....

....

....

....

• When you don't get your way, does it cause you pain? How might this pain be put to spiritual use, allowing you to become more like Jesus?

....

....

....

....

....

....

....

APPLY: From the time we were babies, we've been crying and frustrated every time we couldn't get our own way. As we've grown older, we may have learned to disguise this better. We may have figured out other ways aside from yelling and having a tantrum to get what we want, but we still really want what we want!

Even Jesus struggled with this. That's why He prayed in the garden, sweating drops of blood as He begged His Father to find another path for Him to take, one that didn't lead to the cross. And yet, regardless of His natural longing to escape suffering and death, again and again He placed the entire situation back in His Father's hands. *"Not My will,"* He said, *"but only Yours."*

Do we have the courage to follow His example?

_____

_____

_____

_____

_____

_____

_____

_____

_____

_____

_____

_____

_____

PRAY: *Free me, Jesus, from the tyranny of my selfishness. Wean me from the babyish habit of wanting my own way. Keep me wide awake and alert to the Spirit, as You were when You prayed in the garden. Amen.*

Day 132

TRUE REPENTANCE

READ JOEL 2

KEY VERSE: *Rend your heart and not your garments. Return to the L*ORD *your God, for he is gracious and compassionate, slow to anger and abounding in love, and he relents from sending calamity.* JOEL 2:13 NIV

UNDERSTAND:

• Have you ever truly felt brokenhearted over your own sin?

....

....

....

....

....

....

• In Joel 2:13, what adjectives are used to describe God's reaction to one who returns to Him? In other words, to one who repents of sin.

....

....

....

....

....

....

APPLY: How easy it is for us to stand in judgment of the Israelites as we read the stories of how quickly they forgot God's blessings. But we do the same, do we not?

When you sin, God is watching your reaction to that sin. He knows you will fall. We are living in a fallen world. But do you try to hide your sin? Do you diminish it, thinking to yourself, *Well, compared to this other person, I am not much of a sinner at all?*

Sin should break our hearts. God desires to see more than an outward expression of this brokenness. At the time of Joel, the people tore their clothing to express sorrow over sin. True repentance involves an inner sorrow, a tearing of the heart. God is quick to forgive when we come before Him broken and sorry for our sin.

PRAY: *God, examine my heart. Show me if there is any attitude about my sin that displeases You. If I am quick to dismiss it as "not so bad," humble me. Remind me that You are holy and that sin is sin. Break my heart over my sin that I might truly repent and know Your gracious compassion in my life. Amen.*

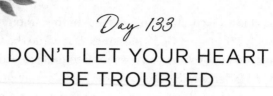

Day 133

DON'T LET YOUR HEART
BE TROUBLED

— READ JOHN 14:1–27 —

KEY VERSE: *"I am leaving you with a gift—peace of mind and heart. And the peace I give is a gift the world cannot give. So don't be troubled or afraid."* JOHN 14:27 NLT

UNDERSTAND:

• How does the promise of Jesus preparing a place for you in heaven help keep your heart from being troubled here on earth?

....

....

....

....

....

• Do you relate to Thomas, Philip, or Judas in this passage? Why?

....

....

....

....

....

....

....

APPLY: Some of Jesus' disciples were clearly confused here in this passage. That's kind of comforting, isn't it? These men had spent so much time with Jesus. They had sat under His teaching. They had seen Him perform miracles. Time and again He had proven for them that He is God, and yet they still doubted and questioned! That ought to give you comfort and peace when you are doubting and questioning too. Thomas, Philip, and Judas had spent time with Jesus in the flesh. Here we are, thousands of years past when our Savior lived and taught in person on the earth, and yet we hold on dearly to our faith in Him. So, if Jesus patiently, lovingly answered *their* questions, surely He has even more patience and love for *ours*. Maybe some nights you are praying questions like Thomas, Philip, and Judas asked. In those times, remember the answers Jesus gave: He is the way, the truth, and the life. He is God. He reveals Himself to those who seek after Him, obey Him, and love Him. He has sent the Holy Spirit to live in us and help us and remind us of everything He taught. And He offers peace that is out-of-this-world awesome!

PRAY: *Dear Jesus, thank You for Your patience and love for those who question and doubt like I do sometimes. Through Your Holy Spirit who is in me, remind me of all You have taught and promised. Please lead me and guide me in Your Word, reveal Yourself to me, and fill me with Your extraordinary peace. Amen.*

Day 134

HE IS ALWAYS KIND

—— READ TITUS 3:3–8 ——

KEY VERSES: *When God our Savior revealed his kindness and love, he saved us, not because of the righteous things we had done, but because of his mercy. He washed away our sins, giving us a new birth and new life through the Holy Spirit.* TITUS 3:4–5 NLT

UNDERSTAND:

• How have you tried to earn God's favor?

....

....

....

....

....

....

....

• Why is trying to earn God's favor a futile endeavor?

....

....

....

....

....

....

....

....

APPLY: Of all the characteristics of God, His kindness toward us is one that we should praise Him for every day. Kindness seems like such a simple thing, but it goes hand in hand with His passionate love for His children. His kindness allows us to approach Him when we know we've messed up. His care for us helps us to be confident that He will not condemn us in our sin when we sincerely repent and ask for forgiveness. His kindness was what resulted in His plan for our salvation through Jesus Christ.

We can't earn His kindness. He cannot be kinder to us or love us more if we say the right things or act a certain way. He loves us so much that He offers us new life in the Holy Spirit.

Your kind Father is waiting to hear from you. What is on your heart today that you'd like to tell Him? He will not judge you. He will respond in love. . . and in kindness.

PRAY: *Father, when I think of all the ways You demonstrate how You love me, I realize just how kind You are to me. You bless me in so many ways, and You give me an identity in Christ that is perfect and whole—not dependent on my own goodness or abilities. Give me opportunities to show Your kindness to others today. Amen.*

Day 135

USABLE, IN SPITE OF

———— **READ 1 TIMOTHY 4** ————

KEY VERSE: *Don't let anyone look down on you because you are young, but set an example for the believers in speech, in conduct, in love, in faith and in purity.* 1 TIMOTHY 4:12 NIV

UNDERSTAND:

• Have you ever felt unqualified for a task? How did you manage to overcome those feelings of inadequacy?

....

....

....

....

....

....

• Think of the names of a few people who have encouraged you along the way and who have said, "You've got this!"

....

....

....

....

....

....

....

APPLY: Timothy was relatively young (probably in his twenties) when he took on the role of evangelist. Some would argue that he hadn't done his time, that he didn't have enough notches on his belt, that he needed more life experience when the call of God propelled him into ministry.

Maybe you can relate. Maybe God called you at a young age or when you didn't feel psychologically ready. Maybe inadequacies or anxieties arose. Maybe folks nearby whispered, "Why did she get picked? I'm a better candidate."

It's hard to know how and why God chooses the ones He does, but you can trust in the choosing. If the Lord calls, He will equip. It's that simple. So rest easy! The task ahead might seem daunting. You might think you don't have the goods. Today God wants you to know that He does. He's got all you need and more.

PRAY: *Lord, I rarely feel completely adequate or prepared for the tasks You put in front of me. Many times, I think You've called the wrong person. But today I choose to submit to the task. If You've called me, Lord, I know You will equip me. I'm trusting in that promise today. Amen.*

Day 136
I'M PANICKED

──────── **READ PSALM 91** ────────

KEY VERSE: *This I declare about the LORD: He alone is my refuge, my place of safety; he is my God, and I trust him.* PSALM 91:2 NLT

UNDERSTAND:

• How do you think panic is different from other kinds of fear? What in your life makes you panic?

....

....

....

....

....

....

• How might scripture be the antidote for panic's poison? Consider writing some of the verses in this passage of scripture on a note card or in your phone, somewhere you can refer to them whenever panic threatens to overcome you.

....

....

....

....

....

....

APPLY: The original meaning of *panic*, dating back a few hundred years, had to do with the sort of contagious, unreasoning fear that can sweep through a herd of cattle—or a crowd of people—causing them to run into even worse danger. In fact, the original thing that triggers panic is often not even an actual danger; it might be merely a sudden loud sound or an event that startles us. Panic can be personal, but it can also sweep through an entire society, creating a state of fear that's so overpowering, we lose our ability to think clearly.

Panic is destructive—but we don't have to let it control our lives. Instead, as soon as we notice panic's poisonous touch, we can turn immediately to the only One who can hold us steady. He is our refuge, our place of safety. We can rest in His shadow.

PRAY: *Cover me with Your feathers, almighty God. Shield me with Your wings. Protect me with the armor of Your faithfulness. When panic threatens to grab me in its grasp, remind me that You are with me, saving me from every danger—including the ones that exist only in my imagination! Amen.*

Day 137

LIVE IN THE LIGHT

READ 1 JOHN 1-2

KEY VERSE: *But if we live in the light, as God is in the light, we can share fellowship with each other. Then the blood of Jesus, God's Son, cleanses us from every sin.* 1 JOHN 1:7 NCV

UNDERSTAND:

• What is the opposite of light?

....

....

....

....

....

....

....

• What do you think it means to live in the light versus to live in the darkness?

....

....

....

....

....

....

....

....

APPLY: As Christians, we have found the light, but the world around us still dwells in darkness. Darkness comes in many forms, but it is always the opposite of God's best. God is light. He exposes darkness with light.

Those who are spiritually blind walk in darkness. They are on a sinful path. If they had the light, they would turn and take another path—the path that leads to heaven. But as it is, they are on the path to hell.

At times, you may feel as if you are in the dark. Depression may overtake you. You may feel that God has left you. He hasn't. It is at those times that you must rely on the truth of scripture. God has promised to never leave you. He has rescued you from sin and set you on a path of righteousness. Remember in the darkness what you know to be true in the light.

PRAY: *Lord, help me always to walk in the light as You are in the light. Keep my heart and mind pure even as I live in the midst of an evil culture that promotes sin. Father, when I feel that I am in the dark, remind me that I am a child of the light. I know You, and I am forever saved from sin and destruction. In the powerful name of Christ I pray. Amen.*

Day 138
CHOSEN

─────── **READ 2 KINGS 2:1-22** ───────

KEY VERSE: *As they were walking and talking, a chariot and horses of fire appeared and separated Elijah from Elisha. Then Elijah went up to heaven in a whirlwind.*
2 Kings 2:11 NCV

UNDERSTAND:

• How did Elijah go to heaven?

....

....

....

....

....

....

• Who had remained very close to Elijah until he was taken up into heaven?

....

....

....

....

....

....

....

APPLY: Elisha had refused to leave Elijah until the very end. He had stuck to him like glue, a faithful friend. Perhaps he wanted to see Elijah taken up into heaven in order to confirm and strengthen his own faith. Perhaps he just wanted to be with him as long as he possibly could. What we do know is that he remained faithful. He refused to leave Elijah's side.

When Elijah asked Elisha what he could do for him, the only desire Elisha expressed was to have a double portion of his spirit. He didn't want wealth or fame, only to be very well equipped to serve God.

Do you stand by and support your spiritual mentors, those who are teaching and preaching the gospel as Elisha supported Elijah? Do you stick closer than a brother? And what is your desire in doing so? Do you desire to learn as much as you can and to serve God in an even greater way?

Consider your loyalty and your motives. You will be blessed if they are pure before God.

PRAY: *Lord, I do not understand the mystery as to why Elijah was lifted into heaven as he was. Make me as faithful as Elisha to the work of Your Kingdom. Help me not to desire any other thing than more of Your Spirit, greater ability to serve and love You better. Amen.*

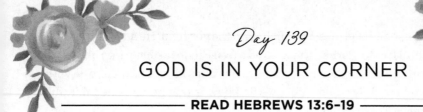

Day 139

GOD IS IN YOUR CORNER

───── **READ HEBREWS 13:6-19** ─────

KEY VERSE: *So we say with confidence, "The Lord is my helper; I will not be afraid. What can mere mortals do to me?"* HEBREWS 13:6 NIV

UNDERSTAND:

• Can trust in God and fear exist at the same time? Why or why not?

....

....

....

....

....

....

• When anxiety starts to creep in, what can you do to remember that God is on your side?

....

....

....

....

....

....

....

APPLY: Confidence is such an attractive quality, isn't it? Whether it's someone who can easily command the attention of the room or speaks in public flawlessly or simply excels at their job, it's inspiring and motivating to see someone who has it all figured out. Spoiler alert: The truth is that most of the time, even confident people have real fears.

Real, lasting confidence isn't something that comes from within us and our abilities. And confidence that truly conquers fear is rooted in the fact that, as Christians, we have God on our side. He is fighting for us, protecting us, and making us strong in spirit, heart, and mind.

Where in your life do you need an extra dose of confidence? The Lord is your helper. All you need to do is ask for His guidance and His help. With Him in your corner, you can overcome anything!

PRAY: *Father, I need Your help. I trust You, but fear keeps trying to force its way into my heart and mind. I can't shake these feelings of uncertainty. My brain keeps fretting over scenarios that I know will probably never happen, but I can't stop the thoughts by myself. Fill me with Your peace. Give me the confidence that You are in control and You want the best for me. Amen.*

Day 140
HE'S GOT YOU COVERED

─────────── **READ RUTH 3** ───────────

KEY VERSES: *"Wash, put on perfume, and get dressed in your best clothes. Then go down to the threshing floor, but don't let him know you are there until he has finished eating and drinking. When he lies down, note the place where he is lying. Then go and uncover his feet and lie down. He will tell you what to do."* RUTH 3:3–4 NIV

UNDERSTAND:

- Through good times and bad, God's got you covered. Think of a time when He proved this to you.

....

....

....

....

....

....

- Has anxiety ever left you feeling vulnerable? How did God cover or protect you during this vulnerable season?

....

....

....

....

....

....

....

APPLY: The story of Ruth and Boaz is one that brings great hope to those who feel lost and alone. Precious Ruth lost her husband at a young age. Her mother-in-law, Naomi, slipped into the role of mentor and friend. The two became so close that Ruth clung to the older woman, even returning to Naomi's homeland with her after the family tragedy.

When push came to shove in Ruth's life, she continued to look to Naomi for advice. Through Naomi, she eventually found her husband-to-be, Boaz, a man who swept her into his fold and covered her with the edge of his robe.

Do you have a Naomi or Boaz in your life? Who covers you, shields you when you're vulnerable? Have you become that person for others? Perhaps there's a friend, mentor, family member, or coworker who shares her thoughts with you. Or, maybe you've become a Naomi to a younger woman in your world.

This special bond between younger woman and older is so precious. God wants all His girls—regardless of age—to learn from one another and to grow in the faith as their friendships grow as well.

....

....

....

....

....

....

....

....

....

PRAY: *Lord, thank You for placing godly women in my life—women I can learn from, bounce ideas off of, and share personal concerns with. It's difficult to be anxious with so many friends cheering me on. I'm so grateful for them, Lord. Amen.*

Day 141

I'M AFRAID TO TRUST YOU, GOD

— READ 1 JOHN 4:13–21 —

KEY VERSE: *There is no fear in love. But perfect love drives out fear, because fear has to do with punishment. The one who fears is not made perfect in love.* 1 John 4:18 NIV

UNDERSTAND:

• How are trust and love related?

....

....

....

....

• Are you afraid of God? If so, do you really believe He loves you, unconditionally, just as you are?

....

....

....

....

• What connection between the love of God and the love of others does this passage indicate?

....

....

....

....

APPLY: The message woven throughout this entire book is this: trust in God is what gives us the courage and strength to face life's difficult times. But what if we're simply too afraid to trust?

To some extent, trust is an act of will, a moment-by-moment decision to commit everything to God. But God does not want us to have to grit our teeth and screw up our courage every time we come near Him. What He really wants with us is an intimate love relationship. Trust naturally thrives in that state of mutual intimacy.

How can we build that relationship with God, Someone we can neither see nor touch? John tells us the way in verse 17 (NIV): "In this world we are like Jesus." In other words, if we act as Jesus would, demonstrating love to everyone with whom we come in contact, we will become so confident of God's love that we will forget all our fears.

PRAY: *Teach me to trust You more, Lord, by turning me outward, away from my fears, so that I can give to others—and enter into a new relationship with You. Draw me so close to You that there's no more room for fear inside my heart. Amen.*

Day 142
GOD SEES THE HEART

───── **READ 1 SAMUEL 16** ─────

KEY VERSE: *But the L*ᴏʀᴅ *said to Samuel, "Do not look at his appearance or at his physical stature, because I have refused him. For the L*ᴏʀᴅ *does not see as man sees; for man looks at the outward appearance, but the L*ᴏʀᴅ *looks at the heart."* 1 Sᴀᴍᴜᴇʟ 16:7 ɴᴋᴊᴠ

UNDERSTAND:

- What are some common methods that we as humans use for judging others? (For example, by social class, by level of education, by race. . .)

....

....

....

....

....

....

- According to 1 Samuel 16:7, how does the Lord judge a person?

....

....

....

....

....

....

....

....

APPLY: Young man after young man paraded before Samuel. Their father, Jesse, probably watched Samuel expectantly. Don't you imagine he looked for a sparkle in Samuel's eye or a nod of his head to indicate the son who would be chosen to serve as king? And yet, Samuel said again and again, "This is not the one the Lord has chosen."

Jesse couldn't imagine that the chosen one could be the youngest, David, who was tending the sheep.

When young David stood before Samuel, the Lord pronounced him the chosen one. David was anointed with oil, and the Spirit of the Lord came upon him.

How do you see those around you? Or even yourself? Do you judge by the outward appearance or by the heart? God sees the heart.

....

....

....

....

....

....

....

....

....

....

....

....

PRAY: *Help me, Lord, not to judge a book by its cover. While a person may do or say all the right things, it is their heart that You see. The race, social status, and even personality of a person is not what You see. You see the heart. Help me to follow Your example in this. Amen.*

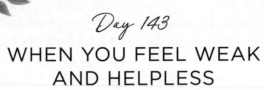

Day 143

WHEN YOU FEEL WEAK
AND HELPLESS

—————— **READ JUDGES 6–7** ——————

KEY VERSE: *The LORD turned to [Gideon] and said, "Go with the strength you have, and rescue Israel from the Midianites. I am sending you!"* JUDGES 6:14 NLT

UNDERSTAND:

- Gideon questioned God and told Him he felt abandoned by God. How did God respond to Gideon?

....

....

....

- Can you relate to feeling abandoned by God and questioning Him? If so, how has God responded to you?

....

....

....

....

- Have you ever asked God for a sign like Gideon did? Do you think Christians today should do that? When and why? Or why not?

....

....

....

....

....

APPLY: Despite his reservations, Gideon eventually obeyed and let God use him to lead in the defeat of a powerful enemy. Through God's great power, Gideon and an army that had dwindled to only three hundred men rescued Israel from the Midianites. Are you in a situation where you wish you could jump in and come to someone's rescue? Yet you feel helpless with no heroic qualities—and maybe you even feel like the weakest and worst, just like Gideon did? But the angel of the Lord had called Gideon a mighty hero because the Lord was with him, making him the hero. According to His will, God can use you in mighty and heroic ways if you simply obey and open yourself to letting Him do His good work through you.

PRAY: *Heavenly Father, I want to be available to You for any task, no matter how big or small, heroic or ordinary. Show me how You want me to serve You and others. Any good thing I am capable of and any good work I do are all because of Your love and power working through me. My life is from You and for You, Lord. I love and trust You! Amen.*

Day 144
A NEW YOU

READ 2 CORINTHIANS 5:11–21

KEY VERSE: *Therefore, if anyone is in Christ, he is a new creation. The old has passed away; behold, the new has come.* 2 CORINTHIANS 5:17 ESV

UNDERSTAND:

- In what ways do you try to change yourself for the better? Physically? Mentally? Emotionally? Spiritually?

....

....

....

....

....

....

- Many fairy tales deal with transformation (Cinderella, the Little Mermaid). Why do these stories resonate with us at any age?

....

....

....

....

....

....

....

APPLY: There's something thrilling about an extreme transformation. From a professional makeover to a weight loss in the triple digits, we cheer for the individuals in these stories as they seek to change themselves for the better. To gain more confidence. To get healthier. Their improved selves are revealed, and they often are empowered by the change.

These kinds of physical changes are well and good, but they aren't eternal. Only God can truly transform us into new creations, perfectly forgiven because of the sacrifice of Jesus on the cross. Our old, sinful selves *die*. We are no longer who or what we were, and God's great mystery of new creation happens. We're not a better version of ourselves, we are made *new*. And whole. And perfectly loved.

Have you grasped fully the fact that you are new, sister? You aren't used, washed up, or a secondhand treasure. Your new self is *here* now. Today, celebrate your newness in Christ!

....

....

....

....

....

....

....

....

....

....

PRAY: *Thank You, Lord, for making me new. You did not leave me in my own sinfulness, and You have such abundant life for me to live out as Your loved child. I want to live each day in eager anticipation of new experiences with You. Draw me close, Father. Continue to make me more like You. I long for continued transformation! Amen.*

Day 145
CONSOLATION

— READ JEREMIAH 31 —

KEY VERSES: *The LORD appeared to us in the past, saying: "I have loved you with an everlasting love; I have drawn you with unfailing kindness. I will build you up again, and you, Virgin Israel, will be rebuilt. Again you will take up your timbrels and go out to dance with the joyful."* JEREMIAH 31:3–4 NIV

UNDERSTAND:

• Have you ever walked through a season where you felt inconsolable? How did you get through it?

....

....

....

....

....

....

....

• How has God used you to console a friend or loved one?

....

....

....

....

....

....

....

APPLY: Jeremiah is known as the weeping prophet. Maybe you can relate to that description. Perhaps you're the sort of person who feels things deeply, who has a hard time hiding your emotions.

The truth is Jeremiah had a lot to weep over. He faced persecution from those who disagreed with him, conflicts with false prophets, and untold plots against him.

Perhaps you've felt like that at times, like the whole world is conspiring against you. Maybe you've adopted a "What's the point?" attitude. Things are just too hard. The pressure is too great. Your anxieties have gotten the best of you.

If so, then look up! Your redemption is drawing near. Jeremiah's story ended triumphantly, with God's assurance that He would turn mourning into dancing. He will do the same in your life. No matter what you're going through right now, redemption is coming. God will rebuild, restore, and renew your life and give you purpose once more.

....

....

....

....

....

....

....

....

....

....

....

PRAY: *Thank You for restoring my life, Lord. I don't want to live in defeat. I want to lift my eyes, dry my tears, and give every anxiety to You. I know I can trust You, Father. Amen.*

Day 146

I FEEL SO LOST!

──────── **READ LUKE 15:4–7** ────────

KEY VERSES: *"When he has found it, he lays it on his shoulders, rejoicing. And when he comes home, he calls together his friends and his neighbors, saying to them, 'Rejoice with me, for I have found my sheep which was lost!'"* LUKE 15:5–6 NASB

UNDERSTAND:

- Feeling lost can be caused by a variety of circumstances. What is making you feel lost?

....

....

....

....

- Can you imagine yourself as a lost sheep—and picture God as a shepherd who will never stop searching for you until you are safe in His arms?

....

....

....

- Do you think we are ever *really* lost to God?

....

....

....

....

APPLY: In the Gospels, Jesus tells three little stories that are all similar. In this story, a shepherd searches for a lost sheep. In another story, a woman searches her house for a lost coin until she finds it, and then she shares her joy with her friends. In the third story, a man's son runs away from home—and then comes home at last, where he is greeted with love and celebration. In each of these stories, where God is represented by a shepherd, a housewife, and a father, Jesus never implies that God blames the lost one for going astray. And He makes it clear that the joy of being found is one that's shared throughout the entire kingdom of God.

When we feel lost, we can rest in the assurance that God is searching for us. He will find us, and when He does, even the angels will rejoice.

PRAY: *Thank You, Jesus, that You do not blame me for all the ways I lose myself. I am so grateful I can trust You to bring me back home. Amen.*

Day 147

GOD'S ECONOMY

—— READ PSALMS 113–114 ——

KEY VERSES: *He raises the poor from the dust and lifts the needy from the ash heap, to make them sit with princes, with the princes of His people.* PSALM 113:7–8 NASB

UNDERSTAND:

- How did Jesus humble Himself when He came to earth? Why did He do this?

....

....

....

....

....

....

- God often chooses the lowly over those with wealth or power. Name some examples of this from the Bible.

....

....

....

....

....

....

....

....

APPLY: In this world, often those with power or money appear to end up on top. They drive the fancy cars, have the best jobs, and experience all the luxuries this life has to offer. In God's economy, things are quite different. He often chooses to exalt the humble.

God chose a prostitute named Rahab to provide protection for some of His men. He even sent His own Son to earth to be born in a manger and to be raised in the home of Joseph, a carpenter. Jesus called fishermen as His closest disciples, those who "did life" with Him throughout His earthly ministry!

Praise God today for being God. There is no other like Him, as Psalm 113 declares. Thank Him for seeing the hearts of men and women rather than just the exterior. Remember to see others as God sees them. They are precious in His sight regardless of their status or state.

PRAY: *Lord, You are able to turn things around in our lives. Psalm 113 states that You give barren women children. You seat the poor at Your table as guests. Thank You for loving us so. Amen.*

Day 148

LET THE LORD REFRESH YOU

READ ISAIAH 58

KEY VERSE: *The Lord will always lead you. He will meet the needs of your soul in the dry times and give strength to your body. You will be like a garden that has enough water, like a well of water that never dries up.* ISAIAH 58:11 NLV

UNDERSTAND:

• What makes your soul feel dry at times? How do you let God refresh you?

....

....

....

....

....

....

....

....

• How do you apply verses 13–14 in your life?

....

....

....

....

....

....

....

....

APPLY: Do you have plants in your home that are near death because no one remembers to water them? They start to look pretty sad, don't they? Or think of your lawn or garden in the middle of a hot summer with no rain. Sometimes we start to feel dry and ugly like that in our souls when we aren't spending good time with God. We need to read His Word and pray and worship Him so that He can lead and refresh us. We also need to fellowship with other believers who regularly do these things. God gives the kind of living water that makes us never feel thirsty again. When Jesus spoke to the woman at the well, He meant it for us too: "Whoever drinks the water I give them will never thirst. Indeed, the water I give them will become in them a spring of water welling up to eternal life" (John 4:14 NIV).

PRAY: *Lord, please lead me. Meet the needs of my soul in dry times, and give strength to my soul. Thank You for refreshing me and restoring me with Your extraordinary living water! Amen.*

Day 149

GOD'S GOOD CREATION

READ PSALM 19:1–6

KEY VERSE: *The heavens are telling of the greatness of God and the great open spaces above show the work of His hands.* PSALM 19:1 NLV

UNDERSTAND:

• When has God's creation awed you so much that you couldn't help but worship?

....

....

....

....

• What does God's creation reveal to you about His character? His aesthetic preferences?

....

....

....

....

• What one thing do you think is most interesting or fascinating in all of God's creation?

....

....

....

....

....

APPLY: Our God delights in transformation. From the caterpillar changing to the butterfly to the seasonal cycles of the leaves of deciduous trees, creation constantly changes according to His masterful plan. The sky—what Psalm 19 refers to as "the heavens"—may be the best example of constant change. Consider how the sunrise's Creator uses different palettes of color and varying brushstrokes each day to fill the sky with beauty. And the night sky is no different as God directs the moon's phases and lights up the vast expanse with innumerable pieces of light.

The heavens say so much about God's greatness without using a single word.

Today, really look at God's creation. Raise your eyes to the sky. Kneel to be eye level with a child. Notice a flower or a bird's song or a dog's bark. He created our world—including you—for His pleasure and for our blessing.

PRAY: *Creator God, today I am celebrating Your artistry throughout all of Your creation. Even in nature around me every day, I can learn much about You. Give me Your eyes to appreciate and delight in the things You delight in. I praise You for the Master Artist You are. You have made all things good and pleasing in Your sight. Amen.*

Day 150

MIXED MESSAGES

READ GENESIS 11:1-9

KEY VERSE: *That is why it was called Babel—because there the Lord confused the language of the whole world. From there the Lord scattered them over the face of the whole earth.* Genesis 11:9 niv

UNDERSTAND:

- The world sends so many mixed messages. Which ones confuse you the most?

....

....

....

....

....

....

- Why do you suppose God chose to confuse the language and scatter people across the face of the earth?

....

....

....

....

....

....

APPLY: Not long after Adam and Eve left the garden, an unusual event took place. The people (who had everything in common, including their language) began to build a tower to make a name for themselves. When God saw what they planned to accomplish, He chose to shake things up a bit. He confused their language and scattered the people.

Strange, right? God is usually all about unity, not division. Why split up the people? Why scatter them across the globe? The truth is these folks were getting a little too puffed up. They were looking at themselves as heroes, saviors. Yes, they were working together, but only to bring glory to themselves.

Maybe you've been in a similar situation where a team effort ended up being about personal glory. Or maybe you've experienced excessive pride in a coworker or someone on a sports team. We can all get a little puffed up at times. As believers, we send a mixed message when we begin to tout ourselves instead of the Lord. It's time to refocus on Him, to take our eyes off ourselves so that He can be magnified.

PRAY: *Father, I want to give all the glory to You. You're the only Savior I'll ever need. If I begin to sing my own praises, stop me, I pray. May I only live to praise You. Amen.*

Day 151

I FEEL REJECTED

READ JOHN 15:18–27

KEY VERSE: *"If the world hates you, remember that it hated me first."* JOHN 15:18 NLT

UNDERSTAND:

- Have you ever considered how rejected Jesus must have felt when He hung on the cross? He was rejected not only by humanity but even by His heavenly Father.

....

....

....

....

....

....

- How do you think the Holy Spirit might help you face the pain of rejection?

....

....

....

....

....

....

....

APPLY: The Greek word in this Gospel passage that has been translated "world" refers to the entire system of reality in which we live—the physical world, human society, the invisible spiritual world. . .the whole kit and caboodle. So, when Jesus says that the world hated Him, He's saying that all of reality rejected its own Creator.

No rejection we experience will ever be as immense or total as that, and yet Jesus isn't saying to us, "You think *you've* got it bad—look at what *I* had to go through!" No, instead He's saying, *"I know how rejection feels. But the rejection I experienced wasn't deserved, and neither is yours. What's more, I love you so much, I don't want you to have to face rejection alone. That's why I'm sending the Spirit to you. Even though I can't be with you now in physical form, the Spirit will tell you about Me—so that you can tell others."*

PRAY: *Jesus, I am so sorry that You had to endure the world's rejection. Help me to face the smaller rejections in my own life with Your Spirit of love and gentleness. Amen.*

Day 152
PERFECT TIMING

───── **READ JOHN 11:1-44** ─────

KEY VERSES: *When Mary reached the place where Jesus was and saw him, she fell at his feet and said, "Lord, if you had been here, my brother would not have died." When Jesus saw her weeping, and the Jews who had come along with her also weeping, he was deeply moved in spirit and troubled. "Where have you laid him?" he asked. "Come and see, Lord," they replied. Jesus wept. Then the Jews said, "See how he loved him!"* JOHN 11:32–36 NIV

UNDERSTAND:

• When have you felt that God failed to show up or was too late to help you?

....

....

....

....

....

• Have you heard it said that God's timing is perfect? What evidence from scripture gives this statement validity?

....

....

....

....

....

....

....

APPLY: Mary and Martha grieved the recent loss of their beloved brother, Lazarus.

The sisters, known from Luke's Gospel to be different in nature, had one thing in common here. They knew if Jesus had been there sooner, Lazarus would not have died.

This statement, which both Mary and Martha make in the passage, reveals much. They had faith that Jesus could heal. They knew He was the only hope. And neither saw how this story could have a happy ending. Their brother was dead.

Jesus was not late to the scene. The Messiah did not check His watch, realizing too much time had passed. Jesus, as always, was right on time.

A greater miracle than healing took place that day in Bethany. Lazarus rose from the grave after being dead for four days. He came forth at the sound of the Master's voice. And that day, the angels in heaven surely rejoiced because many believed.

PRAY: *Jesus, when it seems You are taking too long, remind me that Your timing is perfect. You are never too early or too late. You are always right on time. Grant me faith in the waiting and in the times I cannot understand Your ways. Amen.*

Day 153

NO FAKES

READ PSALMS 115–116

KEY VERSES: *Our God is in the heavens. He does whatever He wants to do. Their gods are silver and gold, the work of human hands. They have mouths but they cannot speak. They have eyes but they cannot see. They have ears but they cannot hear. They have noses but they cannot smell. They have hands but they cannot feel. They have feet but they cannot walk. They cannot make a sound come out of their mouths. Those who make them and trust them will be like them.* PSALM 115:3–8 NLV

UNDERSTAND:

• What fake gods are most popular in today's culture?

....

....

....

....

....

....

• Are you ever tempted to worship a fake god? How do you fight that temptation?

....

....

....

....

....

....

APPLY: This scripture compares our one true God with the fake gods of the world that some people make for themselves. It describes how silly those fake gods are, with useless mouths, eyes, ears, noses, hands, and feet. But people often make fake gods because they don't really want to serve or worship anyone but themselves. So they will end up as useless and meaningless as those fake gods. But to trust, worship, and obey our extraordinary God is to live the life you were created for, with love, hope, and peace forever.

....

....

....

....

....

....

....

....

....

....

....

....

....

....

PRAY: *Heavenly Father, I want to trust and worship You alone! Please help me keep far away from fake gods. Please help me to keep living for You and sharing You with others. Amen.*

Day 154

HE THINKS OF YOU

──────── **READ MATTHEW 10:24–31** ────────

KEY VERSES: *"Are not two small birds sold for a very small piece of money? And yet not one of the birds falls to the earth without your Father knowing it. God knows how many hairs you have on your head. So do not be afraid. You are more important than many small birds."* MATTHEW 10:29–31 NLV

UNDERSTAND:

• If you've ever been forgotten or overlooked, how can it change your perspective to know that God thinks about you?

....

....

....

....

....

• How does it make you feel that God knows you so well that He has the hairs on your head numbered?

....

....

....

....

....

....

....

APPLY: Our God is not some far-off, cosmic force who created us and then sat back to watch us implode. Even in the middle of our own self-implosion (sin), God is there, loving us back to Himself so we can be in a right relationship with Him.

Maybe today you're feeling forgotten by friends or family. Rejected, overlooked, unloved. When other humans fail us, God is steadfast in His care. He celebrates with us in our victories and comforts us in our tragedies. He rejoices when we make good choices and lovingly disciplines us back to the right path in our failures. We are on His mind and constantly in His heart.

Today, relax in His constant care. Thank Him for knowing you and loving you so perfectly. You are priceless to Him.

....

....

....

....

....

....

....

....

....

....

....

....

....

PRAY: *Father, sometimes I feel overlooked, unloved, and forgotten by others. I try not to dwell on it, but it hurts me deeply. Help me to remember that I am always in Your thoughts. You love me with a fierce love. When it comes down to it, God, You are all I need. Amen.*

Day 155

WALK IN WISDOM

──── READ 1 KINGS 3:16-28 ────

KEY VERSE: *Solomon said, "Don't kill the baby." Then he pointed to the first woman, "She is his real mother. Give the baby to her."* 1 KINGS 3:27 CEV

UNDERSTAND:

- Solomon was quick on his feet! He came up with the perfect solution to the problem, didn't he? Can you think of a time when you were quick on your feet?

....

....

....

....

....

....

- Where do you need the most wisdom—at home, work, or school, or with your relationships?

....

....

....

....

....

....

....

....

APPLY: Perhaps you've heard someone say, "You have the wisdom of Solomon." Maybe you've wondered what that meant. What gave Solomon the edge wasn't just his wisdom, but his ability to discern a situation and then make decisions based on his discernment.

Two women showed up with one baby, each arguing that the baby belonged to her. How would Solomon solve the problem? In a very interesting way! He instructed them to cut the baby in half. Of course, the real mother cried out in anguish while the wannabe mom agreed to Solomon's terms. It was obvious in a flash who the real mom was.

Maybe you want the wisdom of Solomon. It's easy to acquire. The Bible tells us that we're all able to tap into that well. But while you're at it, also ask the Lord for discernment. Wisdom and discernment work hand in hand, after all.

PRAY: *Lord, thank You for discernment and wisdom. I can't drum these things up on my own, but You freely give them to me when I ask. Today, I ask. Fill my cup, Lord. Amen.*

Day 156

I RESENT SOMEONE

READ MARK 11:22–25

KEY VERSE: *"When you assume the posture of prayer, remember that it's not all asking. If you have anything against someone, forgive."* MARK 11:25 MSG

UNDERSTAND:

- If you've allowed resentment to take root in your heart, have you noticed that it hinders your ability to pray? Are you able to come into God's presence with the same sense of intimacy you once had?

....

....

....

....

....

....

- In the words of *The Message*, Jesus asks us to "embrace this God-life" (verse 22). What does the term "God-life" convey to you? How might you embrace it?

....

....

....

....

....

....

....

....

APPLY: "Help me with this, Lord," we pray. "Give me that. Do this; do that." We have so many directions for the Creator of the universe! And yet God loves to know we trust Him enough to bring our petitions to Him. Most of all, He simply loves to hear our voices.

But Jesus reminds us in these verses that prayer is more than asking God for something. We might think His next words will be a reminder to praise God—but no, Jesus turns our attention to our relationship with others. We can't be in an intimate relationship with God, He tells us, if we've put up walls between our hearts and another's.

Resentment is one of the highest walls we erect against the people in our lives. It's built out of the unwillingness to forgive. Ultimately, it will not only separate us from others; it will also separate us from God.

Time to tear down that wall!

....

....

....

....

....

....

....

....

....

....

....

....

PRAY: *Knock down the walls in my heart, loving Lord. Show me how to truly embrace the God-life You want to share with me. Amen.*

Day 157

DISCERNMENT
THROUGH THE SPIRIT

───────── **READ 1 CORINTHIANS 2** ─────────

KEY VERSES: *This is what we speak, not in words taught us by human wisdom but in words taught by the Spirit, explaining spiritual realities with Spirit-taught words. The person without the Spirit does not accept the things that come from the Spirit of God but considers them foolishness, and cannot understand them because they are discerned only through the Spirit.* 1 Corinthians 2:13–14 NIV

UNDERSTAND:

• Who is able to understand things that come from the Spirit of God? Who is not able to accept these things?

....

....

....

....

....

• What is the difference between these two types of people, and which type are you?

....

....

....

....

....

....

APPLY: The things of God seem foolish to those who do not have the Holy Spirit. When you accepted Christ, you were sealed with the Holy Spirit. This enables you to understand and apply God's Word and His ways.

Don't be surprised if unbelievers argue with you about the validity of scripture. They are wearing spiritual blinders. They are unable to see or comprehend scripture.

The Holy Spirit is our Comforter and our Counselor. The Holy Spirit enables us to understand and apply God's Word. Praise God that you do not wear a veil that keeps you from taking in His Word. Pray diligently for those you know who have not yet come to know Christ. Their lives depend upon the shedding of those spiritual blinders. They need the freedom that comes through the Spirit. They need Jesus.

PRAY: *Heavenly Father, I thank You that I have the Holy Spirit. I am so thankful that I am able to understand Your Word and apply it to my life. It saddens me that so many see spiritual things as foolishness. I pray for repentance in their lives that they might accept Christ and receive the blessings of the Holy Spirit. Amen.*

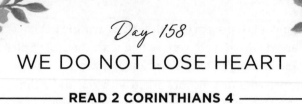

Day 158

WE DO NOT LOSE HEART

---------- **READ 2 CORINTHIANS 4** ----------

KEY VERSES: *Therefore we do not lose heart. Though outwardly we are wasting away, yet inwardly we are being renewed day by day. For our light and momentary troubles are achieving for us an eternal glory that far outweighs them all.* 2 CORINTHIANS 4:16–17 NIV

UNDERSTAND:

• What are the hardships weighing on you tonight? What do you need to cry out to God about them?

....

....

....

....

....

....

• How are you seeking God's power to keep you from losing heart and being defeated by your suffering? How are you being renewed day by day?

....

....

....

....

....

....

....

APPLY: Some days we feel exactly like verses 8 and 9 of this passage describe—hard-pressed on every side, perplexed, persecuted, and struck down. Anyone who says the Christian life should be all good all the time clearly does not read their Bible entirely and in context! We should not run from or deny the hurts and hardships we experience. Feeling all of the awful weight and pain of them and grieving them before God are what leads us to remember the powerful truth in that passage: Yes, we are hard-pressed, *but we are not crushed.* Yes, we are perplexed, *but we are not in despair.* Yes, we are persecuted, *but we are not abandoned.* Yes, we are struck down, *but we are not destroyed.* How is that possible? Because God will never leave us or forsake us. He holds us up and strengthens us through the power of His Holy Spirit living in us. Jesus suffered and died for us, and we grow closer to Him as we share in suffering. At the same time, we show off His eternal life–giving power to others when we suffer but are never defeated—until one day in heaven when we learn the purposes of our hardships and we see the amazing rewards they were gaining us!

....

....

....

....

....

....

....

....

PRAY: *Heavenly Father, please help me to see the value in these hardships I'm experiencing. They help me to know and to show off Your power and love as You strengthen and uphold me. I trust that they are achieving rewards for me so awesome that my mind cannot even imagine them. I am fully depending on You alone, Father, and I love You! Amen.*

Day 159

YOU ARE YOUR
FATHER'S DAUGHTER

—— READ 1 JOHN 3:1-10 ——

KEY VERSE: *See how very much our Father loves us, for he calls us his children, and that is what we are!* 1 JOHN 3:1 NLT

UNDERSTAND:

- When you are getting to know someone, how do you explain and define yourself to them?

....

....

....

....

- In what ways do you struggle with your identity?

....

....

....

....

- How has your identity changed throughout your lifetime?

....

....

....

....

APPLY: Who are you? Mom, grandmother, daughter, granddaughter, niece, aunt, wife? Do you identify yourself as your occupation or a hobby or volunteer work or ministry?

All these things are good, and they do play a part in the way we interact with others, but none of these labels is lasting. Relationships, jobs, hobbies, volunteer opportunities, and even some ministries are part of our lives only for a season. In reality, our identity has nothing to do with what we *do*. Instead, our identity is grounded in the fact that we are handpicked daughters of God the Father. We are sisters to our risen Savior and King, Jesus Christ, and forever counted as forgiven, saved, and standing in the grace of God.

So, when life is in upheaval, when you're not sure who you are, instead remember *whose* you are.

PRAY: *When my life, my roles, and my relationships are in flux, Father, remind me who I am. I am Yours. I am a daughter of the King. I am claimed by Jesus as a sister. I am a vital part of the body of Christ. I am forgiven, cherished, loved, and encouraged in You. Your identity is what I need. When people see me, let me fade into the background, and may Your light shine! Amen.*

Day 160
PRAYER AND PETITION

──────── **READ MATTHEW 6:9–13** ────────

KEY VERSE: *"This, then, is how you should pray: 'Our Father in heaven, hallowed be your name.'"* MATTHEW 6:9 NIV

UNDERSTAND:

- Have you ever had to plead a case in court? What did it feel like, to speak before the judge?

....

....

....

....

....

....

- Isn't it wonderful to know you have instant access to the King of all kings, God Himself? What wows you the most about that idea?

....

....

....

....

....

....

....

APPLY: "Our Father in heaven, hallowed be your name." We know and love those words. They give us power and hope. They connect us to the King of the universe and remind us that He cares about even the smallest of details. Our ability to converse with our Creator, to offer our prayers and petitions, is such a privilege.

Many times, we come before the Lord with requests that seem overwhelming. A friend has a cancer diagnosis. A loved one has been in an accident. A friend's child has died. It's all too much to take in. But God wants us to bring those things to Him, to plead our case (no matter how difficult the need), and to release the burden to Him. For only in releasing the burden can we truly walk in freedom.

What are you holding on to today? What need feels too great? What burden is too heavy? What anxieties are too unnerving? Run to the Lord. Start with the words "Our Father in heaven," and go from there. He longs for you to bare your heart.

PRAY: *Our Father in heaven. . .You are an awesome and amazing God! Thank You for Your willingness to listen to my pleas and move on my behalf. I'm so glad I can cast my cares on You, Lord. Amen.*

Day 161

I CAN'T STOP CRYING

──────── **READ REVELATION 21:3-5** ────────

KEY VERSE: *"He will wipe every tear from their eyes."* REVELATION 21:4 NLT

UNDERSTAND:

• What situation is bringing the tears to your eyes today?

....

....

....

....

....

....

....

• Can you believe that God is able to comfort you—even if you have to wait until you experience eternity?

....

....

....

....

....

....

....

....

APPLY: In this world, death and loss are unavoidable. Every phase of life comes to an end, and each of the people we love will one day die. Tears are a very real part of human life.

This passage in the book of Revelation is describing a different reality, one that we've never experienced in this life. In this new reality, God dwells visibly with us, joined with us in an intimate relationship of belonging. We will no longer have any need for tears because pain and death will have no place there.

It sounds too good to be true, doesn't it? God understands that feeling. Maybe that's why He told John, "Write this down, for what I tell you is trustworthy and true" (verse 5 NLT). Every tear we shed in this world will be comforted in heaven.

PRAY: *I'm tired of crying, God. I feel as though all my tears should be gone by now, and yet they continue to fall. Thank You that You are here, even now in my sorrow. I give You my tears (right now, I have nothing else to give You), knowing that one day You will wipe them all dry. Amen.*

Day 162

THE WAY, THE TRUTH, AND THE LIFE

— **READ JOHN 14** —

KEY VERSE: *Jesus said to him, "I am the way, and the truth, and the life; no one comes to the Father but through Me."* JOHN 14:6 NASB

UNDERSTAND:

• What three things does Jesus claim to be in this verse?

....

....

....

....

....

....

• What does it mean that no one "comes to the Father" except through Jesus?

....

....

....

....

....

....

....

....

APPLY: Throughout the Gospel of John, we find Jesus using the statement "I am" seven times. Jesus was bold to use this phrase because the name for God that meant "I Am" was so sacred to the Jews that they would not even utter it. Jesus claimed to be God because He is God. Jesus said, "I am the bread of life" (John 6:35). He also said, "I am the good shepherd" (John 10:11) and "I am the Light of the world" (John 8:12).

This powerful "I Am" statement in John 14:6 declares that the only way to get to God is through Jesus. Other religions teach that good works will allow people to reach God. Some believe that God is in everything or that humans themselves are God. Christianity alone teaches that Jesus is the only way to the heavenly Father. Take comfort in the fact that you may come into the presence of God because you are a believer in the one who is the way, the truth, and the life: Jesus.

PRAY: *Jesus, You are the way, the truth, and the life. I am so thankful to know You as my Savior. Thank You for dying on the cross for my sins, bearing them for me. Thank You for providing a way for me to spend eternity with God. Amen.*

Day 163

GOD'S MAGNIFICENT CREATION

---- **READ GENESIS 1:1–2:3** ----

KEY VERSES: *So the heavens and the earth were completed, and all that is in them. On the seventh day God ended His work which He had done. And He rested on the seventh day from all His work which He had done.* GENESIS 2:1–2 NLV

UNDERSTAND:

• Why do you think the phrase "God saw that it was good" is repeated throughout Genesis 1?

....

....

....

....

....

....

• Why are people different from the rest of creation?

....

....

....

....

....

....

APPLY: Spending time outdoors in God's magnificent creation can surely help release any anxiety and fill you with peace. When you look at a beautiful sunset, when you go for a hike in a thick forest or on a majestic mountain trail, when you swim in a rippling lake, when you pick a gorgeous wildflower, when you do anything that makes you focus on and appreciate nature, praise your amazing Creator God! The natural world He designed and gave us is truly extraordinary. It reminds us in countless ways how awesome He is. He planned and created land and air and sea and plants and animals with incredible love, detail, beauty, and purpose. And if He created all that so marvelously, how much more did He create you, who are created in His image, with incredible love, detail, beauty, and purpose? Rest well tonight, dreaming of creation and about how dearly loved you are by your Creator.

PRAY: *Heavenly Father, thank You for Your awesome creation. It reminds me every day how incredible You are and how dearly loved I am. I praise You and I love You! Amen.*

NEW CLOTHES

────────── **READ COLOSSIANS 3:1–14** ──────────

KEY VERSE: *Therefore, as God's chosen people, holy and dearly loved, clothe yourselves with compassion, kindness, humility, gentleness and patience.* COLOSSIANS 3:12 NIV

UNDERSTAND:

• When you experience God's compassion, how does that influence the compassion you show to others?

....

....

....

....

• Of the list of compassion, kindness, humility, gentleness, and patience, which is the easiest for you to demonstrate?

....

....

....

....

• Which is the most challenging for you to demonstrate?

....

....

....

....

APPLY: How much time do you take to choose an outfit each day? Do you lay it out the night before, complete with specific accessories? Or do you tug on whatever smells cleanest from the hamper?

Just as our physical clothes can say something about who we are, Paul is urging his readers in Colossians 3 to clothe themselves with the attributes of Christ Jesus: compassion, kindness, humility, gentleness, and patience. Why does Paul use the clothing analogy? Because clothing is something that we must intentionally put on; we come out of the womb without wearing a stitch!

Which articles of Jesus' clothing does today call for? All these things layer well and help prepare you for any climate. Best of all, when you dress yourself in these clothes, you're looking even more like the love of God.

Today, take stock in the ways that God shows you compassion, kindness, gentleness, and patience. Ask Him for opportunities to show these to others as well.

PRAY: *God, I want to be more like You. You shower me with compassion and kindness. But my own selfishness gets in the way of being like You—I am proud and impatient with others. Help me to realize how much I have been forgiven, how much You love me, so that I can show this same love to others. Amen.*

Day 165

FOOD FOR DAYS

───────── **READ 1 KINGS 17:7–16** ─────────

KEY VERSE: *"For this is what the Lord, the God of Israel, says: 'The jar of flour will not be used up and the jug of oil will not run dry until the day the Lord sends rain on the land.'"* 1 Kings 17:14 NIV

UNDERSTAND:

- Have you ever been through a season of lack, where provisions were in short supply? What did you do?

....

....

....

....

....

....

- How do you garner the faith to believe for the impossible during lean seasons?

....

....

....

....

....

....

....

APPLY: Imagine the plight of that poor widow woman. A child to feed. No way to replenish what little food she had in the house. And then, on top of everything, the man of God wants her to share? Must have felt impossible. And intrusive.

Now imagine how she must have felt, meal after meal, day after day, as the flour and oil replenished themselves. Surely she blinked, stared at her ingredients to make sure she wasn't losing her mind, and then blinked again. Wow!

Maybe you've been in her place. Your provisions were low. You wondered where the next meal was going to come from. From out of nowhere, a bag of groceries appeared on your doorstep. A gift card arrived from a friend. An unexpected check showed up in the mailbox.

God loves to replenish your storehouse, and His methods are always imaginative and fun. So don't fret. Don't be anxious about tomorrow. You won't go hungry. He's got this one covered.

PRAY: *Thank You for Your provision, Lord. You've seen me through every lean season, making sure I had everything I needed and more. I'm so grateful. Amen.*

Day 166

THE FUTURE SCARES ME

READ PSALM 139:3–15

KEY VERSE: *I look behind me and you're there, then up ahead and you're there, too—your reassuring presence, coming and going.* PSALM 139:5 MSG

UNDERSTAND:

- When you look back on your life, can you see the way God has been with you ever since your conception in your mother's womb? Does this help you face the future with greater confidence?

....

....

....

....

....

- Do you truly believe that God has the future in His hands—or do you doubt His power to manage all of time, past, present, and future? How might your feelings change if you could truly trust in God's presence throughout all time?

....

....

....

....

....

....

....

....

APPLY: A children's picture book, *The Runaway Bunny* by Margaret Wise Brown, tells a similar story as the first verses in this passage of scripture. The little bunny thinks of one situation after another where he might escape his mother's love. He imagines himself becoming a bird or a fish or a boat—and each time, his mother assures him that whatever he becomes and wherever he goes, she will be right there with him, fitting into the scenario in whatever way is required for her to stay close to him.

God's love for us is the same as the mother bunny's for her child. No matter what happens to us in the future, no matter where we go or what we become, He will be there, present in the circumstances. He sees our future as clearly as He sees in the past—and He is already there, up ahead, waiting for us.

PRAY: *Thank You, Spirit of love, that the future can take me nowhere that will ever lead me out of Your presence. Amen.*

Day 167
DO NOT GO ON SINNING

—— READ JUDE ——

KEY VERSE: *I say this because some ungodly people have wormed their way into your churches, saying that God's marvelous grace allows us to live immoral lives. The condemnation of such people was recorded long ago, for they have denied our only Master and Lord, Jesus Christ.* JUDE 4 NLT

UNDERSTAND:

• Have you ever heard something that you instantly knew did not align with God's Word?

....

....

....

....

....

• What would you say to someone who said that because of God's grace we can live however we desire?

....

....

....

....

....

....

....

APPLY: The author of Jude urgently warns about ungodly people who have "wormed their way" into the churches. He does not want anyone to be led astray by them. These people said that due to God's grace, it was fine to go on sinning. Sin was covered by the grace of God anyway.

What a dangerous way to live! And what backward thinking! The apostle Paul taught in the book of Romans that our sinful lives were crucified with Christ and we were set free. Romans 6:18 (NLT) states, "Now you are free from your slavery to sin, and you have become slaves to righteous living."

Are there people in your life who claim to be Christians and yet live a sinful lifestyle? Just as the author of Jude warns the people of his day, be warned. It is often easy to be led astray by such people. You want to surround yourself with friends who point you toward godly living.

PRAY: *Lord, please give me the discernment I need to distinguish the godly from the ungodly. I never want to be led astray by those who think of Your grace as a sort of insurance plan, assuring them of forgiveness no matter how they live. I want to honor You and live a godly life. In Jesus' name I pray. Amen.*

Day 168
WALK FAITHFULLY

———————— **READ GENESIS 6:1–9:17** ————————

KEY VERSES: *Noah found favor in the eyes of the* LORD. *This is the account of Noah and his family. Noah was a righteous man, blameless among the people of his time, and he walked faithfully with God.* GENESIS 6:8–9 NIV

UNDERSTAND:

- What was most familiar to you about the story of Noah and the ark? What had you never heard of or thought much about before?

....

....

....

....

....

....

- What do Matthew 24:37–39 and 1 Peter 3:18–22 add to the story of Noah?

....

....

....

....

....

....

....

....

APPLY: Have you ever found yourself on a path that you're sure God led you to, but as you keep walking it, things start feeling really strange? You're afraid you've misunderstood what you were once certain was God's crystal-clear direction. Noah must have felt that way too sometimes. He was righteous and blameless and walked faithfully with God, but you have to wonder if he started shaking his head in confusion at times when God gave instructions to build a giant boat, fill it with two of every animal on the earth, and then wait while rainwater flooded and destroyed the earth. Bewildered or not, Noah continued to obey God, and that took steadfast faithfulness and courage. In the end, God did exactly what He had said He would—He destroyed the earth with a great flood. Only Noah and his family and the animals they had gathered survived, safe inside the ark. Noah could be extremely grateful that he faithfully obeyed God whether he felt confused or not. If you find yourself trying to follow God's leading even when it doesn't make much sense, let Noah's story give you peace tonight. Let it remind you that with faithful, patient obedience, you will see God's hand and His rescue in His perfect timing.

....

....

....

....

....

....

....

....

....

....

PRAY: *Heavenly Father, please give me the peace and patience I need to keep obeying You even when I don't fully understand where You are leading and what You are doing. No matter what, I want to trust and follow You! Amen.*

Day 169

LIVE EVERY DAY IN AWE

—— **READ PSALM 33:1–15** ——

KEY VERSE: *Let all the earth fear the Lord; let all the inhabitants of the world stand in awe of him!* Psalm 33:8 ESV

UNDERSTAND:

• When was the last time you were awestruck by God?

....

....

....

....

• Why is God worthy of our awe?

....

....

....

....

• Do you think it's possible to increase your awe of God in your everyday life? Why or why not?

....

....

....

....

APPLY: If you ever doubt the power of words, remember this: Our Creator God spoke the world into being (Psalm 33:9). "Let there be light," He said in Genesis 1:3, and light appeared. From His infinite mind and artistic sensibility, He formed each mountain and star, each creature with its unique look and role in His plan. And then He sculpted us, the most beloved of His creation, intricate and beautiful living beings made in His own image.

He gave us free will and hearts geared toward relationship—with Him and with other humans. And He loved us with a love so great that He would sacrifice everything to allow us to be with Him after we messed up our perfect relationship with Him.

The whole earth is filled with awe-inspiring reminders of God's majesty. Today, pray and ask God to open your eyes to see the reminders as they truly are and stand in awe of Him.

....

....

....

....

....

....

....

....

....

....

....

PRAY: *My Creator and King, show me the wonder of Your creation. In the life-giving nourishment of rainfall, in the majesty of a sunset, in the twinkling of points of light in the heavens, I am amazed. You provide everything I need, and what's more, You have made all things beautiful as well. Thank You, God. Amen.*

BE HAPPY ATTITUDES

READ MATTHEW 5:1–12

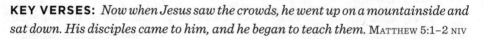

KEY VERSES: *Now when Jesus saw the crowds, he went up on a mountainside and sat down. His disciples came to him, and he began to teach them.* MATTHEW 5:1–2 NIV

UNDERSTAND:

- The Beatitudes give us all we need to live a happy, fulfilled life. Which one speaks to you the most, and why?

....

....

....

....

....

....

- Why do you suppose God is concerned with blessing us and making sure we experience happiness in this life?

....

....

....

....

....

....

....

APPLY: Have you ever wondered why Jesus took the time to deliver the Sermon on the Mount or to include the Beatitudes as part of His message? If He had skipped over them, we might never have known that we are blessed when persecuted or comforted when mourning. Maybe we'd never realize that the meek would inherit the earth or that the merciful would be shown mercy.

These few lines of scripture are filled with promises from on high. They bring hope to the hopeless and joy to the downtrodden. They remind us that any anxious thoughts can dissipate in the presence of the Lord.

Some people refer to the Beatitudes as the "be happy attitudes." When you apply them to your life, they bring peace and, ultimately, happiness.

Which beatitude are you leaning most heavily on at this point in your life? Remember, Jesus took the time to insert that line of scripture so that you would know His peace and joy.

_____

_____

_____

_____

_____

_____

_____

_____

_____

_____

_____

PRAY: *Thank You for shifting my attitude with these scriptures, Lord! I'm so glad You included them in Your text. You think of everything, Father. Amen.*

Day 171

MY IMPULSIVENESS HAS GOTTEN ME IN TROUBLE—AGAIN!

———— READ 1 THESSALONIANS 5:4-8 ————

KEY VERSE: *Let's keep our eyes open and be smart.* 1 THESSALONIANS 5:6 MSG

UNDERSTAND:

• Can you identify what is at the root of your impulsiveness? Is it pride...
genuine concern for others...or just sheer carelessness?

....

....

....

....

....

• *The Message* version of these verses says that since we are "sons of Light" and
"daughters of Day" we live under "wide open skies" (verse 5). What images do
these words shape in your mind? How might you use them to remind yourself
to think more carefully the next time your impulsiveness threatens to lead
you astray?

....

....

....

....

....

....

....

APPLY: "I didn't mean any harm," we sometimes say. "I just acted impulsively." We seem to assume that our failure to think carefully about our behavior will excuse any hurtful consequences of our actions. Deep down, though, doesn't acting impulsively imply that we think we can do whatever we want? Even if we say we were motivated by love or kindness or pure excitement, acting without thinking is selfish. It can cause great damage to ourselves and others.

We're not walking through life asleep or inebriated, our senses inoperative or dulled. God gave us brains, expecting us to make use of them. He doesn't want us stumbling around in the dark, following every whim that crosses our minds. Instead, He wants us to walk carefully, soberly, clothed in His love.

PRAY: *Lord, forgive me for acting so impulsively yet again. Teach me to discipline myself so that I always take time to think before I act. Strip me of my headstrong pride so that You can dress me in faith, love, and the hope of Your salvation. Amen.*

Day 172
BUILDING YOUR HOME

——— READ PROVERBS 14 ———

KEY VERSE: *The wise woman builds her house, but the foolish tears it down with her own hands.* PROVERBS 14:1 NASB

UNDERSTAND:

- Proverbs 14 provides a contrast between two types of individuals. What are they?

....

....

....

....

....

....

- What are the verbs, or action words, in Proverbs 14:1? Consider the meaning of each. Which one do you spend most of your time doing?

....

....

....

....

....

....

....

APPLY: The home is a haven for a family. It's a place of peace where a family seeks refuge from the world. There are women who get this right and those who don't.

More often than not, the woman of the house sets the tone for the home. Are you setting a tone of peace or of strife? How do you greet your husband and children at the end of a long day? Do you instantly launch into a to-do list? Do you scold? Or do you provide warmth, nurturing, and acceptance?

The wise woman seeks to meet the needs of her family. She is conscientious with finances. She encourages and builds up her husband and kids. She manages things rather than just letting them go. A home should not be a place of disorder and disarray.

Seek to honor God by being a builder rather than a destroyer of your home.

PRAY: *Lord, forgive me for the times when I have forgotten the importance of my role. I want to be categorized as a wise woman and not as one who tears down her own home. Help me to be a student of my husband and children, learning them well, that I might know the ways I may build them up and encourage them best. Amen.*

Day 173
WATCHING OVER YOU

───────── **READ PSALM 71** ─────────

KEY VERSES: *For You are my hope, O Lord God. You are my trust since I was young. You have kept me safe from birth. It was You Who watched over me from the day I was born. My praise is always of You.* Psalm 71:5–6 NLV

UNDERSTAND:

• What are your earliest memories of being aware God was watching out for you?

....

....

....

....

• What times in your life has God seemed closest to you? Why?

....

....

....

....

• What times in your life has God seemed far away? Why?

....

....

....

....

APPLY: You've had lots of people in your life who have taken care of you over the years—parents, grandparents, husband, siblings, aunts and uncles and other relatives, friends, teachers, coworkers, school staff, coaches, doctors, nurses, and on and on. As an adult, you take care of yourself more, of course, but you still need plenty of people in your life to call on for help with all kinds of things. Ultimately, though, God is the one who constantly watches over you. Praise and thank Him for His extraordinary care. It is God working through all of those who take care of you and help you when you need it. And He will for all of your life, like Psalm 23:6 (NLV) says: "For sure, You will give me goodness and loving-kindness all the days of my life. Then I will live with You in Your house forever."

PRAY: *Heavenly Father, thank You so much for watching over me and guiding me through many people in my life. I trust that You will always provide the right people in the right places at exactly the right times when I need them. Amen.*

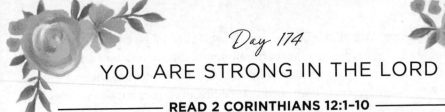

Day 174

YOU ARE STRONG IN THE LORD

READ 2 CORINTHIANS 12:1-10

KEY VERSES: *Each time he said, "My grace is all you need. My power works best in weakness." So now I am glad to boast about my weaknesses, so that the power of Christ can work through me. That's why I take pleasure in my weaknesses, and in the insults, hardships, persecutions, and troubles that I suffer for Christ. For when I am weak, then I am strong.* 2 Corinthians 12:9–10 NLT

UNDERSTAND:

• Why does Paul admit to weakness in this passage?

....

....

....

....

....

....

....

• What challenges do you have that only God can overcome?

....

....

....

....

....

....

....

....

....

APPLY: The apostle Paul is a giant of our Christian faith. This man with a miraculous conversion story (see Acts 9) went on to preach the gospel, greatly encourage congregations to the ends of the earth, and pen thirteen of the books in the New Testament. By anyone's standards, Paul had much to boast about.

But here in 2 Corinthians 12, Paul downplays his accomplishments and instead focuses on his own weaknesses. We don't know what his specific difficulty was, but it was something that he could only overcome with God's help. And God's strength, Paul says, is best displayed through human weakness.

Where are your weaknesses, your struggles? Whether it's something physical, spiritual, mental, or emotional, turn it over to God. With the power of the Holy Spirit inside of you, His strength will be made perfect in your weakness.

PRAY: *God, when this world tells me to be empowered by my own strength, remind me that I am nothing without You. It feels strange to say it, but I thank You for my weak spots. Fill those gaps with Your power, dear Lord, and I will be strong in You today and forever. Amen.*

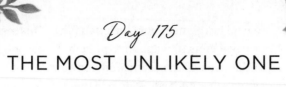

Day 175

THE MOST UNLIKELY ONE

—— READ 1 SAMUEL 16:1–13 ——

KEY VERSES: *So he asked Jesse, "Are these all the sons you have?" "There is still the youngest," Jesse answered. "He is tending the sheep." Samuel said, "Send for him; we will not sit down until he arrives." So he sent for him and had him brought in. He was glowing with health and had a fine appearance and handsome features. Then the* Lord *said, "Rise and anoint him; this is the one."* 1 Samuel 16:11–12 NIV

UNDERSTAND:

• God's ways are not our ways. Sometimes He chooses the most unlikely person. Have you ever been that person? If so, how did He call you out of your comfort zone?

....

....

....

....

....

• It's not always easy to submit to the authority of someone younger than yourself. Have you ever been in a situation (on the job or at church) where someone younger took a position of leadership? If so, how did you respond?

....

....

....

....

....

....

APPLY: Think of young David, the shepherd boy, tending sheep in the field. Just an ordinary day. Nothing big on the horizon.

Enter Samuel, the man appointed by God to seek out the future king. David could not have known that Samuel would point a finger in his direction and say, "Him! He's the one." David was, after all, just a boy. And just a lowly shepherd at that.

Aren't you glad God looks at the heart, not outward appearance? If He judged based on human criteria, David would never have made the cut.

God wants to use the ordinary people of this world to do extraordinary things. His ways are not our ways. But don't be surprised when He interrupts your run-of-the-mill day to call you to that next big task. But no worries. Push those anxieties aside! If He calls, He will equip. So hang on to your hat. There are big things ahead!

PRAY: *Lord, I don't know what You have for my future, but I know I can trust You. There are days when I feel like David—lowly and plain. But I know You have big things ahead for me. I wait with expectancy, Father! Amen.*

Day 176

I TOLD A LIE—AND
NOW I'M SORRY!

— READ PSALM 51:1–12 —

KEY VERSES: *Wash me throughly from mine iniquity, and cleanse me from my sin. For I acknowledge my transgressions: and my sin is ever before me.* PSALM 51:2–3 KJV

UNDERSTAND:

- Why do you think the psalmist said that his sin was against God rather than the persons involved in the situation? Do you feel that your lie hurt God more than it did anyone else? Why or why not?

....

....

....

....

- What motive lay behind your lie?

....

....

....

....

- In verse 6 (KJV), the psalmist said that God desires "truth in the inward parts." What do you think he meant by that?

....

....

....

....

APPLY: Lies can slip out so easily. We stray from the truth for all sorts of reasons—to make ourselves look better to others or to hide another worse sin. Sometimes we lie simply to make our conversation more interesting (we think) or to soothe another person's ego.

But the psalmist knew that truth is important to God, and he stressed that it's *inner* truth that's most vital for our relationship with God. Perhaps that's because we may begin to believe our own lies, creating a false self that doesn't match who we really are on the inside. How can we be close to God—or anyone else—when we're hiding ourselves?

The first step back to that inner truth is to acknowledge our lies and ask God's forgiveness. He is the only one who can wash away the falsehoods we've hidden behind.

PRAY: *Create in me a clean heart, God, and renew a right spirit within me. Don't cast me away from Your presence, and don't take Your Holy Spirit from me. Restore to me the joy of Your salvation, and hold me up with Your Spirit. Amen. (See verses 10–12 KJV.)*

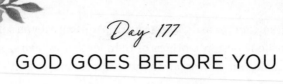

Day 177

GOD GOES BEFORE YOU

———— READ DEUTERONOMY 31 ————

KEY VERSE: *"The LORD himself will go before you. He will be with you; he will not leave you or forget you. Don't be afraid and don't worry."* DEUTERONOMY 31:8 NCV

UNDERSTAND:

• What are the promises packed into the key verse for today?

....

....

....

....

....

....

• What challenge will you face less afraid knowing that the Lord goes before you?

....

....

....

....

....

....

....

APPLY: Regardless of the fact that God had promised them the land of Canaan, the Israelites of the past had been too afraid to enter. They feared the giants who lived in this amazing land. After a period of forty years in the wilderness as God's punishment for their lack of faith, this new generation was ready to go in. It was critical that they hear the words of Moses or they too might forfeit the land that flowed with milk and honey.

They were not to fear. God was with them. He would not leave them or forget them. They were commanded not to worry.

Where are you hesitant? Where do you need to step out in faith? When we shrink back from taking a step of faith where God is clearly leading us, we forfeit amazing blessings. Claim these promises in your own life today. God is with you. He goes before you. He will not leave or forget you. Trust Him.

PRAY: *Heavenly Father, I will go where You lead. Help me to lay down fear and worry. I want to trade those hindrances for Your help and Your faithfulness. I know that You go before me. Wherever You may lead, I will follow in faith. Amen.*

Day 178

ABOVE AND BEYOND

—————— **READ LUKE 5:1–11; JOHN 21:1–14** ——————

KEY VERSES: *When He had finished speaking, He said to Simon, "Push out into the deep water. Let down your nets for some fish." Simon said to Him, "Teacher, we have worked all night and we have caught nothing. But because You told me to, I will let the net down." When they had done this, they caught so many fish, their net started to break. They called to their friends working in the other boat to come and help them. They came and both boats were so full of fish they began to sink.* LUKE 5:4–7 NLV

UNDERSTAND:

• What does Peter's first reaction to the miracle in Luke 5:8 tell you about his character?

....

....

....

....

• In John 21:7, Peter jumped out of the boat and into the water as soon as he realized it was Jesus. Do you think you would have done the same? Why or why not?

....

....

....

....

....

APPLY: In Luke 5, at the very beginning of Jesus' earthly ministry, He helped the fishermen catch far more than they could have imagined. They had just spent the whole night fishing and had caught nothing, but Jesus only had to say the words and suddenly the fish were everywhere—enough to break their nets and sink their boat! And in John 21, we read how Jesus did a similar miracle, and this time it was part of how He was showing Himself alive again after His death and resurrection. Both times, the disciples must have been so amazed and overjoyed—and especially so after they had believed Jesus to be dead! Don't ever forget that God is able to provide so much more than you can possibly fathom—including eternal life! Keep trusting Him and asking Him for everything you need.

PRAY: *Loving Savior, You go above and beyond to show how You love to provide. Thank You for meeting my day-to-day needs with plenty of extra blessing, and thank You especially for giving eternal life! Amen.*

Day 179

UNDERSTANDING
OUR FREEDOM

—— READ 2 CORINTHIANS 3:7–18 ——

KEY VERSES: *For the Lord is the Spirit, and wherever the Spirit of the Lord is, there is freedom. So all of us who have had that veil removed can see and reflect the glory of the Lord. And the Lord—who is the Spirit—makes us more and more like him as we are changed into his glorious image.* 2 Corinthians 3:17–18 NLT

UNDERSTAND:

• How does your life reflect the glory of the Lord?

....

....

....

....

....

....

• In what ways is the Spirit making you more like God?

....

....

....

....

....

....

....

APPLY: To really understand the freedom we have in Christ, we first must understand just how restrictive the old covenant was. Open your Bible to books like Leviticus, and you'll see lists of ceremonial, sacrificial, and moral laws. In order to be right with God, His people had to follow *each* of these laws. Break just one, and they were out of God's good favor. Living under the law was oppressive and exhausting, but the faithful also understood the effort was worth it—a blameless life meant fellowship with God—intimate friendship like Moses experienced on the mountain (see 2 Corinthians 3:13).

Under the new covenant of Christ, Jesus came to earth to satisfy all these laws and be the ultimate sacrifice for the sins of the world. No longer do we need to work to earn the Father's approval and to be His friend. All we must do is accept the free gift of grace that He offers. We don't have to climb a mountain to reflect the glory of God. We can experience His full life here, now, today!

PRAY: *God, because of Jesus and the gift of Your Spirit, I know I live in freedom. Teach me how to live fully free and more like You each day. Amen.*

Day 180

DO IT GOD'S WAY

───────── **READ GENESIS 16:1-15** ─────────

KEY VERSE: *So after Abram had been living in Canaan ten years, Sarai his wife took her Egyptian slave Hagar and gave her to her husband to be his wife.* GENESIS 16:3 NIV

UNDERSTAND:

• Sometimes, when our anxieties are high and our faith is low, we step out on our own and take matters into our own hands. Have you ever done that? How did it work out?

....

....

....

....

....

• Who was most to blame in this situation—Abraham, Sarah, or Hagar? Have you ever been in a situation where everyone involved got ahead of God?

....

....

....

....

....

....

....

APPLY: It doesn't take much effort to see that Sarah got ahead of God in this twisted tale. When she saw that she could not provide a child for her husband, she went to her maid and concocted a plan to keep Abraham's lineage going. Can you even imagine Hagar's shock at Sarah's suggestion?

Now picture the jealousies that surely arose when Hagar's son, Ishmael, was born. Sarah, the very one who came up with the plan, was riddled with jealousy. If she had just waited, if she hadn't jumped the gun, she would have seen the fruition of God's plan in her own life. She should have waited on Isaac.

Maybe you know what it's like to get antsy, to feel like you need to come up with your own plan because God isn't moving fast enough to suit you. You let your fears and anxieties get the better of you. Anytime you do that, you're stepping out from under the umbrella of His protection and safety. It's better to hang on to your faith and believe that He will come through for you, even if circumstances make you feel otherwise.

PRAY: *Lord, I don't want to get ahead of You! I don't want to take off down the road, thinking I've found a better way. Stop me in my tracks, I pray. Quiet my heart. May I stick close to You and trust in Your plan. Amen.*

Day 181

MY MIND IS FULL OF DOUBTS

───────── **READ MARK 9:17–29** ─────────

KEY VERSE: *"I believe. Help me with my doubts!"* Mark 9:24 msg

UNDERSTAND:

- In this passage from the Gospel of Mark, Jesus seems exasperated by the father's willingness to put up with his son's illness—but does He seem angry about the man's lack of faith?

....

....

....

....

....

....

- Do you think the man's doubts ever completely disappeared?

....

....

....

....

....

....

....

....

....

APPLY: In this passage of scripture, Jesus shows human emotion in response to a situation. "How many times do I have to go over these things?" He says in *The Message*. "How much longer do I have to put up with this?" (verse 19). Most parents have said something similar to their children at one time or another!

And yet, reading this story nearly two thousand years after the event took place, we still don't understand what Jesus meant. We know that children continue to suffer illness, and God does not always heal them, even when their parents have a strong faith. Given the reality of our world, it's no wonder we still have doubts. The Bible is filled with promises of blessing and healing—but how can we believe those promises when we see so much suffering in our lives and in our world?

Perhaps the real message contained in this story is the example the father gives to us. He admits his doubt—and surrenders it to Jesus.

PRAY: *Jesus, like the father in this story, I am troubled and full of doubts. I need Your healing hand to touch a situation in my life. I believe in You—and I give You all my doubts. Amen.*

Day 182
NEVER LOOK BACK

──────── **READ GENESIS 19:1–26** ────────

KEY VERSE: *But Lot's wife looked back, and she became a pillar of salt.* Genesis 19:26 NIV

UNDERSTAND:

• After becoming a believer, have you ever been tempted to "look back" at something Jesus called you to lay down? What was it? How did you respond to the temptation?

....

....

....

....

....

• Why do you think God imposed such a harsh punishment on Lot's wife just for looking back as she was leaving Sodom?

....

....

....

....

....

....

APPLY: Not unlike the call to evacuate before a hurricane (although much stronger!), Lot's family received a warning from angels to get out of Sodom before God destroyed the entire city.

Lot's wife, a Sodomite, looked back as they were leaving. On her way out of the city, the memory of sinful pleasures she had enjoyed there cost her everything. Like the lure of a county fair's music and the scrumptious scent of delicious foods, Sodom beckoned her. Just one glance back was all she took. But it was enough for our holy God to turn her instantly into a pillar of salt.

Don't spend time looking back. Whether it's past sin that calls your name or a past relationship or status, resist the urge to dwell in the past. A wise man once said, "If you live in the past, you will miss the present and therefore, you will have no future."

God provided an escape route from sin. His name is Jesus. Follow Him, and never look back.

PRAY: *Heavenly Father, I pray that You will keep me from the snares of temptation. May my eyes be so focused on Your will and Your ways for my life that I might never look back. You have promised me hope and a future (see Jeremiah 29:11). Please never let my heart stray from Your best for me. Amen.*

Day 183

LIE DOWN AND
SLEEP IN PEACE

—————————— **READ PSALMS 3–4** ——————————

KEY VERSES: *Let the light of Your face shine on us, O Lord. You have filled my heart with more happiness than they have when there is much grain and wine. I will lie down and sleep in peace. O Lord, You alone keep me safe.* PSALM 4:6–8 NLV

UNDERSTAND:

• What causes you to shake with anger (Psalm 4:4)? Do you have any sin to confess because of that anger? How do you practice self-control to let God be the one to deliver justice?

....

....

....

....

....

• What does it mean to "look into your [heart] and be quiet" (Psalm 4:4 NLV)?

....

....

....

....

....

....

....

APPLY: The New Life Version of the Bible titles Psalm 3 a Morning Prayer of Trust and Psalm 4 an Evening Prayer of Trust. They timelessly give us courage today—if we meditate on them and pray them day and night as well. No matter the number or power of our enemies, they cannot compare to God's sovereign protection over our lives. No matter who is running after lies and spreading them like wildfire, God's truth prevails. No matter what is going on around us, we can lie down and sleep in peace because almighty God keeps us safe. We cry out to Him, and He hears our prayers. He shows us what is truly right and good.

PRAY: *Heavenly Father, yes, please let the light of Your face shine on me. In a world full of evil and lies, I need to see Your goodness and remember Your truth every moment, day and night. Please lift my head when I am discouraged, and hear my prayers when I am crying out to You. I trust in You alone to give me rest and keep me safe. Amen.*

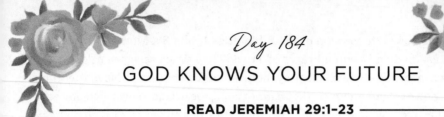

Day 184

GOD KNOWS YOUR FUTURE

—— READ JEREMIAH 29:1-23 ——

KEY VERSE: *"For I know the plans I have for you," says the* LORD. *"They are plans for good and not for disaster, to give you a future and a hope."* JEREMIAH 29:11 NLT

UNDERSTAND:

• When in the past did God work in a way that you did not expect?

....

....

....

....

....

....

....

• What do you fear about the future? Are your fears rational or irrational, and do you have any control over the outcome you fear?

....

....

....

....

....

....

....

APPLY: Whether we admit it or not, we all like to be in control. From deciding whether or not to buy a house to determining at what temperature to set the thermostat, there's nothing too big or too small that we'd like to have our say in.

What does the future hold? We may have plans and hopes and dreams, but the truth is we have little control over what happens today, tomorrow, or a decade from now. Left unchecked, our desire for control can cause sleepless nights or even strife in our relationships, and worry may spiral into despair.

But God, in His infinite wisdom and knowledge of all that has been and all that will be, cares about your future. Even when you are struggling with stress and uncertainty, God is working out your today for a hope-filled tomorrow. Live in His goodness, in His grace, and in His love.

....

....

....

....

....

....

....

....

....

....

....

....

....

PRAY: *God, I give my future to You. Forgive me for acting as if I am in control, because I'm not. You're much better at it. I believe You have good plans for my today and my tomorrows. Align my desires with Your will so that I am living today and every day in You. Please be the Lord of my life, Father. Amen.*

Day 185

SUPERNATURAL PEACE

—— READ ACTS 16:16–40 ——

KEY VERSES: *About midnight Paul and Silas were praying and singing hymns to God, and the other prisoners were listening to them. Suddenly there was such a violent earthquake that the foundations of the prison were shaken. At once all the prison doors flew open, and everyone's chains came loose.* ACTS 16:25–26 NIV

UNDERSTAND:

- Maybe you're like Paul and Silas. Maybe you've been through a situation where you were falsely accused or held accountable for something you weren't responsible for. How did God come to your rescue? Did He give you peace in the middle of the situation?

....

....

....

....

....

- Worship plays a major role in breaking free from the past. How has God used songs of praise to encourage your heart?

....

....

....

....

....

APPLY: Don't you love this story of what happened to Paul and Silas while in prison? Perhaps you're struck by the fact that they were singing worship songs to God—right there, behind prison bars. (It takes a lot of faith to worship your way through a tough situation, doesn't it?) These men were seemingly undeterred by their plight as they lifted their voices in a mighty chorus to the Lord.

What God did next was rather astounding! He shook the earth, rattled their chains, threw open the doors, and released them from their imprisonment. Wow!

But you rarely hear of a prison story ending like this. Paul and Silas could have run for the hills. Instead, they took the time to minister to their jailer and lead him to the Lord. What an amazing night that must have been!

PRAY: *Lord, thank You for the reminder that I can praise my way through the darkest night. When I lift a song to You, anxieties have to go! Even when I'm feeling trapped or imprisoned by a situation, You give me a song of praise. I'm so grateful. Amen.*

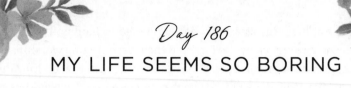

MY LIFE SEEMS SO BORING

──────── **READ EPHESIANS 3:14-21** ────────

KEY VERSES: *And I ask him that with both feet planted firmly on love, you'll be able to take in with all followers of Jesus the extravagant dimensions of Christ's love. Reach out and experience the breadth! Test its length! Plumb the depths! Rise to the heights! Live full lives, full in the fullness of God.* EPHESIANS 3:17–19 MSG

UNDERSTAND:

• Do you feel that a life of "extravagant dimensions" is available to you? Why or why not?

....

....

....

....

....

• When you feel bored with your life, ask yourself, "Are my feet planted firmly on love? And if they're not, where *are* they planted?"

....

....

....

....

....

....

....

APPLY: We have an extravagant God. In the words *The Message* uses for this passage of scripture, God "parcels out all heaven and earth" (verse 15) with a generous hand. Think about the vast range of God's creation—from amoebas to whales, from African savannahs to the frozen arctic regions, from lakes, rivers, and seas that teem with life to the intricacy of human life. We live in a world of rich variety and infinite beauty, where all creation reflects the Creator's loving hand.

And yet in the midst of this wealth, we still manage to be bored. Our eyes grow blind to the wonder of the world. We lose the childlike attitude that looks at the world with curiosity and delight. Paul, the author of this letter to the church at Ephesus, tells us that the antidote to our numbed grown-up lives is one we may not have expected. We need to find a new perspective, one that is firmly planted in love.

PRAY: *Heavenly Friend, I ask that You restore to me a child's eyes and ears so that, even in the midst of a life that seems boring, I may perceive the wonder, mystery, and beauty of Your creation. Help me to take root in Your love so that I may grow into the person You want me to be. Amen.*

Day 187

GOD WILL MAKE
ALL THINGS RIGHT

———————————— **READ 2 SAMUEL 7** ————————————

KEY VERSE: *"Your house and your kingdom will endure forever before me; your throne will be established forever."* 2 SAMUEL 7:16 NIV

UNDERSTAND:

• To whom does God reveal information about David in 2 Samuel 7?

....

....

....

....

....

....

• How does knowing that Jesus eventually comes from the line of David change the way you interpret God's promises to David in these verses?

....

....

....

....

....

....

APPLY: In the Garden of Eden, man made a choice to turn away from God. This is known as the fall. Because of the fall, we have death in the world. There was no physical death prior to it. We also have shame. Adam and Eve clothed themselves with fig leaves to hide from the Lord after they had sinned against Him. As a result of the fall, things are not right in the world. Things are not as God designed and desired.

When God put King David on the throne, a promise was revealed. It was a promise that God was establishing a throne that would endure forever. How is that? Because Jesus Himself would come from the line of David.

Way back in 2 Samuel, God was working out a plan of restoration. Through Christ, we are reconciled with God. And one day, God will once again make all things right in His world. Heaven will be even grander than Eden!

PRAY: *Heavenly Father, I thank You that on my darkest day and when I face my deepest disappointment, I can remember that You have overcome this world. You are working out Your plans just as You were in 2 Samuel. One day You will make all things right again. Amen.*

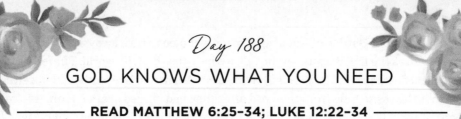

GOD KNOWS WHAT YOU NEED

———— READ MATTHEW 6:25-34; LUKE 12:22-34 ————

KEY VERSE: *"Look at the birds of the air; they do not sow or reap or store away in barns, and yet your heavenly Father feeds them. Are you not much more valuable than they?"* MATTHEW 6:26 NIV

UNDERSTAND:

- What similarities and differences do you find in the two passages?

....

....

....

....

....

....

- What do you find yourself worrying about lately? How do these passages speak to those worries?

....

....

....

....

....

....

....

APPLY: What will we eat, what will we drink, what will we wear? Do you relate sometimes to the tone of that rather frantic series of questions? Maybe it's not literally food, beverage, and clothing that fill your mind with concerns right now, but the general idea could be the same. Most of our worries boil down to taking care of ourselves and our loved ones, both now and in the future. The higher our expectations and standard of living, the greater those worries might be because we'll have more to lose the more we expect and possess. So, we are wise to live as modestly as possible and hold gratefully and loosely to extra blessings beyond our most basic provisions. When we picture the refreshing simplicity of birds and flowers having beautiful purpose and being perfectly provided for, seemingly without a care in the world, we can be inspired to solely trust our Creator like they do. We are created in His image and are far more cherished and valued by Him. When we seek to know and love Him above everything else, we realize how everything we have is ultimately a gift from Him. He will never stop loving and caring and providing for us here on earth, and He is keeping all the very best gifts and treasures for us to enjoy perfectly forever in heaven.

....

....

....

....

....

....

....

PRAY: *Heavenly Father, again and again I need to release my worries about my needs and the needs of my loved ones to You. No one sees and cares and provides as well as You do. Please help me remember to trust that. Thank You for all You have already provided for me. Help me to realize how so much of what I have is extra blessing on top, and help me to strive to be as generous to others as You are to me. Amen.*

Day 189

YOU ARE NEVER ALONE

———— **READ JOHN 14:15-26** ————

KEY VERSES: *"And I will ask the Father, and he will give you another Helper, to be with you forever, even the Spirit of truth, whom the world cannot receive, because it neither sees him nor knows him. You know him, for he dwells with you and will be in you."* John 14:16–17 ESV

UNDERSTAND:

• What does the Holy Spirit mean to you?

....

....

....

....

• Does the Spirit ever seem dormant inside you? Why do you think that is?

....

....

....

....

• What is one practical way you can engage with the Holy Spirit today?

....

....

....

....

APPLY: Jesus' disciples must've felt panicked. Their beloved Rabbi had said repeatedly He would soon leave them. And if He was sincere in His promise, what would they do without Him, the Son of God who guided them on the path of truth, answered their questions, challenged them, and comforted them?

They couldn't understand it then, but the Helper that Jesus promised His Father would send would be so much more. Jesus came to earth to be God with us. The Spirit arrived to be God *in* us. Think of it! The same almighty, powerful God who spoke the world into existence has taken a home in your heart. . .forever!

You are not alone. You cannot be separated from God's love any more than you can be separated from His Spirit. Don't let this magnificent Helper go unnoticed today! Breathe in the Spirit, and ask for help to live out God's plan today.

PRAY: *Spirit of God, sometimes You are a mystery to me. But I long to know You better. Come alive in my heart today and make Your presence known. Jesus said You are my Helper. So I am asking for Your help. Help me even when I act like I don't need it. Amen.*

Day 190
GIFTED TO SERVE

---— **READ 1 CORINTHIANS 12** ———

KEY VERSE: *Now to each one the manifestation of the Spirit is given for the common good.* 1 Corinthians 12:7 niv

UNDERSTAND:

- When you look over the list of spiritual gifts, which ones stand out to you? Why?

....

....

....

....

....

....

....

- Is there an area of your life where you excel? What is your strongest gift, and how have you used it?

....

....

....

....

....

....

....

....

APPLY: If you've ever done a Bible study of the spiritual gifts, then it's likely you've taken a test to see which ones you possess.

Which gifts are your strongest? Are you called to minister through words of wisdom or knowledge? Do you have a prophetic gifting or the ability to pray for healing? There are so many ways to reach out to others using these gifts.

When you realize that God is the one working through you—that you don't have to figure it out on your own—then your anxieties are squashed. There's no need to fret. God's got this.

Open your heart to be used by God in the gifts of the Spirit; then watch as He touches others in a supernatural way. . .through you.

PRAY: *Lord, how amazing! You've given me gifts to be used to reach others. Today I lay down my fears, my concerns, and choose to operate in those gifts, Lord. Use me, I pray. Amen.*

Day 191

I'M NOT SURE I BELIEVE IN GOD ANYMORE

──────── **READ LUKE 24:36-43** ────────

KEY VERSES: *"Don't be upset, and don't let all these doubting questions take over. Look at my hands; look at my feet—it's really me. Touch me. Look me over from head to toe."* LUKE 24:38–39 MSG

UNDERSTAND:

• What makes you doubt God's reality? Are your doubts intellectual (based on things you *think*), or are they emotional (based on your inability to *feel* God)?

....

....

....

....

• Does your doubt make you feel guilty? Do you think God is angry with you if you doubt?

....

....

....

....

• How might you "touch" God in order to reassure your doubts?

....

....

....

....

APPLY: We all have doubts sometimes about God's reality. Doubt is normal. It's no sin to doubt. But doubt that continues for a long time can cause us pain. It can rob us of the peace and joy God wants us to experience. It can hamper our ability to be the people we want to be (the people God wants us to be).

You might think that the disciples, who had seen Jesus work miracle after miracle, would no longer doubt Him. That wasn't the case though. Like all human beings, they could be filled with faith and love at one point in their lives—and then be terrified and doubting at another. And yet Jesus did not scold them for their doubt. Instead, He showed them Himself.

He longs to do the same with us. When doubts overcome us, He holds out His hands and says, "See? It's *Me*!"

....

....

....

....

....

....

....

....

....

....

....

....

....

PRAY: *Jesus, show me Yourself. Use even my doubts to draw me closer to You. Amen.*

Day 192

A WISE MOTHER

———— **READ PROVERBS 1** ————

KEY VERSES: *My child, listen when your father corrects you. Don't neglect your mother's instruction. What you learn from them will crown you with grace and be a chain of honor around your neck.* PROVERBS 1:8–9 NLT

UNDERSTAND:

- What do the first seven verses of Proverbs 1 state that the proverbs are intended for?

....

....

....

....

....

- If you are a mother, are you teaching and correcting your children in such a manner that grace and honor will be their reward if they heed your words?

....

....

....

....

....

....

....

APPLY: What are you teaching your children? Do you correct them when their behavior or attitudes are not godly? If you do, be encouraged. You are the type of mother that is spoken of in Proverbs 1:8–9.

As a parent, you have an obligation to grasp teachable moments with your children. You are responsible for teaching them God's ways. You are also held accountable for correcting them and disciplining them as necessary.

Too many mothers these days let their children rule the roost. This is not of God. Be certain that as you are training and disciplining your children, you are thinking of their future. What will serve them best—to be coddled or to be taught? To be allowed utter freedom or to learn self-restraint? Be sure that you are mothering your children in God's way.

Godly parenting will pay off. Proverbs says your children will receive grace and honor as rewards for following your instructions.

PRAY: *Help me, Lord, to be a mother who corrects and trains my children. Where I have been lazy, give me a renewed focus. Where I have allowed too much freedom, remind me that my children long for boundaries. I want to be a godly mother whose children will benefit from my teaching. Amen.*

Day 193
A SECOND CHANCE

--- **READ JONAH 1-3** ---

KEY VERSES: *Then the L*ord *spoke to Jonah a second time: "Get up and go to the great city of Nineveh, and deliver the message I have given you." This time Jonah obeyed the L*ord*'s command and went to Nineveh, a city so large that it took three days to see it all.* Jonah 3:1–3 nlt

UNDERSTAND:

• Have you ever had a Jonah type of experience in your life?

....

....

....

....

....

....

• How have second chances from God helped you develop more faith and gratitude?

....

....

....

....

....

....

....

APPLY: Jonah is a great story to revisit when you feel like you've been called by God to a place or situation you don't really want to be in. Just like Jonah, you might be tempted to go in "the opposite direction to get away from the LORD" (Jonah 1:3 NLT). That's what Jonah did, and the consequences are an unforgettable lesson. None of us wants to end up in the belly of a whale, literally or figuratively, for disobeying God. But the best part of the lesson is remembering God's great love and gracious mercy toward us, evidenced especially in Jonah's prayer in chapter 2: "I cried out to the LORD in my great trouble, and he answered me. I called to you from the land of the dead, and LORD, you heard me!" (verse 2 NLT). Our holy God had every right to ignore Jonah for his disobedience, but instead He listened. He loved Jonah and had mercy on him, and you can feel Jonah's gratitude and praise in the words of his prayer. God gave Jonah a second chance, and the story reminds us that God loves to give us second chances as well.

PRAY: *Heavenly Father, help me to remember Jonah when I'm feeling like I don't want to obey. Remind me of the lessons he learned. Thank You for Your grace and mercy to give me many second chances as well. Amen.*

Day 194
COUNT IT JOY

─────── **READ JAMES 1:2–18** ───────

KEY VERSES: *Count it all joy. . .when you meet trials of various kinds, for you know that the testing of your faith produces steadfastness. And let steadfastness have its full effect, that you may be perfect and complete, lacking in nothing.* JAMES 1:2–4 ESV

UNDERSTAND:

• Does the promise of a stronger faith after enduring trials make it easier to endure them? Why or why not?

....

....

....

....

• What difficulties have you come through that resulted in a greater faith?

....

....

....

....

• How can you encourage someone who is going through a difficult time?

....

....

....

....

....

APPLY: It's easy to live a joyful life when the birds are singing, there's a spring in your step, and all is right with the world.

But this is real life, and if those carefree seasons come, they are woefully short-lived.

James encourages us to count every difficulty, every bump in the road, and every dead end a joy. Why? Because challenges, frustrations, and disappointments grow our faith and dependence on God. He will strengthen you through anything life can throw at you and your family; and when you emerge on the other side, James says your faith will be greater, more perfect, and complete.

Are you in a difficult season now? Hold on, don't give up, and find joy in the fact that God is working. He will bring you through to a better tomorrow.

....

....

....

....

....

....

....

....

....

....

....

....

PRAY: *Almighty Father, I long to experience Your joy. But it is hard to be joyful when everything is so difficult right now. Help me to look past the challenges of today to see what You're doing in my life and in my current situation. I love You and I trust You. Amen.*

Day 195
CAST THOSE CARES

—— **READ JOHN 21:1-14** ——

KEY VERSE: *He said, "Throw your net on the right side of the boat and you will find some." When they did, they were unable to haul the net in because of the large number of fish.* John 21:6 NIV

UNDERSTAND:

• Have you ever held on to your cares unnecessarily? When God asks you to toss them overboard, go for it!

....
....
....
....
....
....

• Can you think of a time when God told you to "fish" on the other side of the boat? He's in the provision business and wants to bless you.

....
....
....
....
....
....
....
....

APPLY: When Jesus instructed the disciples to cast their nets on the opposite side of the boat, He was giving them several opportunities at once: to obey, to trust, and to prosper. Maybe He's given you similar challenges at times. He was also giving them the option of doing things His way instead of their own.

It's not always easy to do things God's way, but when you do, your burdens are lifted. As you cast that net on His side of the boat, you're releasing the cares and anxieties that came with trying to do things your own way.

What is God asking you to trust Him with today? Can you cast your net on His side of the boat, let go of your worries, and trust Him to give you a large haul? Get ready to obey, and you will see amazing results!

PRAY: *Lord, today I choose to obey You—to toss my net on Your side of the boat that I might see a haul. I release my cares, my anxieties, and my need to control, and I choose to trust You instead. Praise You, Father! Amen.*

Day 196

MY MOTHER IS
DRIVING ME CRAZY

———— **READ EPHESIANS 4:23–32** ————

KEY VERSE: BE ANGRY, AND *YET* DO NOT SIN. EPHESIANS 4:26 NASB

UNDERSTAND:

- The New Testament has many verses about how we are to interact with others within the body of Christ. Have you ever considered that these words apply to your relationship with family members as well?

....

....

....

....

....

....

- How might you handle your anger without sinning? What do you think Paul meant when he gave that advice?

....

....

....

....

....

....

APPLY: Of course, it may not be your mother who annoys you. It could be your mother-in-law or your sister. It could be some other family member. But most of us have at least one close relation who just drives us crazy!

When Paul wrote this letter to the church at Ephesus, he had a good understanding of human nature. He knew how people act when they are in close relationship with one another, and he knew that it's not all happy, fuzzy feelings—not by any means! Inevitably, we're going to get angry with the people we love.

But Paul reminds us that anger does not have to lead to sin. We don't have to allow it to hurt others. Instead, day by day, as we interact with family members, we need to be "renewed in the spirit of [our] mind," putting on the "new self" He has called us to be (verses 23–24 NASB).

PRAY: *Give me more patience with this person, Lord. Help me to be kinder, more tenderhearted, forgiving her for her foibles as You have forgiven me (verse 32). Amen.*

HEAVEN IS MY HOME

READ PHILIPPIANS 3

KEY VERSES: *But our citizenship is in heaven. And we eagerly await a Savior from there, the Lord Jesus Christ, who, by the power that enables him to bring everything under his control, will transform our lowly bodies so that they will be like his glorious body.* PHILIPPIANS 3:20–21 NIV

UNDERSTAND:

• What does it mean that your citizenship is in heaven?

....

....

....

....

....

....

• What will our bodies be like one day after the return of Jesus?

....

....

....

....

....

....

....

APPLY: Do you ever feel like you don't belong here? That's because you don't! As Christ followers, we are aliens in this world. We're just passing through. Our real home is heaven. So if you feel out of place in the culture in which you are stuck, get used to it. Though we are in the world, we are not of it. We are bound for a greater place, and we will dwell there with new bodies that are like that of our Savior.

While we don't know all there is to know of heaven, we know that our new bodies will be better than our current ones. We know there will be no more tears or death there. We know we will reign forever with our God.

When you don't fit in, it's okay. You are not meant to. Embrace it as homesickness. You are longing for paradise. One day you will feel right at home because you will be with your God in heaven.

....

....

....

....

....

....

....

....

....

....

....

PRAY: *Lord, there are so many bad things on the news every night. People are hurting one another. This culture is upside down, calling sin okay and persecuting those who seek to be godly. Help me to recognize that I am in this world for a purpose but my real home is heaven. I look forward to the day I can be there with You. Amen.*

THE MIGHTY VOICE
OF THE LORD

──────── **READ PSALMS 27–29** ────────

KEY VERSES: *The voice of the* Lord *is over the waters; the God of glory thunders, the* Lord *thunders over the mighty waters. The voice of the* Lord *is powerful; the voice of the* Lord *is majestic.* Psalm 29:3–4 NIV

UNDERSTAND:

• How do these three psalms speak into your life and give you peace?

....
....
....
....
....
....

• In what concerns are you needing to clearly hear God's voice? Are you doing well in giving His voice the most attention?

....
....
....
....
....
....
....

APPLY: With so much social media and the entire internet carried around on our phones in our pockets and purses, we have constant, sometimes overwhelming, input into our lives from all kinds of sources, opinions, and persuasions. This can be a good thing when used wisely and a terrible thing without limits. It's easy to let far too many voices speak into our lives, especially when sometimes the loudest worldly ones are the worst kind of influence. It can be a struggle to let God's voice be the one we give the most attention to. So, we have to constantly go to His Word, putting it above all other influence. Psalm 29 describes the great power of God's voice, and we can focus on this psalm as we ask God to speak more boldly and loudly into our minds and hearts than any other voice. He is our loving, guiding shepherd. We should constantly strive to know and listen to His voice and follow Him alone (John 10:27).

PRAY: *Heavenly Father, please speak boldly and clearly to me. I want to hear Your voice above all others. Please help me to use wisdom and limits on how much I listen to other voices, and help me to give Yours top attention. Amen.*

Day 199

GOD'S FAITHFULNESS
HAS NO END

—————— **READ DEUTERONOMY 7:6–9** ——————

KEY VERSE: *Know therefore that the L*ORD *your God is God; he is the faithful God, keeping his covenant of love to a thousand generations of those who love him and keep his commandments.* DEUTERONOMY 7:9 NIV

UNDERSTAND:

• How do you know you can trust God to keep His word?

....

....

....

....

....

....

• When has God been faithful to you despite your own unfaithfulness?

....

....

....

....

....

....

....

APPLY: We humans are a fickle bunch. We go from one fad diet to the next. Today's stunning interior design is tomorrow's cheesy, dated look. From today's bestselling author to tomorrow's newest big celebrity, our attention spans grow shorter by the minute.

Thank goodness our steady God doesn't follow whims or popular thought. When we have exhausted ourselves by trying to keep up with current trends and schools of thought, the Lord is steadfast in all things, not the least of which is that He will faithfully keep His promises to His children.

Maybe what you really need today is mental rest from chasing after the newest thing. Your loving Father provides that in His faithfulness. You don't need to wonder what He's thinking or what He's doing. He will not suddenly change His expectations or stop caring about you and move on to someone else. You have His love, and you have it forever.

....

....

....

....

....

....

....

....

....

....

....

PRAY: *Father God, I praise You because of Your faithfulness. You are my rock and my strong fortress that cannot be moved. I don't have to fretfully wonder what You're doing in my life because I trust You fully. Infuse my spirit with steadfastness in my relationships. I want to shine Your light of faithfulness to others in everyday life. Amen.*

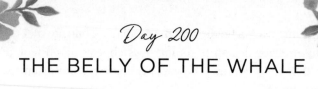

Day 200

THE BELLY OF THE WHALE

READ JONAH 1–2

KEY VERSES: *From inside the fish Jonah prayed to the LORD his God. He said: "In my distress I called to the LORD, and he answered me. From deep in the realm of the dead I called for help, and you listened to my cry."* JONAH 2:1–2 NIV

UNDERSTAND:

- Jonah's disobedience had consequences. He landed in the belly of a whale. Has your disobedience ever landed you in an awkward place?

....

....

....

....

....

....

- What do you suppose Jonah was thinking while inside the fish?

....

....

....

....

....

....

....

APPLY: Jonah didn't want to go to Nineveh. It's as plain and simple as that. He knew that confronting the Ninevites about their sinful condition would likely result in kickback. (After all, who wants to be reminded of their wickedness?) So he ran in the opposite direction. As a result, he found himself in a jam, one unlike any other in history before or after.

Chances are pretty good you've never landed inside the belly of a fish, but you've probably walked through rebellious seasons where your disobedience resulted in harsh consequences. Like Jonah, you were trapped in a prison of your own creation.

God loves it when He's got our full, undivided attention. No matter where you're sitting, He longs to speak to you, to give guidance and direction. Whether you're in a prison cell, a quiet bedroom, or the belly of a fish.

No running in the opposite direction! Even if His instructions are difficult, God will give you everything you need, as long as you stay on the right path. Otherwise, you might just end up in a place you really don't want to be.

PRAY: *I'll admit it, Lord. . .sometimes I run. I do the opposite of what You ask me to do. I let fear get the best of me. Then I suffer the consequences. Today, give me the courage to do all You ask, that I might live in safety. I trust You, Father. Amen.*

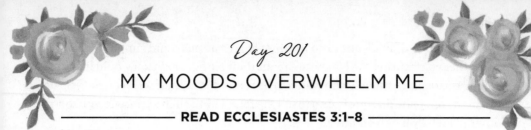

Day 201
MY MOODS OVERWHELM ME

READ ECCLESIASTES 3:1–8

KEY VERSES: *To every thing there is a season, and a time to every purpose under the heaven: . . .a time to weep, and a time to laugh; a time to mourn, and a time to dance.* Ecclesiastes 3:1, 4 KJV

UNDERSTAND:

• What does this passage of scripture say to you about the interplay between positive and negative emotions in our lives?

....

....

....

....

....

....

• Do you feel guilty for having certain negative emotions? Why or why not?

....

....

....

....

....

....

APPLY: Somehow, we've gotten the impression that strong people don't experience strong emotions. The Bible never tells us that. The great heroes of the faith, including Jesus, experienced boisterous moods. They were swept with rage, they wept with sorrow, they danced with joy, and they shouted with laughter.

There's nothing wrong with having moods! In fact, since they're a part of normal human life, it's safe to say that they're a gift from God, one He intended to enrich our lives. That doesn't mean, of course, that we should let our moods have more power over us than God does or that we should allow them to rob us of our confidence in His love. But as this scripture tells us, there is a time and place for everything. Each season of our lives—each circumstance and each emotion we feel in response—can teach us something about ourselves and the God who loves us.

PRAY: *Lord of both joy and sorrow, remind me that You created my emotions. I pray that my moods might not control me—but that they will give You glory. Amen.*

Day 202

FOLLOWING GOD'S CALL

──────── **READ JONAH 1–2** ────────

KEY VERSES: *Now the* L*ord* *provided a huge fish to swallow Jonah, and Jonah was in the belly of the fish three days and three nights.* J*onah* 1:17 NIV

From inside the fish Jonah prayed to the L*ord* *his God. He said: "In my distress I called to the* L*ord*, *and he answered me. From deep in the realm of the dead I called for help, and you listened to my cry."* J*onah* 2:1–2 NIV

UNDERSTAND:

• Why did Jonah end up in the belly of a great fish?

....

....

....

....

....

....

• Have you ever turned away and tried to hide from something you felt God calling you to do? How did it turn out?

....

....

....

....

....

....

....

....

APPLY: Jonah avoided God's clear call to Nineveh because he knew God would graciously forgive the Assyrians in Nineveh. Jonah did not think they deserved God's mercy. He fled to a faraway land to hide from God.

Just as his predecessors' attempt to hide from God in the Garden of Eden, Jonah's attempt was unsuccessful. God was with him everywhere he went. He never lost sight of Jonah.

The Lord provided the large fish to swallow Jonah in order to save his life when the sailors cast him overboard. It was not just a physical lifesaving that Jonah received. His heart was changed in the belly of that fish. He reached rock bottom, and he cried out to God.

The next time you clearly sense God calling you to do something, do it. Learn from Jonah. Jonah thought he knew better than God, but God, in His sovereignty, always has a reason for what He asks of His children.

PRAY: *God, I am thankful Jonah followed Your directions in the end. Many came to know You as a result. Help me to trust that while it may not be clear to me in the moment, You know the plans, and my job is simply to obey. Make me ever sensitive to Your voice that I might hear Your call upon my life. Amen.*

NO ONE ELSE LIKE JESUS

———— **READ HEBREWS 7** ————

KEY VERSES: *We need such a Religious Leader Who made the way for man to go to God. Jesus is holy and has no guilt. He has never sinned and is different from sinful men. He has the place of honor above the heavens. Christ is not like other religious leaders. They had to give gifts every day on the altar in worship for their own sins first and then for the sins of the people. Christ did not have to do that. He gave one gift on the altar and that gift was Himself. It was done once and it was for all time.* HEBREWS 7:26–27 NLV

UNDERSTAND:

• Have you experienced opposition for your faith in Jesus? How does this passage help you handle opposition to your faith?

....

....

....

....

....

• How do verses 23–25 help give you great peace and gratitude?

....

....

....

....

....

APPLY: Throughout your life, people will challenge your faith in Jesus Christ and try to dissuade you, but belief in Jesus as God and the one and only Savior is the only religion that is right and true. We should share our faith peacefully and lovingly, never forcefully. Jesus alone was perfect and holy and without sin. He gave His own life once for all people of all time, and no other religion offers that kind of gift and love and miracle! To know Jesus as Savior is to simply believe in Him and accept the awesome gift He gave of grace and eternal life. He took our sins away when He died on the cross for them and then rose to life again. Hold fast to this awesome truth, and let God fill you with peace as you trust in Him.

PRAY: *Loving Savior, thank You for giving Your life to save everyone who believes in You! There is no one else like You! You are God and You are Savior, and I am so grateful for You! Amen.*

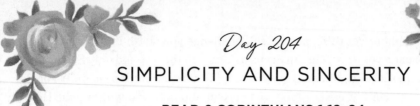

SIMPLICITY AND SINCERITY

—— READ 2 CORINTHIANS 1:12–24 ——

KEY VERSE: *For our boast is this, the testimony of our conscience, that we behaved in the world with simplicity and godly sincerity, not by earthly wisdom but by the grace of God, and supremely so toward you.* 2 CORINTHIANS 1:12 ESV

UNDERSTAND:

• Why do you think Paul is urging Christians to live with "simplicity and godly sincerity"?

....

....

....

....

• What pitfalls can come with living by "earthly wisdom"?

....

....

....

....

• In what ways can you simplify and live a more sincere life?

....

....

....

....

APPLY: It can be exhausting to try to keep up with current popular thought. From health and nutrition studies to politics and science, everything, it seems, is in a constant state of flux. It's impossible to know what the world sees as right and wrong, what's up and down, what's left and right.

While we should be aware of what's going on around us (we do live as nomads on earth, after all), Paul urges us not to get caught up in "earthly wisdom" but rather live simply and with godly sincerity. What does this look like? When we follow Christ's commands—love God and love others—we are shining the light of the Father in a dark and confusing place. And reflecting a sincere heart in everything we do shows the world that we are focused and grounded in a life-giving faith. Living such a life will attract others to the saving grace of Christ!

....

....

....

....

....

....

....

....

....

....

PRAY: *Jesus, I've tried for too long to live the way the world tells me I should. It's exhausting trying to have it all, understand it all, do it all, and look flawless in the process. Give me Your wisdom to know what is essential: love, generosity, truth, forgiveness. Help me to live a life of simplicity and sincerity rooted in You. Amen.*

A RAINBOW OF PROMISE

──────── **READ GENESIS 9:1–17** ────────

KEY VERSE: *"I am putting my rainbow in the clouds as the sign of the agreement between me and the earth."* GENESIS 9:13 NCV

UNDERSTAND:

• Have you ever reached the end of a long journey to find a rainbow of hope at the end?

....

....

....

....

....

....

• Why do you suppose God chose to use all the colors of the rainbow to signify hope?

....

....

....

....

....

....

....

APPLY: There are a variety of stories in the Old Testament where God made a covenant with man. Nearly every famous Bible character had some sort of encounter that would fall into this category. For Noah, however, the covenant was very unusual.

After the ark came to a halt on Mount Ararat, a rainbow filled the sky. Clearly, Noah, his wife, his sons, and his daughters-in-law had never seen anything like it. How they must have marveled at the arc of color, shimmering in the sky above. Can you imagine the oohing and aahing?

God promised that He would never again destroy the earth with floodwaters, and He "covenanted" that promise by setting the rainbow in the sky.

Has God made any promises to you? How has He sealed those promises? Does He remind you in the middle of the storms so that you won't give up? He's not a promise breaker, after all.

....

....

....

....

....

....

....

....

....

....

....

PRAY: *Father, I'm so glad You're a promise keeper! If You said it, I know You'll follow through. I'm grateful for the covenants You've made with me, Lord. You are worthy of my praise. Amen.*

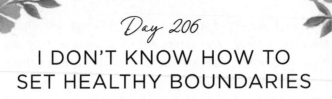

I DON'T KNOW HOW TO SET HEALTHY BOUNDARIES

---------- **READ PSALM 16:1–8** ----------

KEY VERSE: *The boundary lines have fallen for me in pleasant places; surely I have a delightful inheritance.* PSALM 16:6 NIV

UNDERSTAND:

• If setting boundaries—such as saying no to someone's request—makes you uncomfortable, why do you think that is? Do you feel guilty if you don't do what others want? Do you think God expects that of you?

....

....

....

....

• How has your lack of boundaries hurt you? Can you examine your life to see how healthy boundaries would have protected you from unnecessary pain?

....

....

....

....

• What boundaries might God be calling you to put in place in your life? This is something to ponder and pray about.

....

....

....

....

APPLY: Somehow, many of us have gotten confused about the necessity of boundary lines. We assume that Christ's command to lay down our lives for others means we don't have the right to say no to others' requests. We seem to think that God expects us to let others trample over our time and energy, taking whatever they want.

But boundaries are necessary to our emotional, spiritual, and even physical health. They not only help us to keep danger out, but they also allow us to protect the resources we have within, including our relationship with God.

With God's guidance, we can learn to set the boundaries that will define the pleasant places where we can grow, the territory of divine inheritance that will allow us to find safety and refuge. Then, when God calls us to venture out beyond these lines, we can act with strength, with all our God-given resources available for our use.

PRAY: *God, I need Your counsel. Teach me to listen to my own heart. Show me where I should say yes—and when I should say no. I need a safe space where I can be alone with You. Amen.*

Day 207

SUFFER IN HIS NAME

— READ 1 PETER 4 —

KEY VERSE: *But if you suffer because you are a Christian, do not be ashamed. Praise God because you wear that name.* 1 PETER 4:16 NCV

UNDERSTAND:

- First Peter 4 warns believers not to be shocked when trouble comes but to share in the suffering of Christ. Have you ever suffered because you are a Christian?

....

....

....

....

....

- If you have not suffered due to your beliefs, consider this: Are you living in a way that stands out to the nonbelievers in your midst? Or does your life so blend in with theirs that you are never questioned or mistreated for your faith?

....

....

....

....

....

....

....

APPLY: Soldiers wear the uniform of their country. If they die, they are honored to give their lives for the name of their homeland. Are we the same? As believers in Christ, we should stand out as His people. We may meet with persecution in our lifetime for following hard after Him. People may not understand choices we make. They may make fun of us or even try to cause us harm.

Whatever persecution you may bear for the name of Christ, you will be rewarded for it in heaven. God sees and records all suffering in the name of Jesus.

If you do not suffer for the sake of Christ, take inventory. Are you living in such a way that you stand out from the crowd? Be sure you are not so well camouflaged that no one would suspect you are a Christian. Stand up and stand out for Jesus. A day is coming when it will be even more difficult to stand firm in the faith.

PRAY: *Lord, help me to stand up for You and to stand out for You. I am honored to suffer in Your name. I love You, and I want to be known as one who follows hard after You, the one true God, regardless of the cost. In Jesus' name I pray. Amen.*

Day 208

PRACTICAL PEACE

━━━━━━━━ **READ HEBREWS 13** ━━━━━━━━

KEY VERSES: *Now may the God of peace—who brought up from the dead our Lord Jesus, the great Shepherd of the sheep, and ratified an eternal covenant with his blood—may he equip you with all you need for doing his will. May he produce in you, through the power of Jesus Christ, every good thing that is pleasing to him. All glory to him forever and ever! Amen.* HEBREWS 13:20–21 NLT

UNDERSTAND:

- Ponder Hebrews 13:2. Have you experienced a time when you showed hospitality to a stranger who you believed was truly an angel?

....

....

....

....

....

- In what ways can faith and following Jesus get overly complicated unnecessarily?

....

....

....

....

....

....

APPLY: We have ultimate peace with God because of the righteousness we gain when we accept the work of Jesus Christ on the cross to forgive our sins. And we can have plenty of practical, everyday peace in life if we focus on and apply the good instruction given in God's Word—like in the closing of the book of Hebrews. Keep loving each other and showing hospitality, kindness, and compassion to one another, including strangers. Empathize with those who are imprisoned and in pain. Honor and respect marriage with faithfulness and no sexual immorality. Be content with the simple blessings that provide for our needs; do not constantly strive to gain wealth and possessions. Do good works and share with the needy. Respect and follow the example of good faith leaders. Remember there is nothing mere people can do to us, because God never leaves us or lets us down. And breathe deeply with gratitude for the strength of God's grace and the fact that we don't need to get caught up in any new faith fads. We can trust that Jesus Christ is the same yesterday, today, and forever.

PRAY: *Heavenly Father, I am so grateful for Your grace and the practical wisdom and instruction to follow in Your Word. Please help me not to overcomplicate life and faith but simply keep loving and obeying You. Please equip me with all that I need to do Your will. Amen.*

Day 209

GOOD MEDICINE

———— **READ PROVERBS 17:13–28** ————

KEY VERSE: *A joyful heart is good medicine, but a crushed spirit dries up the bones.* PROVERBS 17:22 ESV

UNDERSTAND:

• Who or what can make you laugh no matter what?

....

....

....

....

....

• Who can you be joyously silly with?

....

....

....

....

....

• What situation or friend needs an infusion of joy today?

....

....

....

....

....

APPLY: The writer of Proverbs tucked this little verse in the middle of a string of warnings—hard issues that life throws our way as well as pitfalls and types of people to avoid. From fights and foolish financial decisions to corruption and lying, it's a laundry list of pathways to ruin.

But, the writer seems to say, joy in the middle of all of these things is good medicine—just what the doctor ordered.

Life is hard. Every day brings troubles—Jesus tells us so in Matthew 6:34—but how we choose to view and deal with those troubles is up to us. Look hard enough, and joy can be found in any situation. And viewed at the right angle and with a joyful heart, you may even find bright pockets of laughter in the darkest places.

Do you need an infusion of joy today? Look for the unique ways that God is shining light into your everyday life. And share that joy with others!

....

....

....

....

....

....

....

....

....

....

....

PRAY: *Joyful Father, I am so thankful that You are a God who delights in laughter. You invite me to unburden my spirit (Psalm 55:22), and joy comes rushing in. Show me how to cultivate a heart bursting with Your hope and joy so I can share it with others. Give me pockets of laughter throughout my day. May it be Your soothing cure to my parched spirit and be a good medicine for everyone around me. Amen.*

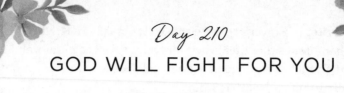

Day 210

GOD WILL FIGHT FOR YOU

───────── **READ 1 SAMUEL 17** ─────────

KEY VERSE: *David asked the men standing near him, "What will be done for the man who kills this Philistine and removes this disgrace from Israel? Who is this uncircumcised Philistine that he should defy the armies of the living God?"* 1 SAMUEL 17:26 NIV

UNDERSTAND:

• Standing up to your enemies (especially the ones who loom over you) is tough! When was the last time you had to stand up to someone? How did the story end?

....

....

....

....

....

• Think of a time when God fought a battle for you.

....

....

....

....

....

....

....

APPLY: If you rewound the story of David and Goliath a bit, you would see a boy on his way to the battlefield with one purpose in mind: to deliver bread and cheese. David didn't head to the army's camp to fight. He was just a delivery boy. When he heard Goliath's taunts, though, everything changed. The delivery boy morphed into a warrior. With renewed vision, he reached for five smooth stones to take down his enemy.

Maybe you've walked a mile in David's shoes. You've somehow meandered into a situation, completely oblivious, never dreaming you'll soon be in the fight of your life. You're not even sure how you jumped from point A to point B, but there you are, standing before a giant. And you're scared. Anxious. Worried.

Isn't it wonderful to realize that God went ahead of young David and fought the battle for him? That's what He'll do for you too. Go ahead and reach for those stones. Equip yourself. But watch as the Lord of hosts fights this one for you.

PRAY: *Thank You for fighting my battles, Lord! With Your help, I'll take down every giant who dares to rear his head against me! I'll praise You in advance for the victory. Amen.*

Day 211

I'M STRUGGLING
WITH HATRED

──────── **READ LUKE 6:27–36** ────────

KEY VERSE: *"Love your enemies, and do good, and lend, expecting nothing in return; and your reward will be great, and you will be sons of the Most High; for He Himself is kind to ungrateful and evil men."* LUKE 6:35 NASB

UNDERSTAND:

- Who are the people in your life you consider to be enemies? Be honest with yourself. Even though you might never label these individuals as enemies, your actions and attitudes may say something different.

....

....

....

....

....

....

- What does it mean to be merciful? Can you list three people you know to whom you might extend mercy today?

....

....

....

....

....

....

APPLY: Sometimes we forget how radical Jesus' message truly is. It turns upside down the way we're accustomed to thinking about things. This passage from the Gospel of Luke is an example of how challenging Jesus can be to our habits and attitudes.

No matter how "Christian" we are, most of us feel justified in holding ourselves apart from those who are unkind to us. Doing so seems like a sensible stance to take. We may extend this attitude even further to those who disagree with us politically or theologically. Why, we may ask ourselves, would God want us to associate with those who are clearly *wrong*?

Jesus' answer is clear. He couldn't care less about right and wrong; if that were the case, He would never have given His life for us. And He expects us to follow His example, loving others, even the unlovable, with no expectation of love returned.

PRAY: *Jesus, I ask Your help today to act in love to everyone, even those who have mistreated me. May I carry Your Spirit out into the world. Amen.*

Day 212
FOR SUCH A TIME AS THIS

---- **READ ESTHER 4** ----

KEY VERSE: *"If you keep quiet at this time, someone else will help and save the Jewish people, but you and your father's family will all die. And who knows, you may have been chosen queen for just such a time as this."* ESTHER 4:14 NCV

UNDERSTAND:

• How might God desire to use you in your current circumstances?

....

....

....

....

....

....

....

• Are you willing to take risks for the kingdom of God?

....

....

....

....

....

....

....

....

APPLY: The story of Esther reminds us of God's sovereignty. Through a series of events, Esther, a Jewish orphan, became a queen of Persia. When the time was right, God motioned Esther onto the stage and used her in a starring role to save the Israelite people.

God has orchestrated your life in a similar manner. Consider the circumstances God has used in order to bring you to this place in life. Do you have a platform you can use for furthering God's kingdom? Do you have authority that enables you to make decisions that honor Him? Perhaps you can look to your left and your right and see others who need to know the Savior.

You are where you are "for just such a time as this." Be a modern-day Esther. Take a risk as she did when she went before the king. There is great reward in knowing you are in the center of God's will.

....

....

....

....

....

....

....

....

....

....

....

PRAY: *Lord, help me to be like Esther as I take risks for Your kingdom. Help me to trust You as she did when she went before the king, knowing that he could choose to end her life. I want to do Your will in my life regardless of the risk. I long to be a part of Your plans. Amen.*

Day 213

NEW HEAVEN AND
NEW EARTH

—————— **READ REVELATION 21** ——————

KEY VERSES: *"Look, God's home is now among his people! He will live with them, and they will be his people. God himself will be with them. He will wipe every tear from their eyes, and there will be no more death or sorrow or crying or pain. All these things are gone forever." And the one sitting on the throne said, "Look, I am making everything new!"* REVELATION 21:3–5 NLT

UNDERSTAND:

- Why do you think God didn't give us more detail about what life will be like in the new heaven and earth?

....

....

....

....

....

- Do you think the details we're given in Revelation are more literal or symbolic? Why?

....

....

....

....

....

APPLY: The Bible gives us some description and detail but doesn't tell us a whole lot about what forever life in the new heaven and earth will be like, probably because our minds couldn't fully understand how awesome it will be. First Corinthians 2:9 (NLT) says, "No eye has seen, no ear has heard, and no mind has imagined what God has prepared for those who love him." But God's Word does tell us everything will be new and spectacular in its architecture and beauty. Even better, there will be no more death or sorrow or crying or pain. Our dear heavenly Father will wipe every tear from our eyes Himself. We will have total peace and joy forever, with God making His home among us. Incredible! A lovely way to end your day is to praise and thank God for the perfect paradise He is creating for you and fall asleep dreaming of what it might be like.

PRAY: *Heavenly Father, I know the new heaven and earth will be incredible. It's beyond anything I can imagine, but it's still so fun to dream about. I thank You and praise You for the perfect forever You are preparing for all who love You and trust Jesus as Savior. Amen.*

Day 214

GOD'S DOING BIG THINGS

————— **READ ISAIAH 43:14–21** —————

KEY VERSE: *"For I am about to do something new. See, I have already begun! Do you not see it? I will make a pathway through the wilderness. I will create rivers in the dry wasteland."* ISAIAH 43:19 NLT

UNDERSTAND:

• Recall a time when you know God moved in a mighty way to make something happen. How does it make you feel to know that He is ready to do something even greater?

....

....

....

....

• What is God doing in your life today?

....

....

....

....

• What's the biggest change for the better you can imagine in your life?

....

....

....

....

APPLY: We all have seasons of stagnation. There are times when we're unsatisfied with the way things are, but we are either unable or unwilling to make the adjustments necessary to change the situation. Maybe you're under an avalanche of debt. Maybe you have a relationship that is strained or breaking. Maybe you need to lose weight for the sake of your own health and your family, but the number on the scale hasn't budged in years.

Whatever situation you're thinking of, God is moving! Just like He did for the Israelites fleeing Egypt, He will make a way across the Red Sea when there seems to be no way. Here's the key: In order to get there, we must be following Him.

Are you willing to take the steps to allow God to change your situation? It may mean seeking help from experts; it may mean your time and resources. It will not be easy; it may not be quick—but God is faithful, and He is doing something new. Can you feel it?

....

....

....

....

....

....

....

....

....

....

....

....

PRAY: *I'm ready for change, God. Lead me through this wilderness to Your promised land. Show me what You will have me do. Amen.*

Day 215

PARTING THE SEA

———— **READ EXODUS 14** ————

KEY VERSE: *Then Moses put out his hand over the sea. And the Lord moved the sea all night by a strong east wind. So the waters were divided.* Exodus 14:21 NLV

UNDERSTAND:

- God moved in a mighty way to protect His children when He parted the Red Sea. What miracles has He performed on your behalf?

....

....

....

....

....

....

- When was the last time you faced a situation that seemed impassable, like Israel and the Red Sea? How did you make it through?

....

....

....

....

....

....

....

APPLY: Talk about an epic scene! This is one for the history books, filled with all the excitement and drama of a Hollywood movie. Picture the Israelites on a trek out of Egypt across the desert. Enter Pharaoh's army, on the move to stop the Israelites in their tracks.

The Israelites come to the edge of the Red Sea. They're trapped, sick with worry and anxiety. There's no way across—no boats, no bridges, nothing. They're trapped, and the enemy is gaining ground. Surely all is about to be lost.

Then, in an astounding move, God pushes back the water. The Israelites pass through on dry land. Their enemy presses in hard behind them. . .and the waters rush over Pharaoh's army, killing them all.

This story of God's miraculous protection of His children should fill your heart with hope. If He was willing to change nature for the Hebrew children, what will He do for you?

....

....

....

....

....

....

....

....

....

....

....

PRAY: *Lord, what a story! I wish I'd been there in person to witness the parting of the sea firsthand. Thank You for protecting Your children, both then and now. I'm so grateful Your protective hand is at work in my life. Amen.*

Day 216

I FEEL LIKE GIVING UP

———— READ JOHN 16 ————

KEY VERSE: *"These things I have spoken to you, so that in Me you may have peace. In the world you have tribulation, but take courage; I have overcome the world."* JOHN 16:33 NASB

UNDERSTAND:

- What circumstances in your life make you feel like giving up?

....

....

....

....

....

....

....

- Compare the meanings of "giving up" and "surrendering." Is there a difference? Why does giving up imply failure—and yet God asks us to surrender everything to Him?

....

....

....

....

....

....

....

APPLY: Can you imagine how Jesus' followers must have felt when they heard that Jesus planned to leave them? Their hearts must have sank within them—and yet they couldn't have imagined all they would be called to face in the years ahead. Jesus knew there would be times when they would feel like giving up, and He wanted to equip them ahead of time to face the hardships that lay ahead so that they would not stumble and fall (verse 1).

The same promises Jesus made to His disciples He makes to us today. He assures us that His peace is available to us, even in the midst of all the challenges life brings. *"Take courage,"* He says. *"Don't give up. I have already overcome all your problems. Just wait and see what I will do."*

....

....

....

....

....

....

....

....

....

....

....

....

....

....

PRAY: *Jesus, may I know Your peace today. Give me the courage I need to keep going. I surrender all my fear and anxiety to You—so that You can give me the strength to never give up. Amen.*

Day 217
THE LORD IS WITH YOU

──── **READ ISAIAH 41** ────

KEY VERSE: *"Do not fear, for I am with you; do not anxiously look about you, for I am your God. I will strengthen you, surely I will help you, surely I will uphold you with My righteous right hand."* Isaiah 41:10 NASB

UNDERSTAND:

• What does "looking anxiously about you" look like in your own life during times of trouble? To who are you tempted to turn to before you turn to God?

....

....

....

....

....

....

• What are God's promises in this one verse?

....

....

....

....

....

....

....

....

APPLY: Break this verse down. He promises that He is with you. He says He is your God. He says He will strengthen you and help you. He promises to uphold you with His righteous right hand. That is a lot of promises for one verse of scripture!

While these promises were originally for an Israelite audience, they are true for all believers, and we can find great comfort in them.

What does God ask of you in this verse? He tells you not to fear and not to look about anxiously. That is a tall order, isn't it? When times of trouble come, it is our human reaction to pick up the phone and call a close friend or relative. Resist this urge. Look first and foremost to your God, who promises to be with you and to help you. Take your fears and worries to Him. He is big enough to handle them all.

PRAY: *Lord, I know that You are with me. Sometimes I look about anxiously, calling on everyone but You. Remind me to seek You first when I am in need. You stand ready to help me. What a blessing! Amen.*

Day 218

GOD GATHERS THE WATERS OF THE SEA

—— READ PSALMS 32–33 ——

KEY VERSES: *The heavens were made by the Word of the Lord. All the stars were made by the breath of His mouth. He gathers the waters of the sea together as in a bag. He places the waters in store-houses. Let all the earth fear the Lord. Let all the people of the world honor Him.* PSALM 33:6–8 NLV

UNDERSTAND:

• How does the truth in Psalm 32:7 give you peace tonight?

....

....

....

....

....

....

....

• How does singing and music such as that in Psalm 33:1–3 bring you peace?

....

....

....

....

....

....

APPLY: Have you ever sat on the beach, just staring and thinking how incredibly endless the ocean seems? Yet this psalm describes how God can gather the water of the sea together as simply as if putting it all "in a bag," as the NLV puts it. The NIV says as if in "jars." Our one true God is so huge and powerful, so far beyond what our minds can imagine. Let that truth encourage you every day, because the same huge and powerful God who gathers up the waters so easily is the same huge and powerful God who can give you extraordinary peace and power for whatever you are facing. Rest well in that truth tonight.

PRAY: *Heavenly Father, I am amazed by Your greatness and power! If You can gather up all the waters of the earth and control them, I trust that You can gather up all my worries and fears and take them away from me. I know You will encourage me and give me peace. Thank You! Amen.*

Day 219

GOD HEARS AND LISTENS

READ PSALM 66

KEY VERSES: *But truly God has listened; he has attended to the voice of my prayer. Blessed be God, because he has not rejected my prayer or removed his steadfast love from me!* PSALM 66:19–20 ESV

UNDERSTAND:

• What is the difference between hearing and listening?

....

....

....

....

....

....

....

• Scripture tells us that God both hears and listens to our prayers. Why are both important?

....

....

....

....

....

....

....

....

APPLY: Moms of young children are expert listeners. A child may talk a mile a minute about a thousand things that seem to have no common thread, but a mommy understands the precious heart behind the words. She can truly listen to the little voice.

God accepts the prayers of His children in an even more intimate way. He hears our voice. He listens and understands our feelings and motivations behind the words. And because He created us, He knows our true heart for the prayers we pray. As imperfect and inarticulate as we often are when speaking to our Father, He welcomes our prayers and showers us in His love.

God is speaking into our lives as well. Do we hear? We must quiet the other voices and noisemakers in our lives and really listen. After speaking to God, sit in silence and ask Him to speak. The Holy Spirit will help you hear, listen, and understand the Father's voice. When you and God are both attending to each other's voice, there's no prayer more powerful!

PRAY: *Father, thank You for hearing and listening to my voice when I call to You in prayer. When You listen, I feel loved, accepted, and understood. Today I am listening for You. Speak, Lord, and I will hear and understand. Amen.*

A VICTORY HYMN

READ JUDGES 4–5

KEY VERSES: *Now Deborah, a prophetess, the wife of Lappidoth, was judging Israel at that time. She used to sit under the palm of Deborah between Ramah and Bethel in the hill country of Ephraim, and the people of Israel came up to her for judgment.* JUDGES 4:4–5 ESV

UNDERSTAND:

- This is one of the few times that a female is listed as a prophetess of God. What do you think of God using women in a role such as this?

....

....

....

....

....

- Why do you suppose Judges 5 recounts the same story as Judges 4, only in poetic form?

....

....

....

....

....

....

....

....

APPLY: Deborah was a prophetess of God and the only female judge ever mentioned in the Bible. (Talk about being a standout!) She sat under a palm tree between Ramah and Bethel in the hill country, where people would come to her for judgment.

Deborah had a strong prophetic gifting. She shared with Barak (a military commander of that time) that God had commanded him to attack Jabin, the king of Canaan, as well as Sisera, Jabin's military commander.

Stop and picture this for a moment. A woman telling a man to attack and kill another man? In biblical times, this was almost unheard of.

Many would say that it should still be unheard of, that women are to be seen and not heard in church. There are a couple of scriptures that seem to lean in that direction. Taken in context (the culture of that day being quite different from today), some would argue that women have a perfect right to minister. Regardless of what you believe on that score, Deborah certainly led the way for godly women.

....

....

....

....

....

....

....

....

....

....

....

PRAY: *Thank You for the reminder that women are usable, Lord! You've never excluded women from Your plan, and I'm so grateful. Amen.*

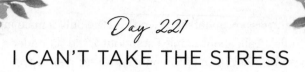

I CAN'T TAKE THE STRESS

—— READ PSALM 55:6–8, 16–17, 22 ——

KEY VERSE: *Cast your cares on the Lord and he will sustain you.* Psalm 55:22 NIV

UNDERSTAND:

- Have you ever wished you could simply fly away, like a bird, from the demands of your life? What circumstances in your life cause those feelings?

....

....

....

....

- How might you find practical ways to cast your cares on the Lord? What actions might that involve?

....

....

....

....

- When the stress in your life seems overwhelming, would it help you to set your phone or computer to remind you to pause, just for a moment, and pray?

....

....

....

....

APPLY: The psalmist expressed in these verses a feeling that most of us have had at one time or another: *If only I could run away from my life! If only I could just be alone somewhere safe and quiet where nothing was expected of me!* Although we do need to find moments to be alone, even in the midst of our busy lives, it's usually not possible to totally escape the stress and pressure each day brings. Apparently, the author of this psalm couldn't escape his life's demands either.

Instead, he shows us another way: Throughout his stressful days—"evening, morning and noon" (verse 17 NIV)—he called to God for help. When the stress in our lives seems unmanageable, we need to follow his example. We don't need to wait to be alone to call out to God. It only takes a moment to cast our stress into God's hands again and again and again throughout our busy days.

PRAY: *Strong Lord, take my stress and carry it for me. May I feel a new sense of lightness even in the midst of my life's demands. Amen.*

Day 222

GOD SINGS OVER YOU

---- **READ ZEPHANIAH 3** ----

KEY VERSE: *"The LORD your God is with you; the mighty One will save you. He will rejoice over you. You will rest in his love; he will sing and be joyful about you."* ZEPHANIAH 3:17 NCV

UNDERSTAND:

• What are the promises found in Zephaniah 3:17? Name each one.

....

....

....

....

....

....

• Which one are you in the deepest need of today?

....

....

....

....

....

....

....

....

APPLY: While this promise was originally for the Israelites, we know that these promises ring true for us today as well. God has saved you if you have put your faith in Christ (see Acts 4:12). You can rest in His unconditional love (see Matthew 11:28–30).

Does it bring you comfort today to know that as you rest in the Lord, He sings over you and takes great delight in you? Have you ever rocked one of your children to sleep, singing over him or her until those little eyelids just cannot remain open? There is nothing more peaceful and delightful than watching your child rest. This is how God feels about you!

Rest in the Lord. Take refuge from the busyness and difficulty of the world. Find peace in His arms, and allow your heavenly Father to sing over you until things seem a bit more manageable.

PRAY: *Lord, hearing that You sing over me makes You seem very close rather than far away. I know that You desire for me to find my rest in You. Help me to trust You enough to relinquish even my deepest fears and sorrows to Your more than capable hands. In Jesus' name I pray. Amen.*

Day 223
GOD SEES

───────── **READ PROVERBS 15** ─────────

KEY VERSE: *The eyes of the Lord are in every place, watching the bad and the good.* PROVERBS 15:3 NLV

UNDERSTAND:

- There is so much pithy, practical wisdom to apply in Proverbs. What verses in chapter 15 have great impact on you tonight?

....

....

....

....

....

....

- When you're tempted to give a harsh word but instead hold your tongue and give a soft answer, what happens? Do you practice this discipline regularly?

....

....

....

....

....

....

....

APPLY: No one has vision like God does. The Bible says He sees and knows absolutely everything in every place. "No one can hide from God. His eyes see everything we do. We must give an answer to God for what we have done," says Hebrews 4:13 (NLV). And Job 28:24 (NLV) says, "He looks to the ends of the earth, and sees everything under the heavens." For people making bad choices and living lives of careless sin, those verses might be scary. But for those who love and want to follow and obey God's Word, they are wonderful and encouraging. God wants us to obey His good ways because He loves us and wants what's best for us. Trust that He always sees you in every moment of your life, and let that give you peace and courage that He's able to strengthen and encourage you at any time and in any situation.

PRAY: *Heavenly Father, please remind me that You are always watching me in every place, in every moment, in every situation. Please let that truth encourage me and give me peace! Amen.*

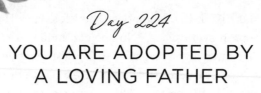

YOU ARE ADOPTED BY A LOVING FATHER

──────── **READ EPHESIANS 1:3–14** ────────

KEY VERSE: *God decided in advance to adopt us into his own family by bringing us to himself through Jesus Christ. This is what he wanted to do, and it gave him great pleasure.* EPHESIANS 1:5 NLT

UNDERSTAND:

• How does knowing that God adopted His children into His family change your perception of your brothers and sisters in Christ?

....

....

....

....

....

• Jesus is God's only Son, but you are an adopted sister to Christ, with full privileges to share in the inheritance of God's kingdom. What does this mean to you?

....

....

....

....

....

APPLY: Adopting a child is a big undertaking. It's not just the time and process—often filled with paperwork and protocol and interviews and red tape—it's also a pricey endeavor, costing anywhere from a few thousand dollars to much, much more.

But for parents who have already taken a child into their heart and family, no paperwork is too lengthy. No red tape is too frustrating. No cost is too high. The child is already perfectly loved, well before signatures are on the adoption papers.

So much more is our heavenly Father's love for you. God set the adoption into motion, and your Savior and Brother, Jesus, cut through the red tape and paid the ultimate price to make sure you could become His sister.

Today, thank God for making your adoption and salvation a family affair, dear one. God's grace and kindness cover you, His daughter.

....

....

....

....

....

....

....

....

....

....

....

PRAY: *Father, I am overwhelmed when I consider the fact that You see me as worthy of being Your adopted, chosen daughter. Because of my Brother, Jesus, You see me as holy and blameless. I don't deserve such favor, but I gratefully accept it. Amen.*

Day 225

WHO ARE THE *THEY*S?

READ LUKE 5:17–26

KEY VERSES: *Some men took a man who was not able to move his body to Jesus. He was carried on a bed. They looked for a way to take the man into the house where Jesus was. But they could not find a way to take him in because of so many people. They made a hole in the roof over where Jesus stood. Then they let the bed with the sick man on it down before Jesus.* LUKE 5:18–19 NLV

UNDERSTAND:

• What amazing friends, to carry their friend all the way to the Healer! Do you have any friends like that?

_____

_____

_____

_____

_____

• How can you be a better friend to someone who struggles with a chronic health issue?

_____

_____

_____

_____

_____

_____

APPLY: *They* brought their friend to Jesus. *They* lowered him through the roof. *They* went out of their way to make sure the one in need had a chance to be seen, noticed.

This story is filled with hints that the one in need had a solid group of friends who cared. Hopefully, you've got a similar group. Who are the theys in your life? Who would move heaven and earth on your behalf?

The truth is we were never meant to do life alone. We all need *theys*. If you're in a lonely season, if the *theys* have vanished, then make up your mind to be a *they* to others. Draw close to one in need—a shut-in, a cancer patient, the woman whose husband left her alone to raise her children without him. Become part of the circle of caring, loving people; then watch as God replenishes your own circle of friends.

PRAY: *I needed this reminder, Lord, that I was never meant to do life alone. Encircle me with people who care, I pray, and help me draw close to others, that I might be a they as well. Amen.*

Day 226

I'M FULL OF ENVY

READ PROVERBS 14:26-30

KEY VERSE: *A sound heart is the life of the flesh: but envy the rottenness of the bones.* PROVERBS 14:30 KJV

UNDERSTAND:

• What do you think is meant by a "sound heart"?

_____

_____

_____

_____

• How might envy rot the "bones" of your being?

_____

_____

_____

_____

• Verse 29 (KJV) speaks of a "hasty spirit." What do those words convey to you? How might you apply them to your own life?

_____

_____

_____

_____

APPLY: Envy and jealousy are often confused, and their meanings are similar. *Jealousy*, however, means we are afraid someone is a threat to something (or someone) we consider to be ours, while *envy* has to do with coveting something that someone else has, something that we lack. The wise author of Proverbs tells us that envy is a destructive emotion that can rot us to the core. According to author Neel Burton, in a 2014 article in *Psychology Today*, over time, envy "can lead to physical health problems such as infections, cardiovascular diseases, and cancers; and mental health problems such as depression, anxiety, and insomnia. We are, quite literally, consumed by envy."

In other words, we might say that envy leads to death. Trust in God (the knowledge that He will give us everything we need) leads in the exact opposite direction. In fact, it's a fountain of life!

PRAYER: *Give me greater confidence in You, Lord, so that I will realize I have no need to envy anyone. After all, You give me everything I need. Amen.*

Day 227

LET YOUR LIGHT SHINE

READ MATTHEW 5

KEY VERSE: *"Let your light shine before men in such a way that they may see your good works, and glorify your Father who is in heaven."* MATTHEW 5:16 NASB

UNDERSTAND:

- Which blessing from the Beatitudes can you relate to? Why does it touch you most deeply?

....

....

....

....

....

....

....

- Why are we to let our light shine before men, according to Matthew 5:16?

....

....

....

....

....

....

....

....

APPLY: There is a children's song sung in many churches that goes like this: "This little light of mine, I'm gonna let it shine. . . . Let it shine till Jesus comes. I'm gonna let it shine."

But what does it mean to let your light shine?

It means you are called, as a Christ follower, to live differently. Your speech should set you apart. Your attitude should distinguish you from others. You should seem almost like an alien living on this earth because, in fact, that is what you are. This is not your home. Your home is in heaven with your Father.

Your good deeds are not to bring glory to yourself but rather to illuminate the path that leads to your Father. When others ask you why you live as you do, point them to God. Let your light shine so that people will come to know Him.

PRAYER: *Lord, give me opportunities today to let my light shine brightly for You. Help me to be bold in my actions and with my words so that others may come to the salvation through Christ. Amen.*

Day 228

CHOOSE WHAT IS BETTER

───────── **READ LUKE 10** ─────────

KEY VERSES: *As Jesus and his disciples were on their way, he came to a village where a woman named Martha opened her home to him. She had a sister called Mary, who sat at the Lord's feet listening to what he said.* LUKE 10:38–39 NIV

UNDERSTAND:

• Do you relate more to Mary or Martha?

....

....

....

....

....

....

• "It will not be taken away from her," says Jesus in verse 42 (NIV). What does that remind you about the things of this temporary world versus spiritual, everlasting life?

....

....

....

....

....

....

APPLY: Martha was very good at hosting and knew all the details of planning and preparing for visitors. Since Jesus was such an extraspecial guest, she wanted everything to be perfect for Him. But Martha grew very frustrated with her sister because, when Jesus arrived, Mary didn't help her with the work of hosting. She simply sat at Jesus' feet to listen to everything He had to say. Both sisters loved Jesus and were showing it in their own ways. But Jesus lovingly told Martha that Mary had chosen what was best, to not fuss much over the details of hosting Him and to simply enjoy His company and listen to His teaching. We women all need that loving, gentle reminder from Jesus at times—to stop fretting and simply relax in the life-giving words and love of our Savior.

PRAY: *Loving Savior, I want to show my love to You in extraspecial details, like Martha, but I want to always choose the best way by enjoying simply being with You and listening to You, like Mary. Please help me to balance this in my life. Amen.*

Day 229

GUARD YOUR TONGUE

— **READ JAMES 3:1-12** —

KEY VERSE: *For if we could control our tongues, we would be perfect and could also control ourselves in every other way.* JAMES 3:2 NLT

UNDERSTAND:

• In what situations are you most likely to lose control of your tongue?

....

....

....

....

• James likens the tongue to a flame of fire (James 3:6). When have you seen words create devastation like an out-of-control fire?

....

....

....

....

• When have you held your tongue despite wanting to say something? How did it make you feel?

....

....

....

....

APPLY: If you're doing this study early in the morning, maybe you haven't had a chance to open mouth, insert foot yet—the day is still young. James 3:8 tells us that unlike all kinds of animals, birds, reptiles, and fish that can be trained and tamed, no one can tame the tongue.

So, if we can't tame it, we must keep it under lock and key.

Proverbs 21:23 (esv) tells us, "Whoever keeps his mouth and his tongue keeps himself out of trouble." Psalm 34:13 (nlt) says to "keep your tongue from speaking evil and your lips from telling lies!" God has given us speech for a reason, and from our words can come encouraging, life-giving hope. But we must learn to listen first, consider second, and answer (when necessary) third. Ask God for the words He would have you say (or not say), and He will help you use your words wisely.

PRAY: *Father, only You can help me get a handle on this powerful muscle in my mouth. My tongue gets me into trouble too often, but I also admit that I too often react with my tongue. Give me the wisdom to know when and what to speak and when to remain silent. Amen.*

Day 230

PREPARE THE WAY

―――――――――― **READ LUKE 3:1-20** ――――――――――

KEY VERSE: *John answered them all, "I baptize you with water. But one who is more powerful than I will come, the straps of whose sandals I am not worthy to untie. He will baptize you with the Holy Spirit and fire."* LUKE 3:16 NIV

UNDERSTAND:

- It's amazing to think that God goes ahead of us, getting things in order even before the need arises. Can you think of a time when you saw His hand at work like that?

....

....

....

....

....

....

- Have you, like John the Baptist, ever gone ahead of a person or situation to prepare the way?

....

....

....

....

....

....

....

....

APPLY: Before Jesus made His way onto the scene in ministry, His cousin John the Baptist carved a path, letting people know He would be coming. When Jesus arrived, advance notice had served its purpose, preparing hearts and minds for the Savior.

In life, we don't always get advance notice. Sometimes no one shows up to prepare the way. We're caught off guard when a loved one is injured in an accident or when a friendship suddenly grows cold. We don't know what hit us when a job loss occurs or a marriage comes to an abrupt end. We crater, our nerves completely shot.

The good news is God is never caught off guard. He knows what's coming, and He is working on our hearts to protect us. He has filled us with His Spirit to guard, comfort, and protect as we navigate through life. In other words, God won't let us down. So rest easy! Let those anxieties go. God has gone ahead of you, and all will be well.

PRAY: *Thank You for going ahead of me, Lord. I know I'm safe because You've already cleared the path. I'm so grateful You've made a way through the wilderness. Amen.*

Day 231

MY FRIEND ANNOYS ME

───── **READ 1 THESSALONIANS 5:15–24** ─────

KEY VERSE: *Make sure that nobody pays back wrong for wrong, but always strive to do what is good for each other.* 1 THESSALONIANS 5:15 NIV

UNDERSTAND:

- What is it about your friend that annoys you so much? Can you get to the bottom of what's *really* bothering you?

....

....

....

....

- Do you think your annoyance might "quench" the Spirit's presence in your life (verse 19 NIV)? If so, why might that happen?

....

....

....

....

- Verse 23 (NIV) speaks of God sanctifying you "through and through." What does that mean to you?

....

....

....

....

APPLY: Even the closest friends can grate on our nerves. Maybe it's the way they eat. . .or talk. . .or behave. Maybe it's simply that their careless words and actions hurt our feelings. Our annoyance can mushroom, expanding larger and larger until we dread being with these individuals. We stop caring very much about what they may need from us, and instead, we focus on how much they bug us. If we keep going in this direction, we may find that we've killed the friendship altogether.

God calls us to turn around before we reach that point. Instead of paying back wrong for wrong, He challenges us to focus on ways we can be of help to our friends. He asks us to pray for them, to rejoice in their unique personalities, and to give thanks for them. And then He promises that He will be the one who will do all this for us, through us.

PRAY: *Jesus, I pray for my friend who annoys me. Remind me of what drew me to this person in the first place. Help me to focus more on my friend and her needs than I do on my irritation. Keep me blameless, spirit, soul, and body, so that my life is an expression of Your ever-faithful friendship. Amen.*

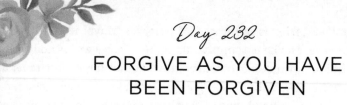

Day 232

FORGIVE AS YOU HAVE
BEEN FORGIVEN

───────── **READ EPHESIANS 4** ─────────

KEY VERSE: *And be kind to one another, tenderhearted, forgiving one another, even as God in Christ forgave you.* EPHESIANS 4:32 NKJV

UNDERSTAND:

- Where will you begin practicing this verse: "Let no corrupt word proceed out of your mouth, but what is good for necessary edification, that it may impart grace to the hearers" (Ephesians 4:29 NKJV)?

....

....

....

....

....

- Compare and contrast the emotions and actions of Ephesians 4:31 with those of Ephesians 4:32. What stands out to you?

....

....

....

....

....

....

....

APPLY: Social media resonates every moment of the day with the attitudes the believers of Ephesus were warned against.

Instead of jumping on the world's bandwagon, believing and declaring your right to hold a grudge, listen to the way of Christ. Let it go. Forgive. Jesus hung on a cross and took our sins upon Himself. God forgave us, and we should forgive one another. We have no right to be angry or seek revenge. That is a worldly belief that is in direct opposition to the teachings of Jesus.

Put away evil speaking as the Ephesians were told to do. Let no unwholesome words come from your lips. Instead, be kind. Be loving. Stand out as a follower of Christ.

When the world says you have every right to be angry or bitter, choose forgiveness. Put off malice, and put on tenderness. It will speak volumes to those around you who do not know Christ.

....

....

....

....

....

....

....

....

....

....

PRAY: *God, I thank You for the forgiveness of my many sins, forgiveness that came to me only through Jesus' death. Put in me a gentle heart where once there was a cold, hard one. Replace my desire to speak ill of others. Help me to build them up instead. May I live according to Your ways and not the ways of the world. Amen.*

Day 233

THE RIGHT PEOPLE, PLACES, AND DETAILS

───────── **READ JOSHUA 2** ─────────

KEY VERSES: *The king of Jericho sent to Rahab, saying, "Bring out the men who have come to you, who entered your house, for they have come to search out all the land." But the woman had taken the two men and hidden them.* JOSHUA 2:3–4 ESV

UNDERSTAND:

• Have you experienced a time when you could clearly see God's hand through the people He made available to you exactly when you needed them?

....

....

....

....

....

• What tiny details have you seen God's hand in as He helps and directs you?

....

....

....

....

....

....

APPLY: The two men Joshua sent to spy on the land of Canaan had to be anxious about their mission. Hopefully, you're not facing anything quite so dangerous as they did; but whatever stressful thing might be weighing heavily on you today, let the story be an encouragement to you. God provides the right people in the right places to help you in your troubles, just like He provided Rahab to help hide and protect the two spies in her home. She told them that she trusted in their God. In turn, the spies promised to help protect Rahab and her family as long as she did not tell anyone about their plans. Then Rahab lowered them by a rope through the window and urged them to hide for three days in the hill country before returning home. Later, with that same red rope, the spies knew where to find her and her family to protect them from being killed when the Israelites took over Jericho.

PRAY: *Heavenly Father, thank You for the way You orchestrate exactly the right people in exactly the right places with exactly the right details to help those who love and follow You. I trust that You do that for me, and I'm so grateful. Amen.*

AVOIDING GOSSIP

──────── **READ PROVERBS 26:17–28** ────────

KEY VERSE: *Fire goes out without wood, and quarrels disappear when gossip stops.* PROVERBS 26:20 NLT

UNDERSTAND:

• Do you find gossip hard to avoid? Why or why not?

....

....

....

• Have you ever been the subject of gossip? How did it make you feel when you found out?

....

....

....

• The Bible uses the metaphor of fire for our tongue and destructive words we speak. What do words and fire have in common?

....

....

....

....

APPLY: Proverbs 26 is chock-full of relational wisdom. From the pitfalls of lying and butting into others' disagreements to warnings against flattery and smooth talking, the overarching message of this chapter is clear: it's often best to mind your own business.

Engaging in gossip—talking about someone behind their back—is the epitome of *not* minding your own business, and it can lead to misunderstanding, broken trust, and damaged relationships. Ah, but those bits of newsy gossip are so delicious, aren't they? Verse 22 (NLT) describes rumors as "dainty morsels that sink deep into one's heart" for good reason.

If you've developed an appetite for gossip, sometimes the easiest and simplest way to kick the habit is to avoid conversations with the person or people who are gossiping. If that's not possible, ask God for the wisdom to tell the others nibbling at the rumor morsels with you that you will no longer engage in it.

PRAY: *Father, I never meant to gossip. It started out innocent enough. A "concern" of a mutual friend masqueraded as a prayer request, and it grew from there. Now feelings are hurt, and I feel terrible. So, I will keep my mouth shut, and Your Word says the fighting will disappear. I'm holding tightly to that truth, God! Amen.*

Day 235

POWER AND AUTHORITY

—————— **READ LUKE 9:1–17** ——————

KEY VERSES: *When Jesus had called the Twelve together, he gave them power and authority to drive out all demons and to cure diseases, and he sent them out to proclaim the kingdom of God and to heal the sick.* LUKE 9:1–2 NIV

UNDERSTAND:

• God has given you authority, just as He gave the disciples. What's the most amazing thing you've witnessed as you've used this authority?

....

....

....

....

....

....

• Have you ever prayed for a sick person and watched that person be healed?

....

....

....

....

....

....

....

....

APPLY: Can you even imagine what the disciples must have been thinking as Jesus spoke words of power and authority over them? Picture yourself in their shoes, with the King of the universe looking you in the eye and saying, *"I give you all power and authority to perform miracles, to drive out demons, to cure diseases, and to proclaim the gospel message!"*

Wow! That will certainly push your anxieties and fears aside, won't it?

Here's the truth: Jesus has spoken those very same words over you. You have that same authority to speak life into situations, to pray over impossible circumstances, and to witness miracles. You have the power to preach the gospel, to share the love of Jesus with the unsaved, and to help those who are caught up in addiction.

Begin to claim that authority. Walk it out. Speak with faith and confidence as you pray in Jesus' name. Then, brace yourself! Miracles are surely on their way.

PRAY: *I'm so grateful for Your authority, Jesus! When I speak in Your name, my words carry a lot of weight. Like the disciples, I will make a difference in my world. Thank You, Lord. Amen.*

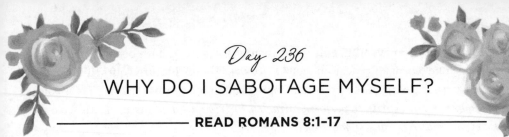

WHY DO I SABOTAGE MYSELF?

———— READ ROMANS 8:1–17 ————

KEY VERSE: *So letting your sinful nature control your mind leads to death. But letting the Spirit control your mind leads to life and peace.* Romans 8:6 NLT

UNDERSTAND:

- Can you identify specific ways that you have sabotaged yourself in the past year?

....

....

....

....

....

....

- What do you think motivates your acts of self-sabotage? Is it fear. . . self-hatred. . .shame. . .or something else? Discussing this issue with someone whose discernment and love you trust may be helpful.

....

....

....

....

....

....

....

APPLY: Self-sabotage makes no rational sense—why would we prevent our-selves from achieving our goals?—and yet most of us have committed this act of self-betrayal at one time or another. We may not be able to see these actions immediately, but we'd be wise to take a closer look. If we can identify behaviors that have led us over and over down the wrong paths, we're probably sabotaging our own growth. This might take the form of getting involved again and again in destructive relationships, or it might show up as a repeated tendency to hesitate at the crucial moment, causing us to lose out on life-giving opportunities.

Whatever form it takes, it's a form of unconscious sin that leads to death rather than the life God wants us to experience. But we don't have to be a slave to it any longer. Jesus has freed us, and His Spirit can lead us down new paths.

PRAY: *Holy Spirit, reveal to me the ways I sabotage myself.*
I don't want to lie to myself any longer. Give me the courage
to become the person You created me to be. Amen.

Day 237

GOD'S STRENGTH

—— READ ISAIAH 40 ——

KEY VERSE: *He gives power to the weak and strength to the powerless.* Isaiah 40:29 NLT

UNDERSTAND:

- Isaiah 40 makes many statements about God. Which one grabs your attention? Why?

....

....

....

....

....

....

....

- What in this fallen world regularly drains you of strength and power?

....

....

....

....

....

....

....

....

APPLY: The prophet Isaiah asks the reader to consider who can be compared to God. He reminds us that God places the stars in the sky and knows them by name. He points out the greatness of God, saying that all the nations are like a grain of sand in God's hand.

In today's key verse, we see that power and strength are gifts from God. God, who is full of power, gifts His children with power. He is the source. We need only to tap into that source in order to be filled with strength.

What drains you? Is it work? A dysfunctional relationship? Caring for your family? Old wounds that never seem to fully heal? Whatever zaps you of your strength, lay it down and ask God to fill you with power. He longs to see you thriving again! Just as the children's song says: "I am weak, but He is strong. Yes, Jesus loves me."

....

....

....

....

....

....

....

....

....

....

PRAY: *Jesus, I am weak, but You are strong. You are powerful, and I need some of that power to make it through the day. Bless me, I pray. Fill me with strength to face this fallen world with confidence and grit. I need You every hour! Thank You for the power source that You are to my life. Amen.*

GOD LEADS THE WAY

— **READ ISAIAH 42** —

KEY VERSE: *"I will lead the blind by a way that they do not know. I will lead them in paths they do not know. I will turn darkness into light in front of them. And I will make the bad places smooth. These are the things I will do and I will not leave them."* ISAIAH 42:16 NLV

UNDERSTAND:

• Isaiah 42:6 says God will take hold of your hand. Are you doing your part by reaching out for Him and letting Him keep your hand in His?

....

....

....

....

....

....

....

• Do you regularly sing to the Lord a new song like verse 10 describes? How does that help fill you with peace?

....

....

....

....

....

....

....

APPLY: Have you ever tripped or stubbed your toe because you were fumbling around in the dark? You might feel as though that is how you are living your life—in total darkness. Maybe you just cannot see the right way to go when making a big decision or facing a big problem in your job or in your marriage and so on. So, trust this scripture, where God promises to turn darkness into light and make rocky places smooth for His people. He will open new paths for you when you don't know what to do or where to go, and He will never leave you! Keep praying and keep trusting!

PRAY: *Heavenly Father, I'm following You even when I cannot see where You are taking me. I trust You to take me on good paths and make all the rough spots smooth. Thank You for leading me and never leaving me. Amen.*

YOU ARE BLESSED TO
BE A BLESSING

────── **READ 2 CORINTHIANS 9:6–15** ──────

KEY VERSE: *You will be enriched in every way so that you can be generous on every occasion, and through us your generosity will result in thanksgiving to God.* 2 CORINTHIANS 9:11 NIV

UNDERSTAND:

• Why does God bless you?

....

....

....

....

• When have you been the recipient of someone's generosity? What did it mean to you?

....

....

....

....

• What needs can you meet today?

....

....

....

....

APPLY: We ask for and eagerly welcome God's blessings in our lives—food, shelter, clothing, money, to name a few—but why does God provide us with these things? One reason is that He enjoys giving good gifts to His children (see Matthew 7:11, James 1:17), but another reason explained in 2 Corinthians 9 is that God blesses us so we can be a blessing to others.

Think of it! God gives us the opportunity to pay forward the good gifts He gives to us. He invites us to follow His example and give generously, which not only blesses the receiver but enriches our lives and results in praise and thanks to God!

Be on the lookout for ways to be generous with your time, talent, and money. And in the meantime, prepare to be generous. Make time to do it. Save money to do it. God is blessing you—to be a blessing!

PRAY: *Lord God, You are so good to me! Today I am not taking for granted everything You give to me. I am so blessed! Show me where You want me to be generous today. Keep my motives pure and my eyes open to Your will. My desire is for Your blessings to not stop here but flow through me. Amen.*

Day 240

BLINDED BY THE LIGHT

READ ACTS 9:1–9

KEY VERSES: *As he journeyed he came near Damascus, and suddenly a light shone around him from heaven. Then he fell to the ground, and heard a voice saying to him, "Saul, Saul, why are you persecuting Me?"* ACTS 9:3–4 NKJV

UNDERSTAND:

• Saul was moving in one direction in his life and then suddenly. . .bam! God stopped him in his tracks and turned his story around. Have you ever had an abrupt change like that?

....

....

....

....

....

....

• Have you known any Sauls, people whose lives were radically transformed?

....

....

....

....

....

....

....

....

APPLY: So many Bible stories (like this one) begin with a person having an ordinary day, doing an ordinary thing. Saul was just walking down the road, something he'd done hundreds of times before. Then, before he knew what hit him, a bright light blinded him and put a halt to his journey.

Saul's loss of vision was just the first of many things that would happen. God spoke very clearly to him and completely shifted his life journey. No longer would he be Saul the persecutor. He would be Paul the evangelist, who would change the course of history and whose name would be known thousands of years later.

Sometimes we have to be blinded in order to see. Maybe you've been there. God had to distract you with a supernatural experience to get your attention. Regardless of His tactic, the Lord has one goal in mind—to put you on the road that will lead to heaven.

PRAY: *Lord, I don't want You to have to intervene in my life in a supernatural way to get my attention. May I be focused on You and moving in the direction You want me to go. Today I recommit my life to You, Jesus. May I only ever follow You. Amen.*

Day 241

I FEEL UNSAFE

READ DEUTERONOMY 31:3-6

KEY VERSE: *"Be strong. Take courage. Don't be intimidated. Don't give them a second thought because GOD, your God, is striding ahead of you. He's right there with you. He won't let you down; he won't leave you."* DEUTERONOMY 31:6 MSG

UNDERSTAND:

• What in your life makes you feel unsafe? Is it an emotional, spiritual, or physical threat?

....

....

....

....

....

....

• What steps can you take to be safe? Can you ask God to guide you to the steps that need to be taken?

....

....

....

....

....

....

....

....

APPLY: Feeling unsafe is a terrible experience. We all need a basic sense of security in order to thrive. It's important to determine where the danger lies (and whether it's real or imagined) and then to take the necessary steps to ensure that we are safe. Often, however, our emotions are what stand in the way of our taking the bold, assertive action that's necessary. We get intimidated, and we freeze in our tracks, afraid to make the necessary moves.

When we're in physical danger, God will be with us, helping us to find ways to protect ourselves (whether that's calling the police, leaving an abusive relationship, or moving to a safer neighborhood). God also wants to protect us from emotional and spiritual danger, guiding us to decisive action that will take us out of danger. He is right there with us, and He will never let us down!

PRAY: *God of courage, guide me to the steps I need to take to protect myself. Thank You that You are already striding ahead of me, ready to show me the way. Amen.*

Day 242

GOOD WORKS
PLANNED IN ADVANCE

—— READ EPHESIANS 2 ——

KEY VERSE: *God has made us what we are. In Christ Jesus, God made us to do good works, which God planned in advance for us to live our lives doing.* EPHESIANS 2:10 NCV

UNDERSTAND:

• How does Ephesians 2:8–9 say that a believer is saved?

....

....

....

....

....

....

• Ephesians 2:10 states that God planned in advance good works for us to do. What have you done in the past year to bring glory to God? The past month? The past week? Today?

....

....

....

....

....

....

....

APPLY: How amazing to think that God was making plans for us in advance! The good works that we take part in are part of His design. We are to live our lives bringing glory to our Creator. One way that we do this is through good deeds.

As you go through life, stop to take inventory of your gifts and passions. Talents and preferences were put in you by the one who knit you together in your mother's womb (see Psalm 139:13). When you use them, it doesn't feel like work because you are in your element. You are serving and giving and doing good deeds in your areas of strength.

You may not consider small acts significant, but they are important to God. The Bible mentions that if you even offer someone a cup of cold water, you are doing it unto Him (see Matthew 10:42). What small act will you do today that brings honor to the Father?

....

....

....

....

....

....

....

....

....

....

....

PRAY: *Lord, it's dangerous to pray for opportunities because then I know You will provide them! I long to serve You and please You through my good works. Show me what good works You planned for me in advance so that I might bring glory to You, my God. Amen.*

Day 243

JOB'S PRAYERS OF PRAISE
AND REPENTANCE

——— READ JOB 1–2 ———

KEY VERSES: *He said, "Without clothing I was born from my mother, and without clothing I will return. The Lord gave and the Lord has taken away. Praise the name of the Lord." In all this Job did not sin or blame God.* Job 1:21–22 NLV

UNDERSTAND:

• What stood out as most familiar to you in the story of Job? What stood out as something you'd never heard of or thought much about?

....

....

....

....

....

....

• Are you holding on to any angry words or attitudes toward God of which you need to repent?

....

....

....

....

....

....

....

APPLY: Job's faith in God was tested in such an incredibly hard way. It's difficult to even imagine the pain and sorrow he endured. Yet after losing so much, Job "fell to the ground and worshiped" (Job 1:20 NLV). However, if you read the whole book of Job, you will find that Job was tested even more, but he did not continue to praise God through it all. In fact, he had quite angry words for a while. In the end, after God reminded Job of His greatness and goodness, Job cried out in repentance, "I hate the things that I have said. And I put dust and ashes on myself to show how sorry I am" (Job 42:6 NLV). Like Job, when we cry out to God with angry words, we should stop and realize God's power and love are over all things in ways we cannot understand. And we must say we are sorry for our disrespect to God. After Job repented, God blessed him again even greater than before.

PRAY: *Heavenly Father, help me to have faith and strength like Job through grief, pain, and hardship. Help me also to learn from Job that if I speak in anger to You, I must apologize and continue to trust in You. Amen.*

Day 244

PRAISE THE LORD IN THE MORNING AND EVENING

───────── **READ PSALM 92** ─────────

KEY VERSES: *It is good to praise the L*ORD *and make music to your name, O Most High, proclaiming your love in the morning and your faithfulness at night.* PSALM 92:1–2 NIV

UNDERSTAND:

• What do you do in the morning to intentionally set the tone for your day?

....

....

....

....

• Why do you think the psalm writer suggests that we proclaim God's love in the morning?

....

....

....

....

• . . .and His faithfulness at night?

....

....

....

....

....

APPLY: For even the most spontaneous, schedule-adverse person, everyone has certain life rhythms. We live by the rising and setting of the sun; we have bookends to each day. This beginning and end is the perfect time to reset our hearts to align with God.

Psalm 92 tells us that it's good to praise the Lord in the morning and celebrate His love. Why? Because throughout the day the world will beat us down with messages that we are unworthy, unqualified, unloved. And starting out the day rooted in the unending love of God will keep us standing strong.

He then goes on to tell us to praise God at night and focus on His faithfulness. Why? Because God showed up throughout the day—in big ways and in small. He kept us going during moments of stress and anxiety, and He kept His promises. Reminding ourselves of His faithfulness helps us remember His unending goodness the next time we're struggling.

Praise Him this morning. Live in His love and faithfulness.

....

....

....

....

....

....

....

....

....

....

....

PRAY: *God of love, thank You for lavishing Your care and devotion on me. I am made whole in Your love this morning. When I'm feeling unloved, unworthy, and forgotten today, wrap Your arms around me and remind me that I am Yours. Amen.*

Day 245

WHEN ALL GOES WELL

READ MATTHEW 21:1-11

KEY VERSES: *Most of the crowd spread their cloaks on the road, and others cut branches from the trees and spread them on the road. And the crowds that went before him and that followed him were shouting, "Hosanna to the Son of David! Blessed is he who comes in the name of the Lord! Hosanna in the highest!"* MATTHEW 21:8–9 ESV

UNDERSTAND:

• It's ironic to think that Jesus was ushered into Jerusalem with such fanfare only to be crucified shortly thereafter. What do you think He went through emotionally?

....

....

....

....

....

• Have you ever walked through a season of favor that was quickly followed by a season of loss?

....

....

....

....

....

....

APPLY: What an amazing day this must have been! Jesus entered Jerusalem, riding on a colt, to a welcoming crowd—one filled with onlookers and fans who cried out, "Hosanna to the Son of David! Blessed is he who comes in the name of the Lord!" They spoke blessings over Him, words of affirmation and adoration.

What different words they shouted a week later as Jesus carried the cross to Golgotha. On that day onlookers jeered, spit on Him, and ridiculed Him.

A lot can change in a week.

Maybe you know what it feels like to be favored one moment then disregarded and cast aside the next. Maybe your husband left you for another woman. Maybe your child stopped speaking to you. Maybe you were overlooked by your boss, passed over for a promotion.

When all goes well, it's easy to shout words of praise. But when things are crumbling around you, depression and anxiety can set in. Today God wants you to know that He's got your back, no matter what you're going through.

PRAY: *I needed that reminder, Lord! I don't want to celebrate only when things are going my way. I want to be found faithful, even during the hard seasons. May I never forget that You won't let me go, Father. Amen.*

Day 246

I'M FRUSTRATED

—— **READ PROVERBS 3:5–8** ——

KEY VERSE: *Trust in the L*ORD *with all your heart and do not lean on your own understanding.* PROVERBS 3:5 NASB

UNDERSTAND:

• Can you see a relationship between frustration and trust? If so, what do you think it is? How does one affect the other?

....

....

....

....

• If you let go of your sense that you are in control of your own life, what happens to your frustration?

....

....

....

....

....

• How might you acknowledge God in all your ways (verse 6)?

....

....

....

....

APPLY: *Frustrate* comes from the same Latin word as *fraud*. Both words originally had to do with being cheated out of something that is deserved. And isn't that what we feel when we are frustrated—that something we *deserved* has failed to happen? Whether it's something we want to do that we just can't seem to accomplish. . .or other people acting in ways we don't like. . .or circumstances not falling into place the way we'd hoped, frustration robs us of our sense of control. We feel as though our lives have gone off course. We believe we *needed* something to happen, but it didn't!

When we're frustrated, though, odds are pretty good that we're leaning on our own understanding rather than God's. Trust means that we put *everything* in God's hands—our abilities, other people's actions, even the weather—allowing Him to straighten things out in His time in His way.

PRAY: *God of wisdom, when I feel frustrated, help me not to rely so much on my own understanding of my life. Remind me to trust You more so that You can make my way lead straight to You. Amen.*

Day 247

THE LOVE OF CHRIST

---------- **READ EPHESIANS 3** ----------

KEY VERSES: *That Christ may dwell in your hearts through faith; that you, being rooted and grounded in love, may be able to comprehend with all the saints what is the width and length and depth and height—to know the love of Christ which passes knowledge; that you may be filled with all the fullness of God.* EPHESIANS 3:17–19 NKJV

UNDERSTAND:

• Through Jesus, we have access to God. What are the words Paul uses when he describes how we may come before God in Ephesians 3:12?

....

....

....

....

....

• What does it mean that Christ's love for you passes knowledge?

....

....

....

....

....

....

....

APPLY: If you are a mother, you have probably worked hard to build confidence in your children. Isn't it your greatest hope that your children know who they are and that they would face the world boldly and with confidence? With the strong roots you give them at home, you've tried to nurture them in such a way that the world cannot shake them.

God loves us in a similar way, yet even far greater. He loves us with an unconditional love that surpasses all knowledge. No one knows a greater love. We are told here in Ephesians that it is very deep and very wide. We are told elsewhere in scripture that nothing is able to separate us from the love of God (see Romans 8:38–39).

Allow God to grow in you a confidence that can take you out into the world. If you are grounded and rooted in Him, nothing can shake you.

PRAY: *Lord, give me boldness and confidence. Help me to know and to feel that I am deeply loved by my Creator God. It brings me great peace to know I will never live one day without Your love, which surpasses all knowledge. In Jesus' name I pray. Amen.*

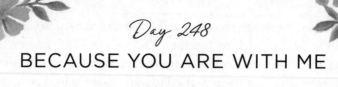

BECAUSE YOU ARE WITH ME

——————— **READ PSALMS 23–25** ———————

KEY VERSES: *The Lord is my Shepherd. I will have everything I need. He lets me rest in fields of green grass. He leads me beside the quiet waters. He makes me strong again. He leads me in the way of living right with Himself which brings honor to His name. Yes, even if I walk through the valley of the shadow of death, I will not be afraid of anything, because You are with me.* PSALM 23:1–4 NLV

UNDERSTAND:

• When have you felt you've truly been in the valley of the shadow of death? How did you feel God's presence with you there?

....

....

....

....

....

• Do you feel hated by anyone like David clearly did in Psalm 25:19? How does this passage help give you peace about that situation?

....

....

....

....

....

....

....

APPLY: One of the most familiar and popular passages of scripture is Psalm 23. Its comfort and peace abound as we picture God caring for us like a good shepherd lovingly cares for his sheep. God never leaves us as He guides, protects, and provides for us, until one day we are safely home with Him forever in heaven. Psalm 24 goes on to praise God for His greatness, glory, and holiness, acknowledging that everything in the world is His. And Psalm 25 pleads with God for direction, protection, and forgiveness of sin, trusting that He gives it and is full of goodness to those who love and obey Him. As you end each day, the praise and prayer in the psalms are beautiful ways to turn your heart and mind to God, letting Him give you the peace you need to rest well and prepare for a new day full of His plans, provision, and mercy.

PRAY: *Heavenly Father, You are my loving Shepherd, and I want to follow Your leading in all things. Please gently prod me back where I belong when I stray from Your good paths and plans for me. Forgive me for my sin and help me to obey You. Amen.*

Day 249
KEEP GOING

──── **READ GALATIANS 6:1–10** ────

KEY VERSE: *Do not let yourselves get tired of doing good. If we do not give up, we will get what is coming to us at the right time.* GALATIANS 6:9 NLV

UNDERSTAND:

- How do you persevere when you feel as though your efforts for God's kingdom are in vain?

....

....

....

....

- How can you know you're spending time on the things God wants you to be doing for Him?

....

....

....

....

- How can you rest without stopping?

....

....

....

....

APPLY: Oftentimes doing good work in the Lord's name is its own reward. Although we aren't saved by our good deeds, when we're demonstrating God's love to others through our efforts, we're helping to further His plan on earth. What could be better?

But other times and in some seasons of life, doing good work may feel like a burden. We may be overextended or putting unrealistic expectations on ourselves and others. The work and our attitude about the work may even be straining relationships with family and friends. Even while doing God's work, it's possible to feel far from Him.

Still, the apostle Paul says, don't give up doing good.

If you're feeling tired of doing good, look at the big picture. Ask God to renew your passion for His work and to show you what He wants you to do. Pause to rest when necessary—not disengaging entirely but allowing yourself to recharge. God will reward your faithfulness!

PRAY: *God, when life gets crazy, I start to develop a bad attitude about the good things You have given me to do. Renew in me a passion for Your work. Give me eyes to see how my efforts play a part in Your plan. And encourage me in my work so I can stay excited and vitalized to do it. Amen.*

Day 250

WATER INTO WINE

─────── **READ JOHN 2:1–12** ───────

KEY VERSE: *"A host always serves the best wine first," he said. "Then, when everyone has had a lot to drink, he brings out the less expensive wine. But you have kept the best until now!"* JOHN 2:10 NLT

UNDERSTAND:

• Why do you suppose the line about the best wine being served first matters in this story?

....

....

....

....

....

....

• Have you ever wondered why Jesus chose to perform His first public miracle at a wedding?

....

....

....

....

....

....

....

APPLY: All the Gospels give us insight into the life of Jesus, starting with His childhood and moving into His ministry years. At thirty years of age, Jesus found Himself at a wedding. The host ran out of wine (a cultural no-no). Jesus' mother came to Him to ask a favor: "Son, do You think You could. . ."

Jesus' first response was to tell her that the time had not come. Then, after thinking it through, He performed His very first miracle—turning water into wine.

There's a lot of debate about why His first miracle took place at a wedding and why He chose turning water into wine. Some would argue that a miraculous healing (restoring sight to the blind, causing deaf ears to hear) might have been more impressive.

But Jesus chose to perform an "everyday" miracle, one that shows us He cares about the little things—when the faucet is leaking, when the car breaks down, when the refrigerator stops working. You can cry out to Him, even in the everyday things, and He's ready with a miracle. What a loving Savior we have.

PRAY: *I'm glad You care about the details, Lord. I can go to You with every concern, every problem. If You took the time to bless a wedding host and his guests, I know You will meet my every need. Amen.*

Day 251
I CAN'T SEEM TO FOCUS

READ PHILIPPIANS 3:12–16

KEY VERSE: *God will clear your blurred vision—you'll see it yet!* PHILIPPIANS 3:15 MSG

UNDERSTAND:

- Goals are good focal points. They can keep us on track, even when we're exhausted or confused.

- What goals are shaping your life? Do they line up with God's will for you—or could some of them be contributing to your lack of focus?

APPLY: A goal is a destination point we've chosen for our lives. The best goals are carefully considered in quiet moments. They're clearly defined, spelled out in concrete terms, so that even in the busiest, most confusing periods of our lives, we can still keep heading in the right direction. Without any goals, we'd just be wandering aimlessly through life.

As Christians, we are following Jesus. He is our goal, the end point we are striving to reach. Remember, though, what happened to Peter when he was walking toward Jesus on the Sea of Galilee—he took his eyes off his goal, and immediately he began to sink. The same thing happens to us, spiritually, when we lose our focus on Jesus. Things start to get blurry. Life seems confusing. We're not sure what we should be doing. We start to sink.

We all have moments like that, but this passage of scripture offers us hope and encouragement. God will sharpen our focus and clear our blurry eyes—so that once again, we can see Jesus.

PRAY: *Jesus, I'm coming to You. Show me the way. When life is confusing, help me to focus only on Your face. Amen.*

AVOID IDOLS

——— READ LEVITICUS 19 ———

KEY VERSE: *"Do not turn to idols or make metal gods for yourselves. I am the LORD your God."* LEVITICUS 19:4 NIV

UNDERSTAND:

- Among the laws laid out for the Israelites, we read that they were not to turn to idols. Why do you think this was, and is, so important to God?

....

....

....

....

....

....

- What is your definition of an idol?

....

....

....

....

....

....

....

....

APPLY: While this law was given in Leviticus, it still applies to believers today. It is repeated in the New Testament, and we know that our God is a jealous God. In 1 Corinthians 10:14, the apostle Paul warns the believers in Corinth to keep away from idols.

Must an idol be fashioned from metal or wood? Do you think that the Lord is also jealous of other types of idols? An idol is anything that we put before God in our lives. Do you spend more time reading the Bible or on social media sites? Do you focus on prayer or TV more often?

Consider today where you're putting most of your time and money. You may find your idols lurking there. Make a conscious effort to turn away from such idols and seek God first and with your whole heart. This pleases the Lord.

PRAY: *Heavenly Father, bring to light anything in my life that I have allowed to become an idol. I may not be constructing other gods of metal or wood, but I am distracted daily by my own idols. Create in me a pure heart that puts You first in all I do. Amen.*

Day 253

GIVE YOUR BURDENS
TO THE LORD

──────── **READ PSALMS 55–56** ────────

KEY VERSES: *When I am afraid, I will put my trust in you. I praise God for what he has promised. I trust in God, so why should I be afraid?* PSALM 56:3–4 NLT

UNDERSTAND:

- What causes you to panic sometimes? How has God shown you He sees and cares?

....

....

....

....

....

....

- Have you ever been totally betrayed by someone you were once close to? What did God teach you through that experience?

....

....

....

....

....

....

APPLY: David's panicky words in Psalm 55:4–6 (NLT) are sometimes oddly comforting in a misery-loves-company kind of way. He says, "My heart pounds in my chest. The terror of death assaults me. Fear and trembling overwhelm me, and I can't stop shaking. Oh, that I had wings like a dove; then I would fly away and rest!" We feel awful for David, yet if we've experienced any kind of horrible upset, we can probably relate. And it's good to know we're not the only ones who've ever felt that way—terrified with a racing heart and wishing we could just fly away quickly to find peace and rest. Like David, we can vent our feelings of total fear and frustration to God. We can tell our heavenly Father about our panic and pain. No one understands and cares like He does. As we cry out, we must hold on to the promise that our good Father sees every one of our sorrows. If we trust in Him, He will guide us to and send us the help we need. He rescues us, defends us against our enemies, and helps us walk confidently in His life-giving light.

PRAY: *Heavenly Father, I relate to David in his panic sometimes. Please calm me with the truth of Your promises. Please send me the help and encouragement I need. Please guide and direct me through Your people, provision, and perfect peace. I trust You, and I love You! Amen.*

Day 254
SPEAK GENTLY

─── **READ PROVERBS 15** ───

KEY VERSE: *A gentle answer turns away wrath, but a harsh word stirs up anger.*
PROVERBS 15:1 NIV

UNDERSTAND:

- In your experience, how has a gentle response defused a tense situation?

....

....

....

....

- In what situations or relationships are you more likely to respond with a harsh word?

....

....

....

....

- Do you think you'd ever regret using gentleness in an exchange?

....

....

....

....

....

APPLY: Words are powerful. Cliché? Yes, but that doesn't make it any less true.

Thoughtless words can unintentionally wreck someone's day. Careless words can lead to confusion and misunderstanding. Intentionally hurtful words can create lasting damage. And words used as weapons to slash at others can take a tense exchange and escalate it to a full-on angry battle.

But thoughtful, gentle words have the opposite effect and can be just as mighty. Words spoken in kindness can *make* someone's day. Encouraging words can start to rebuild a battered self-image. Loving words can mend bridges and tear down walls of resentment. A gentle response can lead to peace.

Today and every day, choose your words carefully. Thoughtfully consider the way you speak to your family, friends, frenemies, coworkers, and even how you speak to yourself. Ask God to fill your heart, mind, and tongue with wisdom to speak gentleness.

PRAY: *God, I need help controlling the words that come out of my mouth. You know the people and the situations that light me up and make me see red. But I have a choice in my reactions and responses. I want to choose gentleness. I want to bring Your peace into every situation. Show me how, because I can't do it by myself. Amen.*

Day 255

PERSISTENCE PAYS OFF

READ 1 SAMUEL 1:1-20

KEY VERSE: *So in the course of time Hannah became pregnant and gave birth to a son. She named him Samuel, saying, "Because I asked the LORD for him."* 1 SAMUEL 1:20 NIV

UNDERSTAND:

• Hannah pleaded with God for quite some time before she conceived Samuel. Have you ever had to have faith for a prolonged time?

....

....

....

....

....

....

• What do you do when you're desperate for a miracle but God is silent?

....

....

....

....

....

....

....

....

APPLY: Poor Hannah. She was loved by God and by her husband, who adored her, but her womb had been closed. Her heart broke over the child she so desperately wanted. And it didn't help matters that her archrival spent much of her time provoking Hannah in order to cause jealousy.

Hannah pleaded her case before the Lord, and God heard her cries. He gave her a son, Samuel, and the course of history was changed because of the role he played in selecting King David.

Have you ever found yourself in Hannah's shoes? You're holding out for a miracle, but someone around you is tormenting you? Ridiculing? Making fun of your dream?

Don't give up, even when anxiety threatens to rear its head. Don't let jealousy enter the picture. Don't get anxious. Keep your heart pure as you wait, and watch what God is about to do. Perhaps, when your dream is fulfilled, it will change the course of history as well.

PRAY: *Lord, I give my hopes, wishes, and dreams to You. I lay down anxieties and say, "In Your time, Father!" I close my ears to the naysayers and keep my focus on You while I'm waiting, Lord. Amen.*

Day 256

I FEEL INADEQUATE

—— READ 2 CORINTHIANS 12:7–10 ——

KEY VERSE: *My grace is sufficient for thee: for my strength is made perfect in weakness.* 2 Corinthians 12:9 KJV

UNDERSTAND:

- Scripture doesn't tell us what Paul's "thorn in the flesh" (verse 7 KJV) was, but we don't really need to know. What is *your* thorn in your flesh? What is it that makes you feel inadequate?

....

....

....

....

....

....

- Look back on your life. Can you see occasions when you experienced God's strength in the midst of your own weakness?

....

....

....

....

....

....

APPLY: No matter how talented, skilled, or intelligent we are, all of us have flaws and weaknesses that hold us back from living our lives the way we wish we could. These weaknesses may get in the way of our personal lives, our professional lives, or our spiritual lives. We wish God would simply take them away from us, and we may even beg Him to do so. But often our prayers seem to go unanswered.

Following Jesus, however, does not mean we will magically become perfect people. All of us will continue to suffer in some way, whether from an illness, a character flaw, or a lack of ability in some vital area of our lives. We ask ourselves, *If God loves me, why won't He step in and take this problem away from me? Hasn't He promised over and over that He will bless me?* But sometimes, strange as it seems, the problem *is* the blessing. It forces us to see how much we need God.

PRAY: *I wish I didn't have to bear this flaw of mine, Lord. But since I do, I'll give it to You. Use me, with all my flaws, however You want. Be strong in my weakness. Amen.*

Day 257

ADOPTED BY GOD

---- **READ GALATIANS 4** ----

KEY VERSES: *But when the set time had fully come, God sent his Son, born of a woman, born under the law, to redeem those under the law, that we might receive adoption to sonship.* GALATIANS 4:4–5 NIV

UNDERSTAND:

• What is your definition of adoption?

....

....

....

....

....

....

• How are believers adopted by God?

....

....

....

....

....

....

....

....

APPLY: You may know a family who chose adoption as a way to expand. Perhaps you yourself were adopted. Adoption is a legal and binding act. It declares one who was not in the family to be part of the family. The adopted individual is given the family's name and all the same rights as a biological child.

God adopted you when you placed your trust in Jesus. You were set free from your sin because Jesus paid the penalty of death for you. You received all the rights of an heir to the kingdom.

The death and resurrection of Jesus happened at just the right time in history. It was God's plan from the beginning to save humanity from sin. Believers have the assurance that they will spend eternity with God the Father. Just as adoptive families celebrate "gotcha day" (the day their child became part of the family), you should celebrate your status as God's beloved child.

PRAY: *Heavenly Father, I thank You for Your plan and for Your perfect timing. Thank You for sending Jesus to save me from my sin. I celebrate the knowledge that through Him I have become part of Your family! In Christ's name I pray. Amen.*

Day 258

SPREAD THE GOOD NEWS

—— READ ROMANS 1 ——

KEY VERSES: *I am not ashamed of the Good News. It is the power of God. It is the way He saves men from the punishment of their sins if they put their trust in Him. It is for the Jew first and for all other people also. The Good News tells us we are made right with God by faith in Him. Then, by faith we live that new life through Him. The Holy Writings say, "A man right with God lives by faith."* ROMANS 1:16–17 NLV

UNDERSTAND:

• How have you shared the Good News lately?

....

....

....

....

....

....

• What sometimes hinders you from sharing the Good News?

....

....

....

....

....

....

....

APPLY: Did you do anything you feel silly or embarrassed about today? Some of us seem to beat ourselves up more than others over those types of things, even though we've all been there, done that. But as Christians, the one thing we should never feel embarrassed or ashamed of is sharing the gospel of Jesus. We should all want to be able to say, like Paul did in Romans 1, that we are not ashamed of the Good News that Jesus came to earth to live a perfect life and teach us, then died on the cross to pay for our sins, and then rose to life again and offers us eternal life too. When we share this Good News with others, we spread God's power to save people from their sins. That should never embarrass us but rather fill us with satisfaction and peace that we are participating in God's purposes and doing the very best work.

PRAY: *Heavenly Father, help me to never be ashamed to share the gospel of Jesus Christ. Thank You for wanting to save all people from their sins! Please empower me and give me great peace as I help to spread the Good News. Amen.*

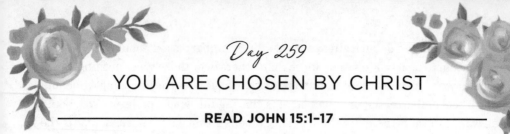

YOU ARE CHOSEN BY CHRIST

—— READ JOHN 15:1–17 ——

KEY VERSE: *"You didn't choose me. I chose you. I appointed you to go and produce lasting fruit, so that the Father will give you whatever you ask for, using my name."* JOHN 15:16 NLT

UNDERSTAND:

- Jesus didn't *have* to choose you; He *decided* to choose you. What does that mean to you?

....

....

....

....

....

....

- Jesus calls His followers His friends in John 15:14. How does friendship with Jesus affect how you think of your relationship with Him?

....

....

....

....

....

....

....

APPLY: We've all felt the sting of rejection. Whether we are overlooked by peers, are passed over for a promotion, or have been abandoned by a friend, insecurities we think we've long laid to rest can resurface in a moment. And we feel useless. Unworthy. Like a failure. Less than others.

Sister, Jesus Christ chooses you.

Today you stand in the love of Christ, who handpicked you before you were born to be His friend. You belong in His family. He invites you to experience the fullness of His Father's kingdom. All you need do is, in turn, remain in His love. Follow Him, obey His commandments, and experience the overflowing joy He offers today. Pray confidently in the name of Jesus, and align your heart to God's wondrous plan for your life.

You are appointed by Christ today. You are chosen. You are loved.

PRAY: *Jesus, "thank You" seems inadequate for my gratitude that You have chosen me. When others have turned their backs, I am confident that You never will. You are the vine, and I am the branch, and I will remain in You all my days. Thank You for remaining steadfast to the work of the Father. Amen.*

Day 260

HOME AT LAST

── **READ LUKE 15:11–32** ──

KEY VERSES: *"'Bring the fattened calf and kill it. Let's have a feast and celebrate. For this son of mine was dead and is alive again; he was lost and is found.' So they began to celebrate."* Luke 15:23–24 NIV

UNDERSTAND:

- Has your family ever dealt with a prodigal? If so, how did it affect the family's spiritual health?

....

....

....

....

....

....

- Think of a time in your life when you wandered from the Lord. How far did you get before He wooed you back home again?

....

....

....

....

....

....

....

APPLY: Perhaps no other story in the Bible has touched the hearts of believers like the tale of the prodigal son. Many relate because they have lived the life of a wanderer. Still others relate because they feel like the older brother.

Regardless of where you find yourself in the story, the outcome is the same: God loves His kids and won't give up on them. He longs for every wandering, broken, anxious heart to turn itself back toward home, for sin and separation to be a thing of the past.

What are you struggling with today? Do you feel like you've wandered too far? Are you, like the older brother, dealing with a judgmental spirit or jealousy? Regardless, God wants to completely heal you, make you whole, and sweep you back into the fold. You are His child, and He adores you.

PRAY: *You're the best Dad ever! No matter how far I stray, no matter how badly I fumble, You're standing there, arms wide open, to welcome me back home. How can I ever thank You, Lord? My heart is filled with praise. Amen.*

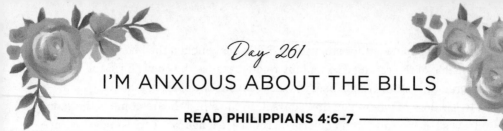

I'M ANXIOUS ABOUT THE BILLS

—— READ PHILIPPIANS 4:6–7 ——

KEY VERSE: *Don't fret or worry. Instead of worrying, pray. Let petitions and praises shape your worries into prayers, letting God know your concerns.* PHILIPPIANS 4:6 MSG

UNDERSTAND:

- Worrying and praying are opposite actions.

....

....

....

....

....

....

- Each time your worries about money come to mind, can you make a conscious effort to pray instead of worry?

....

....

....

....

....

....

....

....

APPLY: When we worry, we imagine a bleak future that doesn't yet exist—that may, in fact, *never* exist. We picture all the terrible things that could happen if we aren't able to pay the bills. We feel inadequate to change things. We dwell on everything that may go wrong. Worry settles like a stone into the pit of our stomach, dulling our appreciation for life and robbing us of sleep at night.

In this passage of scripture, Paul is telling us that there's another option—instead of worrying, we can let petitions and praise shape our worries into prayers. As we make a conscious effort to do this, we will find that the peace of Christ pushes the worry out of our hearts. As a result, we may be able to perceive new solutions to our financial problems. God is concerned with each and every aspect of our lives, and He wants to help us with our money problems.

PRAY: *God, You know how worried I am about money. Help me to use this worry as a tool to turn my heart to You. Each time that worry jabs me again, may it be like a bell that calls my heart to prayer. Amen.*

Day 262

DRAWING BOUNDARIES

—— READ DANIEL 1 ——

KEY VERSE: *God made Ashpenaz, the chief officer, want to be kind and merciful to Daniel.* DANIEL 1:9 NCV

UNDERSTAND:

• What did Daniel ask Ashpenaz for in Daniel 1?

....

....

....

....

• How did God show favor to Daniel in this request?

....

....

....

....

• In your own life, what boundary have you drawn because you are set apart as a child of God?

....

....

....

....

....

....

APPLY: Daniel did not want to eat the food or drink the wine of the king of Babylon because it would make him unclean. He asked permission to abstain, and he found favor with the king's chief officer in this request.

Like young Daniel, an Israelite living in the Babylonian kingdom, you live in a society that is opposed to God's ways. What boundary have you drawn because you are a child of the living God? Have you drawn a boundary regarding modesty in your dress, what movies you watch, or your alcohol consumption? Maybe there is something else that you have drawn a line in the sand regarding.

God caused Daniel to find favor with the chief officer. As you seek to honor God, He will put people and circumstances in place to bless you. Trust Him, and keep living according to His ways despite opposition from those around you.

....

....

....

....

....

....

....

....

....

....

....

....

....

....

....

PRAY: *Lord, thank You for the wonderful example of Daniel in the Bible. His story inspires me to draw boundaries and live according to Your will and Your ways in spite of the culture that is all around me. Give me strength to honor You with my decisions. In Jesus' name I ask. Amen.*

Day 263

AT ALL TIMES

——————— **READ PSALM 34** ———————

KEY VERSES: *I will bless the LORD at all times; his praise shall continually be in my mouth. My soul makes its boast in the LORD; let the humble hear and be glad. Oh, magnify the LORD with me, and let us exalt his name together!* PSALM 34:1–3 ESV

UNDERSTAND:

• How much time do you spend in worship and prayer each day?

....

....

....

....

....

....

• What do you think might change in your life if you increased your worship and prayer time?

....

....

....

....

....

....

....

APPLY: We can alleviate so much of our stress and worries if we make the first few verses of Psalm 34 true of ourselves. If we bless and praise God at all times, boast in His amazing goodness and power, and lift up His name for others to know and honor Him, we don't have much time to focus on problems and pain. Our minds will stay fixed on the one who encamps around us, the one who hears and delivers us from every fear. Name anything you are anxious over, hurting from, or frightened about, and speak praise to God over and above it. Tell God you know that He sees and cares about every detail of the situation and that He is sovereign and good through it all. Describe to Him how you see that He has been caring for you in the midst of it, and trust that He will continue to do so. Breathe deeply as you pray and worship, letting God's peace quiet you and give you rest.

PRAY: *Heavenly Father, You are awesome and mighty in all things. I choose to fix my thoughts and words on You in worship for all that You are and all the good that You do! Please push out every problem and pain from my mind as I praise You! Amen.*

Day 264

STILLNESS BEFORE GOD

---- **READ PSALM 46** ----

KEY VERSE: *"Be still, and know that I am God! I will be honored by every nation. I will be honored throughout the world."* PSALM 46:10 NLT

UNDERSTAND:

• Is being still before God easy for you? Why or why not?

....

....

....

....

....

....

....

....

....

• What's one positive thing you think would come out of meditative stillness?

....

....

....

....

....

....

....

....

....

....

APPLY: When life is particularly chaotic, our minds and hearts tend to shift into chaos mode as well. If you're a natural worrier, your fret level may reach code red. Anxiety may shoot through the roof. You may go into defense mode and put up walls between yourself and the people around you. You may even try to strong-arm the situation and fix it by sheer force of will.

But all these responses mean you've forgotten that God is in control. The fact is nothing can happen in your life that surprises God. He knows what tomorrow will bring. He knows what today has in store. He knows your path in the next hour and even the next minute. And it's all in His capable hands.

Today, stop. Be still and take refuge in the fact that He is God and you are not. He is always ready to help in times of trouble (Psalm 46:1). He is here among us and He is our Fortress (verse 7).

....

....

....

....

....

....

....

....

....

....

....

PRAY: *God, quiet my brain. I am here with You right now in body, mind, and spirit. You are God. You are good. You are holy. You are perfect. You are my rescuer, my redeemer, my shepherd, my friend. I praise You for who You are. I praise You for all You do and all You have yet to do in the world and in my life. Amen.*

THE WALLS COME
TUMBLING DOWN

——— **READ JOSHUA 6** ———

KEY VERSE: *When the trumpets sounded, the army shouted, and at the sound of the trumpet, when the men gave a loud shout, the wall collapsed; so everyone charged straight in, and they took the city.* JOSHUA 6:20 NIV

UNDERSTAND:

• Are there any walls in your life right now, separating you from God or others?

....

....

....

....

....

....

• How is God nudging you to get rid of barriers in your life?

....

....

....

....

....

....

....

APPLY: The walls of Jericho came tumbling down when Joshua took the time to follow God's plan. He could have tried to knock the walls down in his own strength, but that would have taken ages (and the noise would have alerted the enemy). God had a plan to take those walls down instantaneously!

Maybe you can relate to Joshua's story. Maybe there are walls in your life that need to come down—between you and your spouse, between friends or coworkers, perhaps even between you and God. Instead of chipping away at them, ask God to bring those walls down in a flash. Take authority over the situation. March around those walls (spiritually speaking) and let out a shout; then watch as God miraculously takes over.

Walls are no hindrance for God. And, as you watch them tumble, they won't be a hindrance for you either.

PRAY: *I love the story of Joshua, Lord! It's so exciting to watch You move so quickly. I ask You to do that in my life as well. I submit my walls to You, Father. Knock them down, I pray. Amen.*

I FEEL SO HELPLESS

—————————— **READ JOHN 15:1–8** ——————————

KEY VERSE: *"Live in me. Make your home in me just as I do in you. In the same way that a branch can't bear grapes by itself but only by being joined to the vine, you can't bear fruit unless you are joined with me."* JOHN 15:4 MSG

UNDERSTAND:

• What would it look like if you were to make your home in Jesus?

....

....

• Examine your life. Do your helpless feelings come because you have been trying to bear fruit without being joined to Jesus?

....

....

• Jesus speaks in these verses of pruning the vine so that it can bear more fruit. Do you feel that He has "pruned" you? In what ways?

....

....

• Do you think of "pruning" as a negative, painful experience? Does it have to be? Is that what Jesus is indicating in these verses?

....

....

....

APPLY: Again and again, God tells us in the Bible, *"Stop trying to do things on your own! I want to do amazing things in your life—but I need you to get out of My way!"*

Of course, we feel helpless sometimes—because we *are*! No matter how much we try, we are powerless to change certain circumstances. We can keep pulling and tugging, straining with effort day after day, and we'll still accomplish absolutely nothing. It's so frustrating!

But Jesus tells us that's an unnatural way to live. It's like a branch thinking it can continue to bear fruit after it's been cut off from the vine; it just won't happen. The natural way, the way of being we were created to experience, is to simply relax into Him and allow His life to flow through us, out into the world.

PRAY: *Jesus, You know how helpless this situation makes me feel. Help me to stop trying to be in control of the situation so that You can take over. I want to make my home in You so that You can make Your home in me. Amen.*

Day 267
GRIEVE DIFFERENTLY

———— READ 1 THESSALONIANS 4:11–5:28 ————

KEY VERSES: *Brothers and sisters, we want you to know about those Christians who have died so you will not be sad, as others who have no hope. We believe that Jesus died and that he rose again. So, because of him, God will raise with Jesus those who have died.* 1 THESSALONIANS 4:13–14 NCV

UNDERSTAND:

• Who are the dead in Christ, and what does the Bible teach about them?

_____

_____

_____

_____

_____

_____

• How should we grieve differently than the world grieves, and why?

_____

_____

_____

_____

_____

_____

APPLY: As Paul wrote to the Thessalonians, he included some instructions about grief. Believers in Christ in Paul's day, and likewise in the times in which we live, are not to grieve as those who do not know Christ.

Certainly, we are sad when we lose a loved one. But we take comfort in the fact that, if our loved one was a Christian, this is not a real "goodbye" but merely a "see you later." We read in scripture that the dead in Christ shall rise at His Second Coming.

While there remains some degree of mystery about the Second Coming of our Savior, we do know that it is clear that because He died and rose again, those who die "in Him" (as Christians) will rise again as well. Their physical bodies will reunite with their spirits, and they will have a new and complete spiritual body at that time.

Rejoice in the fact that those who know Christ will spend eternity with Him. Death has truly "lost its sting" for the Christian!

....

....

....

....

....

....

....

....

....

....

PRAY: *Lord, I am thankful that even though I grieve the loss of Christian brothers and sisters, I do not have to grieve as the world does. I have hope that I will see them again one day. You have promised me this in Your holy Word. In the name of the risen Christ I pray. Amen.*

Day 268

UNAPPROACHABLE LIGHT

———— **READ EXODUS 33:7-23; 1 TIMOTHY 6:13-16** ————

KEY VERSES: *He who is the blessed and only Sovereign, the King of kings and Lord of lords, who alone has immortality, who dwells in unapproachable light, whom no one has ever seen or can see. To him be honor and eternal dominion. Amen.* 1 TIMOTHY 6:15–16 ESV

UNDERSTAND:

• How do these passages in Exodus 33 and 1 Timothy 6 relate to each other regarding the glory of God?

....

....

....

....

....

....

• What does Exodus 33:20–23 tell you about God's love and care of His people?

....

....

....

....

....

....

....

APPLY: No one yet has ever fully seen God because He is so awesome and incredible that we people are just not able. He "dwells in unapproachable light." It's like trying to look at the sun. We know the sun is there and we can see it and all the good it does, but it's just not possible for our human eyes to look at it directly—it's just too much! Our eyes were not made to look at something so bright and magnificent. But someday, at just the right time, we will get to see God fully, and we will realize how awesome and powerful He is and always has been over everything in all creation. Until then, we keep on loving, following, and serving Him with great hope for our perfect forever in heaven.

....

....

....

....

....

....

....

....

....

....

....

....

....

PRAY: *Heavenly Father, even now on earth while I cannot fully see You, I trust that You are working and You are guiding me. It's amazing to know that one day I will see You fully! I live with great hope for my perfect forever with You! Amen.*

MASTER YOUR TIME

READ EPHESIANS 5:15–20

KEY VERSES: *Make the most of every opportunity in these evil days. Don't act thoughtlessly, but understand what the Lord wants you to do.* EPHESIANS 5:16–17 NLT

UNDERSTAND:

• What do you think Ephesians 5:16 means when it tells you to "make the most of every opportunity"?

....

....

....

....

• Do you consider yourself a good time manager? Why or why not?

....

....

....

....

• What motivates you to act now when you'd rather procrastinate?

....

....

....

....

....

APPLY: In the twenty-first century, we've become expert time wasters. From binge-worthy TV, Pinterest, and video games to social media, internet research rabbit holes, and photo filters, we're willing to let just about any distraction occupy our time—often while avoiding the important things we *should* be doing.

We may treat time like it's an inexhaustible resource, but the truth is our life on earth is fleeting, and that's why Paul in Ephesians 5 is urging us to take hold of opportunities when they arise. The psalmist also understood the urgency when he wrote, "Teach us to understand how many days we have. Then we will have a heart of wisdom to give You" (Psalm 90:12 NLV).

Today, choose the wise path and use your time wisely. Seize opportunities to love others. Spend less thoughtless time staring at your phone and look up. Ask God how He wants you to spend your time. A twenty-four-hour day spent in the Lord's work goes a lot further than does the same amount of time spent surfing the net or bingeing a show.

....

....

....

....

....

....

....

....

....

....

PRAY: *Father, forgive me for wasting Your gift of time. Give me the wisdom to be busy in Your work, moving toward goals that further Your kingdom and draw others closer to You. Make my times of rest holy and refreshing so I can continue to give You my best. Amen.*

Day 270

THE DEATH OF A DREAM

——— READ MATTHEW 27:1–56 ———

KEY VERSES: *Many women were there, watching from a distance. They had followed Jesus from Galilee to care for his needs. Among them were Mary Magdalene, Mary the mother of James and Joseph, and the mother of Zebedee's sons.* MATTHEW 27:55–56 NIV

UNDERSTAND:

• How the disciples must have mourned Jesus' death! And not just for the obvious reasons. Surely they felt it meant the end of a dream. Have you ever watched a dream die?

• Is it possible to have hope in a hopeless situation?

APPLY: It's easy to imagine what must have been going through the hearts and minds of the disciples as they watched their friend, teacher, mentor hanging on the cross. Though Jesus had told them that He would rise again, surely they had their doubts as He breathed His last on the cross. In that moment as heaven met earth for the most sobering moment ever, how they must have mourned the death of a dream. Oh, but the joy of realizing, just a few days later, the resurrection of their hopes and dreams.

Maybe you've watched a dream die. Maybe you've given everything to see it come to pass only to watch it slip through your fingertips. Maybe hopelessness has crept in. Today God wants you to know that He can give you hope even when all around you seems hopeless. He wants to give you resurrection power even in the moments when you're overwhelmed with anxieties.

Don't give up. God has great things ahead for you. This too shall pass, and you'll be on your feet and running again.

PRAY: *Father, it's been painful to watch my dreams die. So many times I've felt like giving up. Thank You for the reminder that resurrection is coming! Amen.*

Day 271

MY PAST IS WEIGHING
ME DOWN

─────── **READ 2 CORINTHIANS 5:17–19** ───────

KEY VERSE: *Anyone united with the Messiah gets a fresh start, is created new. The old life is gone; a new life emerges!* 2 CORINTHIANS 5:17 MSG

UNDERSTAND:

• Can you see ways in which your past is weighing down your present?

_____

_____

_____

_____

_____

_____

• Do you feel that the past is truly gone? Or do you still feel it haunting you, standing in the way of your growth?

_____

_____

_____

_____

_____

_____

_____

APPLY: The Bible's message is truly good news! Rather than being a message of doom and gloom, don't-do-this and don't-do-that, it's full of joy and hope. These verses are wonderful expressions of God's vision for us.

The old life, with all its pain and shame and brokenness, need hold us back no longer. Through Jesus the Messiah (the one anointed by God), we are born anew. We have a fresh start. We can leave the past behind and experience a new relationship both with God and with other human beings.

In the words of *The Message*, "The old life is gone; a new life emerges!"

....

....

....

....

....

....

....

....

....

....

....

....

....

PRAY: *Jesus, thank You for the new life You've given me in You. Help me to step away from my past, with all its destructive habits, behaviors, and attitudes. Make me into a new creature, one who grows more like You with each day we share together. Amen.*

Day 272

SUFFERING

─────── **READ 2 THESSALONIANS 1–2** ───────

KEY VERSES: *Therefore, we ourselves speak proudly of you among the churches of God for your perseverance and faith in the midst of all your persecutions and afflictions which you endure. This is a plain indication of God's righteous judgment so that you will be considered worthy of the kingdom of God, for which indeed you are suffering.* 2 THESSALONIANS 1:4–5 NASB

UNDERSTAND:

• What is your current affliction or pain?

....

....

....

....

....

....

....

• Have you ever suffered for the kingdom of Christ?

....

....

....

....

....

....

....

....

APPLY: Paul was proud of the Thessalonians for loving one another well and for persevering even through trials and hardships. Do you face pain and hardships in your own life? Do you know what it means to suffer?

Know that God sees your suffering. He is near to the brokenhearted. He binds up your wounds. He loves you with an everlasting love and promises to never let you go. One day He will wipe away every tear from your eyes.

There is a better place. It is heaven, and it is our home. We are but aliens here on this earth, in this fallen world, passing through. Make the most of each day. Relinquish your suffering to God. Trust Him for a brighter tomorrow. He has not left you alone. Even your hardships and trials are serving a purpose.

There will be a new order one day. God has promised us this. He will make all things right again, and there will be no more suffering.

PRAY: *Lord, help me to endure my hardships and to maintain a good attitude. Give me the strength I need to persevere. There are days when I feel stronger, but some days I feel so weak. Be my strength. In Jesus' name I pray. Amen.*

Day 273

GODLINESS AND GOOD HEALTH

───── **READ 1 SAMUEL 16:7; 1 CORINTHIANS 6:12-18;** ─────
1 CORINTHIANS 15:35-58; 1 TIMOTHY 4:6-10; 1 PETER 3:1-6

KEY VERSE: *Train yourself to be godly.* 1 TIMOTHY 4:7 NLT

UNDERSTAND:

- How does the comparison of our earthly bodies to our heavenly bodies in 1 Corinthians 15 help you have wisdom about health and appearance goals for your earthly body?

....

....

....

....

....

....

- How do you apply the wisdom of 1 Peter 3:1-6 to the culture you live in today?

....

....

....

....

....

....

....

APPLY: Let God's Word give you peace in a world that focuses far too much on body image. Social media posts, TV, and magazine covers try to make you feel like you are not healthy enough, physically fit enough, pretty enough, and so on. But your heavenly Father wants you to know that "physical training is of some value, but godliness has value for all things, holding promise for both the present life and the life to come" (1 Timothy 4:8 NIV). In other words, maintain the right perspective about keeping your body in good health and appearance. That has value, for sure, and we should want to eat healthy foods, exercise, and take good care of our temples of the Holy Spirit. But we can easily go overboard and let the focus be on pride in ourselves and our looks rather than on honoring God with the care of our bodies. Fix your thoughts and goals on godliness and good health in honor and worship of the one who knows and loves you most of all, from the inside out. Remember that your earthly body, no matter how great it does or does not look and feel right now, is just temporary; but your soul will go on forever in a new heavenly body. And never give control to any other input telling you what you have to look or feel like to fit into the world around you.

PRAY: *Heavenly Father, I want my goals to be about godliness and good health, not worldly appearance and fitness and fashion trends. Please help me to listen to Your voice on these matters more than any other input, and help me to honor You above all. Amen.*

WORK WITH YOUR WHOLE HEART

──────── **READ COLOSSIANS 3:18-25** ────────

KEY VERSE: *Work willingly at whatever you do, as though you were working for the Lord rather than for people.* COLOSSIANS 3:23 NLT

UNDERSTAND:

• When is it easiest for you to work willingly?

....

....

....

....

• When is it difficult for you to work willingly?

....

....

....

....

• What must change for you to work willingly and put forward your best effort in every situation?

....

....

....

....

APPLY: Some tasks are easy and fulfilling and give us great satisfaction to see them completed. Other tasks are impossible and frustrating and leave us feeling drained. Some bosses are motivating, encouraging, and kind. Other bosses are demanding, critical, and harsh.

God doesn't make a distinction between any of these scenarios. His Word tells us to work willingly at whatever is asked of us, knowing that our work in His name is important and necessary and holy and is a blessing in our lives and in the lives of others.

If you're unconvinced that your role in your job, at home with your family, in your volunteer work, or in your ministry can make a difference, consider this: if you surrender your work to God and give it your best effort for His glory, He will bless your work beyond what you could imagine. Roll up your sleeves—the Lord's work needs to be done!

_____

_____

_____

_____

_____

_____

_____

_____

_____

_____

PRAY: *Lord God, I give my job to You. I give my role in my family to You. I give every task and responsibility to You. Bless my boss and the other leaders I work with and for. Let me be an encouragement to them and to others around me. I want to be Your light wherever I am. Amen.*

Day 275

A SECOND CHANCE AT LIFE

—————— **READ JOHN 11:1–44** ——————

KEY VERSES: *When he had said this, Jesus called in a loud voice, "Lazarus, come out!" The dead man came out, his hands and feet wrapped with strips of linen, and a cloth around his face. Jesus said to them, "Take off the grave clothes and let him go."* JOHN 11:43–44 NIV

UNDERSTAND:

• Have you ever felt as if you've been given a second chance at life? What thrilled you the most about tearing off the grave clothes?

....

....

....

....

....

....

• Picture yourself in the crowd as Lazarus burst forth from the tomb. What would you be thinking or doing?

....

....

....

....

....

....

APPLY: Most people look at death as the end of a story. When the last breath is taken, the story has come to its conclusion. The opposite is true with God! At the point of death, things are just getting started! We've got the promise of heaven and life eternal—complete with mansions, streets of gold, and pearly gates.

In the story of Lazarus, however, Jesus decided to change things up a bit. He decided that heaven could wait a little longer for this man of faith. In front of a crowd of witnesses, Jesus cried out, *"Lazarus, come forth!"* The man who had been wrapped in grave clothes for days came out of his tomb and shocked the crowd as he moved toward them. Can you even imagine?

Lazarus was given a second chance at life. Maybe you can relate on a much smaller scale. Maybe you've been given a second chance, a fresh breath. You shocked the doctors when you recovered from a near-death experience. You missed being in an accident by inches. You survived a heart-wrenching breakup. Your grave clothes have now been stripped away, and you're free to begin again.

What will you do with this second chance? How will you live this next phase of your life? Come bursting forth, as Lazarus did, ready to face a new day.

PRAY: *Lord, You are a God of second chances. I've experienced this in my life so many times, and I'm so grateful. Today I burst forth from the tomb, ready for new adventures. Thank You, Lord. Amen.*

Day 276

I'M WORRIED ABOUT
MY PARENTS

—————— **READ ISAIAH 46:3–11** ——————

KEY VERSE: *"And I'll keep on carrying you when you're old. I'll be there, bearing you when you're old and gray."* ISAIAH 46:4 MSG

UNDERSTAND:

• What does it mean to be carried by God?

....

....

....

....

....

....

• When worries fill your mind about your parents, can you imagine them being held in God's arms?

....

....

....

....

....

....

....

APPLY: It's hard to watch our parents age. These were the people who first loved us, who made our lives secure when we were children, and in some sense, they remain the foundation of our lives today. Our world shakes when we see them ill. We know that most of us will have to face our parents' deaths sooner or later, but that doesn't make doing so any easier.

This passage from the book of Isaiah is filled with promises we can apply to the lives of our parents. These promises remind us to look back at the past. No matter what hardships our parents faced, they survived them (or they wouldn't still be here today). God was with them. God carried them on His back since the day they were born—and He's not about to drop them now (verses 3–4).

The promises in these verses apply to us as well. When the day comes to say goodbye to our parents, we will be right where we were all along—safe on God's back. He will not drop us.

_____

_____

_____

_____

_____

_____

_____

_____

_____

_____

PRAY: *Loving Father, I give my parents to You. I know that You have held them in Your arms all along, but I've been trying to pull them into my own arms instead. Help me to show them Your love. I thank You for their lives. Amen.*

Day 277

ITCHING EARS

—————— **READ 2 TIMOTHY 4** ——————

KEY VERSE: *For a time is coming when people will no longer listen to sound and wholesome teaching. They will follow their own desires and will look for teachers who will tell them whatever their itching ears want to hear.* 2 TIMOTHY 4:3 NLT

UNDERSTAND:

- Is there a teacher you have heard on TV or the radio whose words did not seem to line up with scripture?

....

....

....

....

....

....

- Do you like to be told only what you want to hear, or do you seek truth?

....

....

....

....

....

....

....

APPLY: The apostle Paul warns that a time is coming when people will follow their own desires, no longer listen to godly teaching, but instead follow teachers who tell them what they want to hear. Does this sound like the times in which we live?

All you have to do is flip on the TV, step into certain churches, or turn on your car radio. You can hear a message preached in Jesus' name that tells you just about anything you want to hear. Scripture is twisted to fit any situation. Pastors who are filling stadiums are oftentimes preaching a prosperity gospel, full of lies.

Be careful. Test everything with the Word of God. Ask God for discernment. Read and study the Bible. Know it inside and out. Then you will not fall into the trap of following after what your itching ears want to hear. Truth is not always easy, but it is always, always worth seeking.

....

....

....

....

....

....

....

....

....

....

....

PRAY: *God, I do not want to be told what is easy or sounds good. I want to know truth. Give me the discernment I so desperately need in the times in which I live. Help me to sense when something just doesn't line up with Your holy Word. Fill my mind and heart with Your truth, I ask. Amen.*

Day 278

DREAM HOME

— **READ PSALMS 84–85** —

KEY VERSES: *How beautiful are the places where You live, O Lord of all! My soul wants and even becomes weak from wanting to be in the house of the Lord. . . . How happy are those who live in Your house! They are always giving thanks to You.* PSALM 84:1–2, 4 NLV

UNDERSTAND:

- How have you experienced God as your sun and safe-covering as Psalm 84:11 describes?

....

....

....

....

....

- How does Psalm 84:12 help give you peace today?

....

....

....

....

....

....

APPLY: Do you have a dream home you like to imagine living in? It's fun to think about, even while we choose to be content and make our actual homes a restful and comfortable place in which to live. And every woman has different styles and tastes for her home. But better than anything we can dream up and create here on earth is the forever home God is creating for us in heaven. It will be incredible! When we take time to focus on God, praise Him, and hear from Him through His Word, we get little glimpses of how awesomely perfect our forever home will be!

_____

_____

_____

_____

_____

_____

_____

_____

_____

_____

_____

_____

_____

_____

PRAY: *Heavenly Father, thank You for my blessings here and now where I live on earth; but even more, thank You for the perfect forever home with You that You are making for me in heaven! Amen.*

SHAME-FREE

──────── **READ ISAIAH 50:4-9** ────────

KEY VERSE: *Because the Sovereign* Lord *helps me, I will not be disgraced. Therefore have I set my face like flint, and I know I will not be put to shame.* Isaiah 50:7 NIV

UNDERSTAND:

• If you struggle with shame, is it because of your own inner thoughts? Or are you ashamed because of how others perceive you?

....

....

....

....

• Do you think God is ashamed of you? Why or why not?

....

....

....

....

• What is the remedy for shame?

....

....

....

....

....

APPLY: If we're living out God's good plan for our lives, we will sometimes make decisions and take stands that go against the popular opinion of the world. When these times come, it can be downright frightening to open our inner selves to be ridiculed, mocked, and even shamed.

But God is there, and He will help you. Seek wisdom in His Word, talk to believing friends and family, ask for their support, and follow the guidance of the Holy Spirit.

What do you need to take a stand for today? If you've been avoiding it, it's never too late to change course and show God's light and kindness and love in any situation. Scripture tells us that God has not given us a spirit of fear. Rather, He's given us a powerful, loving spirit and a sound mind that can hold fast to His promises (see 2 Timothy 1:7).

PRAY: *Father, I admit that sometimes I don't act because I fear how it will be perceived by others. Forgive me for not trusting that You will keep me from being disgraced. When all is said and done, I know what You think of me is all that matters, but I want to be liked, respected, and accepted by everyone. Show me Your will in all things. Amen.*

Day 280

GET IN THE RIVER

---------- **READ EZEKIEL 47:1–12** ----------

KEY VERSES: *As the man went eastward with a measuring line in his hand, he measured off a thousand cubits and then led me through water that was ankle-deep. He measured off another thousand cubits and led me through water that was knee-deep. He measured off another thousand and led me through water that was up to the waist.* EZEKIEL 47:3–4 NIV

UNDERSTAND:

• As you analyze your walk with God, would you say that you are ankle deep, knee deep, or waist deep?

....

....

....

....

....

....

• Is there anything about the word *surrender* that frightens you?

....

....

....

....

....

....

....

APPLY: If you've ever gone swimming in the ocean, then the story of Ezekiel is probably easy for you to picture. You start off on the shore, toes pressed into the sand. Then, you take those first few steps toward the water. It soon covers the tops of your feet. A few more steps and it's up to your shins. Then your knees. Then your hips. Then, eventually, you're waist deep.

It doesn't take much effort to go deeper in the ocean. The same is true when it comes to your walk with God. He wants to take you much deeper than you are now, to a place of sweet communion and fellowship with Him.

What's holding you back today? Is there a reason you feel safer only wading in up to your ankles? Are you afraid of the commitment? Afraid God will ask you to give up something you love? The truth is God has your best interest at heart. As you go deeper and deeper with Him, you will discover that His love washes over you, removing any worries and concerns you might have had. All He really wants is your heart—your whole heart.

PRAY: *I want to go deeper with You, Lord. Take me well beyond where I am now—not ankle deep or even knee deep. I want to find myself immersed in Your Spirit, Lord, completely overwhelmed by Your presence. My heart is Yours, Lord. Amen.*

Day 281

THIS SECRET IS DESTROYING ME

—————————— **READ HEBREWS 4:12–16** ——————————

KEY VERSE: *Nothing in all creation is hidden from God's sight. Everything is uncovered and laid bare before the eyes of him to whom we must give account.*
Hebrews 4:13 NIV

UNDERSTAND:

• Why do you keep secrets from others (and from God, maybe even from yourself)? Can you identify what motivates you? Is it shame, pride—or something else?

....

....

....

• Do you find it comforting or frightening to be reminded that you can't hide from God?

....

....

....

• What would it cost you to reveal this secret? Do you think it would bring healing—or cause more damage?

....

....

....

....

APPLY: Old things that are left to rot in the dark have a way of seeping into the rest of our life. "Out of sight, out of mind" does not mean powerless! Secrets can be a potent and deadly poison.

We may be hiding the truth out of shame or guilt (which are two different things). Many of us carry within us the secret of either sexual abuse or sexual sin. As terrifying as it may seem to reveal a secret like that, it may be the only way for us to truly heal. What looms in the darkness may prove to be more manageable once it's out in the light of day.

These verses of scripture remind us that nothing is hidden from God. No matter what secrets we are keeping, whether our own or someone else's, He knows all about it—and He longs to lift its weight from our hearts.

....
....
....
....
....
....
....
....
....
....
....
....
....

PRAY: *Thank You, Jesus, that You understand my every weakness. Give me the courage and discernment to know what to do with this terrible secret I've been hiding. I put it in Your hands. Amen.*

Day 282

SECURE IN CHRIST

—— READ PSALMS 91–92 ——

KEY VERSES: *"Because he loves me," says the* Lord, *"I will rescue him; I will protect him, for he acknowledges my name. He will call on me, and I will answer him; I will be with him in trouble, I will deliver him and honor him. With long life I will satisfy him and show him my salvation."* Psalm 91:14–16 NIV

UNDERSTAND:

- Make a list of all the actions God promises to take in Psalm 91. Which ones stand out to you as especially comforting?

....

....

....

....

....

....

- When does God promise to answer prayer in Psalm 91:15?

....

....

....

....

....

....

APPLY: It is often said that a man's greatest need is respect and a woman's is security. Would you agree that you long to feel secure? Most women would answer with a resounding "yes!"

The good news is that whether or not you have a husband, you have a God who is all about protecting you. Under the shadow of His wing, you are safe (see Psalm 36:7).

Psalm 91 is full of strong verbs because they describe your even stronger God. Words like *rescue, save, cover, guard, protect*, and *deliver*—just to name a few—help us to get a clear picture of the security we have in God. He is better than the strongest bodyguard or bouncer on earth!

Psalm 92 describes the righteous as glad, exalted, flourishing, and bearing fruit. If you trust in the Lord for your security, you will never be disappointed. And in the end, you will blossom into the confident woman He so desires you to become.

PRAY: *Help me, Father, to ultimately depend on You for my security. Thank You for Your constant protection. Lead me in Your ways, and help me to revere You and to live in the shadow of Your wing, secure in my faith. Amen.*

Day 283

MARRIAGE MATTERS

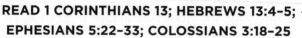

**READ 1 CORINTHIANS 13; HEBREWS 13:4-5;
EPHESIANS 5:22-33; COLOSSIANS 3:18-25**

KEY VERSE: *Love bears all things, believes all things, hopes all things, endures all things.* 1 Corinthians 13:7 esv

UNDERSTAND:

• What is going well in your marriage right now that gives you great peace and joy?

....

....

....

....

• What are areas that might need work in your marriage?

....

....

....

....

• What struggles have you overcome in your marriage, and how does this give you hope and peace for present and future struggles?

....

....

....

....

....

APPLY: The love passage of 1 Corinthians 13 is so popular at weddings, and rightfully so. The basis for a great marriage should be the godly, sacrificial love it describes. If you are struggling with any marriage matters right now, both you and your husband need to sincerely evaluate the way you love each other in light of this passage and all the Bible says about godly love and marriage. It's easier said than done, of course, but prayer is where heart change can begin. Ask God to show you both where you need to adjust and improve. Communicate respectfully with each other first, and get outside godly wisdom and help if you need to. Pray faithfully and continually, even if you don't see answers and improvements right away. Ask for more and more grace, love, and wisdom. Celebrate progress and the things you naturally do well. Most of all, hold fast to your commitment and the sacredness of marriage, and let God bless you as you do.

PRAY: *Heavenly Father, please protect and bring great peace and joy to my marriage as my husband and I seek to honor You most of all with our commitment and relationship. Help us to love each other sacrificially and sacredly. Amen.*

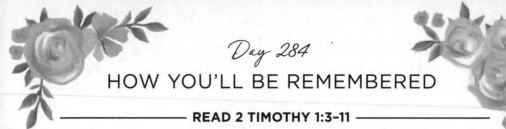

HOW YOU'LL BE REMEMBERED

───────── **READ 2 TIMOTHY 1:3–11** ─────────

KEY VERSE: *I remember your genuine faith, for you share the faith that first filled your grandmother Lois and your mother, Eunice. And I know that same faith continues strong in you.* 2 TIMOTHY 1:5 NLT

UNDERSTAND:

• Who has been instrumental in passing their faith to you?

....

....

....

....

• Who are you passing your faith to?

....

....

....

....

• Someday when people are remembering your legacy on earth, what is the first thing you hope they would say about you?

....

....

....

....

....

....

APPLY: The apostle Paul's young protégé, Timothy, was blessed with a heritage of faith, passed down through multiple generations. Paul writes of Timothy's grandmother and mother as being instrumental in building a strong foundation for his life of service to God.

Whether your family tree is made up of branches strong in faith or you are the first offshoot growing in the Lord, your faith legacy is an important part of your story.

This morning, think about the people who had the most influence in your decision to come to Christ and who have helped you grow. Spend time thanking God for their love and care for you. And then think about whom you are passing your faith to. One of the beautiful things about God's family tree is that it isn't constrained by bloodlines. You can be a spiritual grandmother, mother, or sister to *anyone.* Pray and ask God to show you whom you can pour His love into today.

....

....

....

....

....

....

....

....

....

....

PRAY: *Father, thank You for the heritage of faith in my life. I am humbled when I think about the people who loved me so much that they led me to Your Son. I want to pass on the legacy of Your goodness and salvation to the next generation. Show me who. Show me how. Give me Your heart. Amen.*

Day 285
A FURNACE OF FAITH

READ DANIEL 3

KEY VERSES: *Then King Nebuchadnezzar was astonished and rose up in haste. He declared to his counselors, "Did we not cast three men bound into the fire?" They answered and said to the king, "True, O king." He answered and said, "But I see four men unbound, walking in the midst of the fire, and they are not hurt; and the appearance of the fourth is like a son of the gods."* DANIEL 3:24–25 ESV

UNDERSTAND:

- God protected the three Hebrew men and spared their lives. Has He ever delivered you from a scary situation in a miraculous way?

....

....

....

....

- Who was the fourth man in the fire?

....

....

....

....

....

....

....

APPLY: If you're like most people, you have a healthy fear of fire. The idea of being tossed into a fiery furnace is probably high at the top of your "Please don't ever let this happen to me, Lord" list. It's remarkable to consider the faith of Shadrach, Meshach, and Abednego as flames leaped around them.

Think of the fieriest trial you've ever walked through. In the midst of it, were you afraid the flames would take you down? Did anxieties cripple you to the point where you couldn't function? How did Jesus rush in to meet you in the middle of your trouble? Surely He has delivered you just as He did the men in the fiery furnace.

There will always be trials. We will always have opposition in this life, people like Nebuchadnezzar who think they have a right to inflict pain on us. But take heart! God will be with you, even in your darkest hour. You'll come out of every fiery trial without the smell of smoke!

PRAY: *Father, I'm so relieved to know that You will stick with me, even in the fiery trials I face. I could never make it on my own. Thank You for Your ever-present help in time of trouble. Amen.*

Day 286

I FEEL SHY

───────────── **READ EXODUS 4:1-12** ─────────────

KEY VERSE: *"I will be with you as you speak, and I will instruct you in what to say."* EXODUS 4:12 NLT

UNDERSTAND:

• How does being shy hold you back from doing God's work?

....

....

....

....

....

....

....

• What "staff" might God have given you (verse 2) that He wants to use in some miraculous way you've never imagined? Is there something you've been leaning on, psychologically, that God wants you to surrender to Him—so that He can transform it into something alive and amazing?

....

....

....

....

....

....

....

APPLY: Moses, the great father of the Jewish and Christian faiths, allowed his shyness to get in God's way. He thought he could tell God, "Come on, Lord. You know I'm not good with words. I'm shy. I always have been. That's just the way I am." He seemed to think he knew more about his limitations and abilities than God, his Creator, did.

We often make the same mistake. We act as though shyness is an insurmountable barrier that prevents us from answering God's call on our lives. "Sorry, God," we say. "I'd really like to obey You—but I just can't. I'm too shy."

No wonder God gets exasperated (both with Moses and with us). *"Who made your mouth?"* He asks. *"Who knows better than I what you're capable of doing? Do you think I'd ask you to do something I knew was impossible for you to do?"*

PRAY: *God, You know how my shyness gets in my way. I don't know how to overcome it—so I'm giving it to You. Shy or not, I'll go wherever You want, do whatever You ask, and say anything You tell me to say. Transform me into something You can use to build Your realm on earth. Amen.*

Day 287

REMEMBER WHAT
JESUS HAS DONE

──────── **READ LUKE 8** ────────

KEY VERSES: *After this, Jesus traveled about from one town and village to another, proclaiming the good news of the kingdom of God. The Twelve were with him, and also some women who had been cured of evil spirits and diseases: Mary (called Magdalene) from whom seven demons had come out.* LUKE 8:1–2 NIV

UNDERSTAND:

- Jesus has freed you from sin and promised you eternal life. What is your response?

....

....

....

....

....

- Does your life reflect the magnitude of the gift of salvation?

....

....

....

....

....

....

....

APPLY: Mary Magdalene is mentioned fourteen times in the Gospels. Her name heads the list many times when she is mentioned in connection with other women. She journeyed with Jesus. She was there at the foot of the cross as He bled and died. She was there at the empty tomb. Why was this woman so dedicated to the Savior? She remembered what He had done for her.

We are told in Luke's Gospel that Mary of Magdala had been possessed by seven devils. Jesus drove the demons out of her, and she went from demon-possessed to devoted disciple of the Messiah.

Are we so filled with gratitude that we give to God our very best? Do we show up? Do we serve? Do we use our gifts and resources to bring Him glory? Mary Magdalene did. May we see her example as one worthy of following.

PRAY: *Dear God, make me so thankful for my salvation that I show up. Just as Mary of Magdala showed up at Your cross and Your tomb, may I follow You closely. Thank You for saving me by grace through faith in Jesus. In His name I pray. Amen.*

Day 288

MAKE THE LORD
YOUR REFUGE

—— READ PSALMS 91–92 ——

KEY VERSES: *The Lord says, "I will rescue those who love me. I will protect those who trust in my name. When they call on me, I will answer; I will be with them in trouble. I will rescue and honor them. I will reward them with a long life and give them my salvation."* PSALM 91:14–16 NLT

UNDERSTAND:

- Psalm 91:2 tells us God alone should be our place of refuge. In what wrong places have you sought refuge in the past or have watched other people seek refuge? What did that teach you?

....

....

....

....

....

- When have you sensed God's angels protecting you?

....

....

....

....

....

....

APPLY: Whatever fears are tormenting you lately, let Psalms 91 and 92 quiet them. Trust that as you put your hope in God alone as your refuge, He protects you from absolutely any danger or threat to your life. According to His will for your life here on earth, nothing can ever defeat you. More importantly, through His Son, Jesus Christ, He protects you eternally by giving you life that lasts forever in heaven with Him. Believe in His promises that He has ordered His angels to protect you wherever you go and that He listens to your cries for help and rescues you. Then, as Psalm 92 does, thank and praise God for all His care and protection. Thank and praise Him for the ways He shelters you while arming and strengthening you as He helps you flourish and thrive.

....

....

....

....

....

....

....

....

....

....

....

PRAY: *Heavenly Father, You are the Most High, and I am so grateful to live in Your shelter and find rest in Your shadow. Please quiet my fears with the truth of all Your promises. I proclaim Your love and faithfulness, and I exalt You, God! Amen.*

Day 289

GUILT-FREE

---------- **READ PSALM 103:8–18** ----------

KEY VERSES: *For as high as the heavens are above the earth, so great is his love for those who fear him; as far as the east is from the west, so far has he removed our transgressions from us.* PSALM 103:11–12 NIV

UNDERSTAND:

• What is your favorite word picture for the enormity of God's love?

....

....

....

....

• Why is it essential that we serve a God of extremes and absolutes?

....

....

....

....

• What role should guilt play in our lives as Christians?

....

....

....

....

....

APPLY: Aren't you thankful that our God is a God of extremes? His love for His children knows no bounds—it reaches to the heavens (Psalm 103:11) and is ever-lasting (verse 17). His forgiveness is absolute, and He removes our sins "as far as the east is from the west" (verse 12 NIV).

If we believe these truths, then why do we still struggle with guilt?

One reason is that the prince of this world, Satan, is constantly reminding us of our past. Fleeting thoughts and temptations may trigger memories of who we used to be before we knew Christ. Strongholds of sin that we still struggle with rear their ugly heads. And suddenly we feel unworthy, unloved, and unfit to be a child of the King.

But our extreme God can free us of guilty feelings—right now! Lay your struggles before the throne, and allow His peace to wash over you.

....

....

....

....

....

....

....

....

....

....

....

PRAY: *Father God, I already know I am forgiven, and I believe it when scripture says that You have removed my sins as far as the east is from the west. But I still feel guilt over the past, and I can't seem to shake it. Please take my guilt as far away as my sins. Amen.*

Day 290

HAVE A LITTLE
TALK WITH JESUS

—— READ LUKE 19:1–10 ——

KEY VERSES: *A man was there by the name of Zacchaeus; he was a chief tax collector and was wealthy. He wanted to see who Jesus was, but because he was short he could not see over the crowd. So he ran ahead and climbed a sycamore-fig tree to see him, since Jesus was coming that way.* Luke 19:2–4 NIV

UNDERSTAND:

• Zacchaeus went to great lengths to have a great spot to see Jesus. Have you ever gone to great lengths to spend time with Him?

....

....

....

....

....

....

• Why were the people so irritated with tax collectors like Zacchaeus?

....

....

....

....

....

....

....

APPLY: When you're the local tax collector (a man hated by all), and when you're a wee bit on the short side, you don't press your way through the crowd to see the Savior. You find a way to sneak up, up, up to a safe place to catch a glimpse as He passes through.

Though Zacchaeus thought he was just going to play the role of spectator that fateful day, the Lord had other ideas. Jesus stopped, pointed up to the tree, called Zacchaeus by name, and said, *"Come down! I'm going to your house today!"*

Have you ever felt shunned or unloved like Zacchaeus? Have you ever wondered how—or why—Jesus would pick someone like you to hang out with? The truth is He adores everyone equally—the loved, the unloved, the faithful, the sinner, the whole, the broken. . .everyone. He points His finger, smiles, and says, *"Draw close! I'm going to your house today."*

....

....

....

....

....

....

....

....

....

....

....

PRAY: *I'm grateful You want to spend time with me, Lord. I'm not exactly the most popular person in town. Sometimes I feel like I've been pushed aside, like Zacchaeus. But You welcome me into Your presence, and I'm so happy to spend time with You. Amen.*

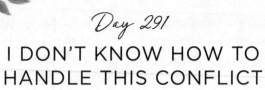

Day 291

I DON'T KNOW HOW TO
HANDLE THIS CONFLICT

READ 2 TIMOTHY 2:23–25

KEY VERSE: *Refuse foolish and ignorant speculations, knowing that they produce quarrels.* 2 TIMOTHY 2:23 NASB

UNDERSTAND:

• Making biased and unfounded assumptions about others leads to conflicts.

....

....

....

....

....

• What assumptions have you made about your current situation? How might these assumptions be contributing to the conflict?

....

....

....

....

....

....

....

....

APPLY: God does not ask us to simply give in to injustice. When Jesus found merchants abusing the temple by selling their wares there, He got angry, and He took action. But that kind of righteous anger has truth as its foundation. It is not the same as being quarrelsome.

Quarrels are generally petty, springing from small irritations that become magnified. They're also caused by our failure to understand another's perspective. (There's a reason why a quarrel is also referred to as a "misunderstanding"!) Instead of waiting to get to the bottom of the situation, discovering the real truth, we leap to conclusions. Then we pass these faulty assumptions on to others, fanning the fires of conflict until the trivial problem grows into a major issue.

God calls us to refuse this kind of thinking and behavior, replacing it with kindness, patience, gentleness, and the willingness to discuss the situation with all the parties who are involved.

PRAY: *Heavenly Lord, this conflict has gotten out of hand. I ask Your forgiveness for all the ways that I have contributed to its growth—and I ask You now to show me opportunities for kindness, patience, and gentleness. May a willingness to listen to each other spread out from me to everyone who is involved. Amen.*

Day 292

LEAVE IT BEHIND

―――――――― **READ JOHN 4:1–38** ――――――――

KEY VERSES: *The woman then left her waterpot, went her way into the city, and said to the men, "Come, see a Man who told me all things that I ever did. Could this be the Christ?" Then they went out of the city and came to Him.* JOHN 4:28–30 NKJV

UNDERSTAND:

• What proves that the woman at the well believed Jesus was the Messiah?

....

....

....

....

....

• What important item did the Samaritan woman leave behind when she went to tell others about her encounter with Jesus?

....

....

....

....

....

....

....

APPLY: Jesus spoke with a Samaritan woman at Jacob's well. This may not seem like such a big deal to us, but Samaritans and Jews did not associate with one another. Certainly, a Jewish man would not be found conversing with a Samaritan woman!

As the conversation unfolded, the woman realized this was no ordinary man. He knew things about her that she had not told Him. He spoke of living water, and He claimed to be the Christ.

In her excitement at having encountered the Messiah, the woman left her water jar and ran into the city to tell others about Jesus. She was, for all practical purposes, the original evangelist!

What is the significance of her leaving the water pot behind? Water was fetched from the well using a clay pot or jar. Water was a necessity for cooking, cleaning, and drinking. What do you consider a necessity that you are willing to lay aside in order to share Jesus with others?

....

....

....

....

....

....

....

....

....

PRAY: *Lord, I cling so tightly to my family and friends. I love the familiarity of home. I even find myself obsessed with material things and social media at times. Please loosen my grip on my "necessities," and make me willing to lay them down in order to share Your good news with those around me. Amen.*

Day 293
A HUNGRY WIDOW

─────── **READ 1 KINGS 17** ───────

KEY VERSE: *"As surely as the Lord your God lives," she replied, "I don't have any bread—only a handful of flour in a jar and a little olive oil in a jug. I am gathering a few sticks to take home and make a meal for myself and my son, that we may eat it—and die."* 1 Kings 17:12 NIV

UNDERSTAND:

• Have you ever chosen to provide for someone else with everything you have, trusting God alone to provide for you?

....

....

....

....

....

....

• In reading verses 17–18 and the widow's questions to Elijah, what do you think happened to her faith and attitude by that point? What did she soon experience and learn despite that?

....

....

....

....

....

....

APPLY: When the prophet Elijah found the widow just like God told him to, she told him she didn't have any bread—just a little bit of flour and oil. She was sure that she was about to make the very last tiny meal for her son and herself and that they would soon starve to death. Maybe you have experienced that kind of desperate resignation, either physically or spiritually. But God can make a way of provision and rescue, like He did through Elijah for the widow of Zarephath. She obeyed the instruction from God through His prophet and chose to trust that He would continue to provide for her and her son, even while she provided for Elijah first. Later, she was rewarded even greater when her son had died and Elijah brought him back to life through the power of God.

....

....

....

....

....

....

....

....

....

....

....

....

PRAY: *Heavenly Father, even when things seem utterly hopeless, remind me that You have the power to provide, restore, and heal in extraordinary ways. Fill me with peace because I trust and hope in You! Amen.*

Day 294

YOU CAN RESIST TEMPTATION

—— READ 1 CORINTHIANS 10:12–31 ——

KEY VERSES: *If you think you are standing strong, be careful not to fall. The temptations in your life are no different from what others experience. And God is faithful. He will not allow the temptation to be more than you can stand. When you are tempted, he will show you a way out so that you can endure.* 1 CORINTHIANS 10:12–13 NLT

UNDERSTAND:

• Do you think the temptations you face are different from others? Why or why not?

....

....

....

....

....

....

• Why is it dangerous to think you are too strong to fall to temptation?

....

....

....

....

....

....

....

APPLY: Temptations come in many forms. Sin-inducing desires happen to everyone—even or especially to the strongest Christians—so that's why the apostle Paul tells us to be careful and realize no one is above falling to temptation.

But, he goes on to say, others have resisted temptation, and so can we because God is faithful to help us stand firm and not give in. Ask Him to show you the people and situations that give you trouble. Ask Him to help you run from anything you know is wrong and choose to do only what is right. Earnestly ask for His help, and seek friends who love God and can offer support when you are tempted.

Paul tells us that our Father will not allow our temptations to be more than we can stand. Today, stand firm in that promise of God's faithfulness.

PRAY: *God, I know when I am tempted to sin that temptation doesn't come from You—it comes from my own selfish desires. Help me to recognize the areas in which I am most vulnerable to temptation, and deliver on Your promise that You will show me an exit to avoid the temptation. Amen.*

A PICNIC OF FAITH

— **READ MATTHEW 14:13–21** —

KEY VERSE: *They all ate and were satisfied, and the disciples picked up twelve basketfuls of broken pieces that were left over.* MATTHEW 14:20 NIV

UNDERSTAND:

• It took the faith of a child to feed five thousand people that memorable day. Have you ever had to exhibit childlike faith in order to see a miracle take place?

....

....

....

....

....

....

• Has God ever performed a "loaves and fishes" miracle in your finances?

....

....

....

....

....

....

....

APPLY: How we love this story of Jesus feeding the five thousand. It reminds us that He has the ability to take our "little" and turn it into a lot. It's also a great reminder that God is our provider. Even when it looks like the cupboard is bare, He's got the ability to fill it in His own miraculous way.

A key player in this story is the young boy who offered up his lunch. If he hadn't let go of what was rightfully his, the others would have gone without. Think about that for a moment. There are times when God asks us to give up the "good" so that He can multiply it and give it back to us as the "best."

Where do you stand today? Are you in need of a "loaves and fishes" miracle? Are you riddled with anxiety while you wait? Then open your hands and get ready to let go of what you've been clinging to. Sure, it might take courage, but when you see God's plan to multiply what you've given Him, you'll be astounded!

PRAY: *There have been seasons in my life, Lord, when I've doubted Your provision. I've looked inside my near-empty picnic basket and panicked. Thank You for the reminder that You can multiply anything I offer You. May I never forget how much You care. Amen.*

Day 296

I FEEL FOOLISH

— **READ GALATIANS 1:10-24** —

KEY VERSE: *Am I now trying to win the approval of human beings, or of God? Or am I trying to please people? If I were still trying to please people, I would not be a servant of Christ.* GALATIANS 1:10 NIV

UNDERSTAND:

- Paul's actions in the past were far worse than mere foolishness. If you had done what he did, do you think you would have had the courage to become a prominent leader of the faith?

....

....

....

....

....

- Does your sense of foolishness hold you back from doing the work of God? If so, in what ways?

....

....

....

....

....

APPLY: All of us feel foolish sometimes. We do things we fear will make us appear stupid. No matter how much we wish we could erase our actions, there they still are, looming in our own minds long after others may have forgotten them. Often, we allow our sense of foolishness to hold us back. We hesitate to call any further attention to ourselves. (In fact, we may wish we could crawl into the woodwork and disappear completely!)

Paul's actions against the early Church weren't mere foolishness; they were violent and hateful. And yet because he was now a servant of Christ, he had to lay aside his worry about others' opinions of him.

That's so hard to do! But we too, like Paul, are called by God to serve Jesus. That means we have to set aside our sense of our own foolishness and instead focus on pleasing Him. His opinion is the only one that matters.

....

....

....

....

....

....

....

....

....

....

....

PRAY: *Today, Jesus, please remind me, again and again, that I am Your servant. Help me to forget what others may think of me. I want to please You—and I want to live in such a way that in the end, regardless of how foolish I am, others will praise You because of me. Amen.*

Day 297

BLOTTED OUT

―――――――――― **READ ACTS 3** ――――――――――

KEY VERSE: *"Repent therefore and be converted, that your sins may be blotted out, so that times of refreshing may come from the presence of the Lord."* Acts 3:19 NKJV

UNDERSTAND:

- To hear that your sins have been blotted out... How does this make you feel?

....

....

....

....

....

....

- What is the source of the "times of refreshing" mentioned in the key verse for today?

....

....

....

....

....

....

....

APPLY: If you are a certain age, you will remember typing on a typewriter before the days of computers. If you made a mistake, it took more than hitting the delete key to take care of the problem. Remember the little strips of correction tape? You had to back up. You had to position that little white strip just perfectly. You had to strike the key again. If everything went perfectly, the error was blotted out, and where that erroneous *k* or *m* had stood, there was just white. Pure white. No letter. No mark. Clean. Ready. As if the mistake had never occurred.

This is a poor analogy, but you get the point: your sins have been blotted out. Christ took them upon Himself when He died on the cross. Your sins are washed white as snow. Just like a perfect correction on that old typewriter, Jesus blotted out your sins. He remembers them no more.

PRAY: *Jesus, thank You for blotting out my sin. Forgiveness is oh so sweet! I am refreshed in Your presence daily. I find strength in Your Word and in quiet meditation. I stand amazed at a Savior who would take my sin upon Himself and die for me. Thank You. Amen.*

Day 298

BEAUTIFUL BEATITUDES

--- **READ MATTHEW 5:1–20** ---

KEY VERSES: *"God blesses you when people mock you and persecute you and lie about you and say all sorts of evil things against you because you are my followers. Be happy about it! Be very glad! For a great reward awaits you in heaven."* MATTHEW 5:11–12 NLT

UNDERSTAND:

• Do you feel truly glad when you suffer for following Jesus? If not, how can you work on changing your attitude about this?

....

....

....

....

....

....

• What ways do you try to shine your light for Jesus for all to see?

....

....

....

....

....

....

....

....

APPLY: Did you know the word *beatitude* means "state of utmost bliss"? What a lovely definition to think of as you read Jesus' Sermon on the Mount and His famous Beatitudes. His teaching here turns most everything that is glamorized in today's popular culture completely upside down. The world doesn't generally glamorize feeling poor and in need of God. Nor does it glamorize mourning, humility, or a hunger for what is right and true. The world also doesn't glamorize being full of mercy, having a pure heart, working for peace, or being persecuted and mocked for doing what is right and following Jesus. Yet Jesus did glamorize and idealize all these things as He promised great blessings and rewards for those who experienced them. As we live out our faith in Him, trusting in the incredible promises of the Beatitudes, we become the salt and light of the earth. We become what the world around us needs to taste and see about God so that they will trust in Jesus as their Savior too.

PRAY: *Dear Jesus, help me to remember Your beautiful teaching in the Sermon on the Mount. I trust in Your salvation and blessings. Help me to display Your dramatic difference in this world, which will point others to wanting to know and love and serve You too. Amen.*

Day 299

YOU CAN REACH YOUR GOALS

—— READ ISAIAH 40:22-31 ——

KEY VERSES: *He gives strength to the weary and increases the power of the weak. Even youths grow tired and weary, and young men stumble and fall; but those who hope in the Lord will renew their strength. They will soar on wings like eagles; they will run and not grow weary, they will walk and not be faint.* ISAIAH 40:29-31 NIV

UNDERSTAND:

• What have you accomplished only because of God's strength?

....

....

....

....

....

• In what area of your life do you need to ask God for strength and stamina?

....

....

....

....

....

....

....

APPLY: You may know in your head and heart there's nothing that God Himself cannot do, but do you realize that He wants to renew your strength so *you* can do great things as well?

What big, audacious dreams do you have? Maybe the burdens of life have buried these goals in your heart, but with God by your side, you can bring them back to life today! Put your hope in the Lord, ask Him to guide your plans, and He will renew your desire.

Working toward a dream isn't easy, but it is achievable. When you start to see results—momentum toward the goal—that's when you will feel as though you are soaring on eagles' wings. With God's help, you will press on and not get tired.

He's here, cheering you on right now. Do you hear that encouraging voice full of love?

PRAY: *God, I have so many dreams and goals, but sometimes I don't know where to begin. Show me what You want for me, and set me on the path toward those goals. Put the drive and tenacity in my heart to make them happen. I give You all the glory for any success I will have. Amen.*

Day 300
SIT AT HIS FEET

──────── **READ MATTHEW 19:1–15** ────────

KEY VERSES: *Then the people brought their little children to Jesus so he could put his hands on them and pray for them. His followers told them to stop, but Jesus said, "Let the little children come to me. Don't stop them, because the kingdom of heaven belongs to people who are like these children."* MATTHEW 19:13–14 NCV

UNDERSTAND:

• Why do you think Jesus has such a special place in His heart for children?

_____

_____

_____

_____

_____

• Have you ever felt like a child, sitting at Jesus' feet?

_____

_____

_____

_____

_____

_____

_____

APPLY: It's so interesting to note that the disciples made an assumption that Jesus wouldn't want the children to gather close around Him. Why do you suppose that was? Perhaps they found it culturally unacceptable. Maybe they felt He had bigger, more important things to do. But Jesus put all those disciples in their place with these words: "Let the little children come to me. Don't stop them, because the kingdom of heaven belongs to people who are like these children."

Don't you love that? Jesus wants the children. He loves the little children. They aren't an annoyance to Him. On the contrary, those babes bring great joy and delight to His heart.

The Bible says that God wants us to come to Him as a little child—with childlike faith and innocence. So run to Him today. Don't worry about what others around you might be saying. Ignore their protests and curl up at Jesus' feet. Release those anxieties. Listen to the cadence of His voice. Feel the joy that radiates from every word.

He loves you, you know—no matter your age. And He wants to spend time with you today.

PRAY: *Jesus, You love the little children! It's more than just a song. You love all the children of the world—every age, every color, every race. Today I come to You with the faith of a child. My heart is wide open, ready to hear what You have to say. Amen.*

I NEED SOME TIME ALONE

──────── **READ MARK 1:32–39** ────────

KEY VERSE: *In the early morning, while it was still dark, Jesus got up, left the house, and went away to a secluded place, and was praying there.* MARK 1:35 NASB

UNDERSTAND:

• Many things that happened in Jesus' life were never recorded in the Gospels—so we have to assume that what *was* recorded was written for a reason. Why do you think the authors of the Gospels tell us again and again that Jesus sought out times to be alone?

....

....

....

....

....

• What relationship do you think existed between Jesus' alone times and His times of ministry?

....

....

....

....

....

....

....

APPLY: The Gospels make it clear that Jesus had an extremely busy life. He and His disciples seemed to travel constantly from one place to another, and always, crowds were following them, pressing around Jesus, clamoring for His attention.

Having just finished a busy day of healing, knowing that another equally busy day lay ahead, Jesus would have needed a good night's sleep. He knew, however, that He also needed something else—time alone—and so He got up very early in the morning in order to have that time.

When our days are busy, we sometimes neglect our times of solitude. *I just don't have time now,* we tell ourselves. *Alone time will have to wait until things calm down a little.* Jesus, however, shows us by example that the busier our lives are, the more we need to include those quiet moments of solitude. Without them, we won't have the strength we need to do His work.

PRAY: *Jesus, help me to remember to make time to be alone with You. I can't face my busy life without You. Amen.*

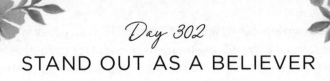

Day 302

STAND OUT AS A BELIEVER

KEY VERSES: *Blessed is the one who does not walk in step with the wicked or stand in the way that sinners take or sit in the company of mockers, but whose delight is in the law of the Lord, and who meditates on his law day and night.* Psalm 1:1–2 NIV

UNDERSTAND:

• What is the difference between walking in step with sinners and standing in the way that sinners take?

....

....

....

....

....

....

....

• How and when do you meditate upon God's Word? If this is not a regular practice for you, how and when will you begin?

....

....

....

....

....

....

....

APPLY: Believers are called to be different. We are to stand out. We are not to look like the world, walk in step with the world, or even get near the road of sin that leads to destruction.

When the jokes become coarse, do you laugh with everyone else? After all, you weren't the one who told the joke. You're just joining in with an innocent giggle.

When gossip is presented to you, do you turn toward it for another juicy morsel, or do you turn away from it, making it clear that you're not interested?

There are opportunities each day for the believer to stand firm and to stand out. Be different. Don't blend in with the crowd.

Be like the tree planted by streams of water. Yield your fruit. Your leaf will never wither. Claim the promise of the one who walks with God.

PRAY: *Lord, make me strong. Give me the boldness to stand for what is right when I am tempted to go in the way of sin. Help me to dwell on Your Word day and night that it might strengthen me. In Jesus' name I pray. Amen.*

Day 303

PERFECT PEACE

---- **READ ISAIAH 26:1-19** ----

KEY VERSES: *You will keep in perfect peace all who trust in you, all whose thoughts are fixed on you! Trust in the LORD always, for the LORD GOD is the eternal Rock.* ISAIAH 26:3-4 NLT

UNDERSTAND:

- Think about a time when the path ahead of you seemed rocky and steep, but you made it through. How did God smooth it for you? Will you trust Him to do that again?

....

....

....

....

....

- Do you sincerely search for and seek God both morning and night? What does that look like in your life?

....

....

....

....

....

....

....

APPLY: Make this song of praise, written by the prophet Isaiah, your personal worship to God. Own what it says in your life. *You* are surrounded by the walls of God's salvation. *You* are kept in perfect peace when you trust in God and fix your thoughts on Him. He is *your* eternal Rock! Are you struggling with pride or dealing with someone in your life who is arrogant? Let God do the humbling that needs to happen. He smooths out the rocky and steep paths ahead of you as you trust in Him, obey His commands, and sincerely seek Him. You might be feeling so discouraged over the evil that others do as they pay no attention to God, but remember that it is His job to defend you and prevail over the wicked—*and He will*, in His timing. Praise God for anything good that you have accomplished in your life, because it is ultimately from Him. And never forget that as you deal with pain and hardship, you can hold fast to the truth that "those who die in the Lord will live; their bodies will rise again" (Isaiah 26:19 NLT).

PRAY: *Heavenly Father, please help me to keep my thoughts fixed on You, and keep me in Your perfect peace! Remind me of the powerful truth from Your Word that puts my attention on who You are, my eternal Rock, and all You are able to do. Amen.*

Day 304

YOU ARE NOT ALONE

─── **READ PSALM 23** ───

KEY VERSE: *Yes, even if I walk through the valley of the shadow of death, I will not be afraid of anything, because You are with me.* PSALM 23:4 NLV

UNDERSTAND:

• Do you believe that, with the Lord as your shepherd, you have everything you need? Why or why not?

....

....

....

....

• When do you feel God's presence most near?

....

....

....

....

• Which word pictures in Psalm 23 are most comforting to you? Why?

....

....

....

....

....

APPLY: From an early age, we're taught to be self-reliant. To work hard and figure it out and provide for ourselves and our loved ones. Plans and hard work are commendable, and scripture encourages us to pursue both (see Proverbs 21:5), but Psalm 23 shows us the picture of God as our shepherd providing everything we need as His sheep.

A shepherd is ever present with his flock, keeping watch over them, leading them to water for refreshment and green grass for nourishment. He keeps his sheep out of danger and walks with them along treacherous paths. He ensures that his sheep are *never alone.*

If you feel alone today, take solace in Psalm 23. The truth is when we *feel* alone, we aren't *actually* alone. Grasp ahold of God's promise that He is with you, and you will have everything you need.

PRAY: *God, I feel alone. But my feelings often can't be trusted. My head and heart know that You are here. You are my vigilant shepherd, and I am Your beloved lamb. Guide me through the dark valleys of life. And please use Your staff to keep me on the path with You. I do not want to stray from Your loving presence. Amen.*

Day 305

RESTING IN HIM

―――――――――― **READ LUKE 10:38-42** ――――――――――

KEY VERSE: *She had a sister called Mary, who sat at the Lord's feet listening to what he said.* LUKE 10:39 NIV

UNDERSTAND:

• Martha wasn't a bad woman. She was simply busy. Have you ever been so busy that you pushed your time with the Lord aside?

....

....

....

....

....

....

• Mary chose the better path—sitting at Jesus' feet, listening to Him as He ministered. Why do you think God prefers her approach to Martha's?

....

....

....

....

....

....

....

APPLY: Let's face it, life can get crazy at times. We've got to get the kids to school, then off to Little League, ballet class, piano lessons, and so on. On top of this, we have bills to pay, appliance repairmen to call, and a job to get to. At the end of the day, we drop into bed, completely exhausted. Somewhere, in the middle of it all, we have to make sure the dishes are washed, the floors swept, and the laundry folded. Whew! Talk about exhausting!

Surely Martha understood this sort of chaotic, anxiety-driven lifestyle. She was a workaholic too. And Jesus (who has nothing against workaholics, by the way) saw her exhaustion. He pointed to her sister, Mary, who had chosen to recline at His feet, and asked Martha to consider resting awhile too.

Maybe you're more Martha than Mary. You have a hard time stopping. You just keep going, going, going, even if it means giving up your quiet time with the Lord. Today He's calling out to you, begging you to cease your labors for a moment and rest at His feet. What have you got to lose? Take a load off and sit for a while.

PRAY: *Father, thank You for the reminder that I need to rest. Sometimes I overdo it. Okay, most of the time I overdo it. But I will do my best to be more Mary than Martha today, no matter what I'm facing. Amen.*

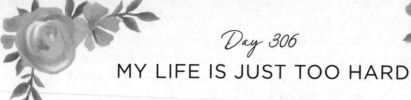

MY LIFE IS JUST TOO HARD

————— **READ JAMES 1:2-6** —————

KEY VERSE: *When your faith is tested, your endurance has a chance to grow.*
JAMES 1:3 NLT

UNDERSTAND:

- How might you consider the troubles that come your way a chance for great joy (verse 2)? Does this seem like a contradiction that's too hard for you to surmount?

....

....

....

....

....

....

- If you had greater wisdom (verse 5), do you think you would be able to better see the joy interwoven with the trouble? Why or why not?

....

....

....

....

....

....

APPLY: Sometimes the Bible seems to ask too much of us. Looking at trouble as an opportunity for joy (verse 2) is over the top!

And yet James, the author of these verses, asks us to consider another perspective. The challenges we face in life often threaten to take from us something we value, whether our pride, our money, or the companionship of people we love. It's natural to value these things, but when we place our faith in any of them rather than in God, we are bound to feel unsettled by life's circumstances. The changing winds of life will blow us back and forth, tossing us and shaking us (verse 6).

When we are truly secure in God, though, we can head into the wind, our course unshaken. Despite any pain, we will still know God's joy, as steady as ever. Our strength and endurance will grow.

PRAY: *God, my life seems too hard to bear right now. Show me Your joy, a steady thread woven through the challenges. Remind me that when my faith is in You, You will make me strong enough to endure whatever demands I face. Amen.*

Day 307

SHARE JESUS:
STEP OUTSIDE THE BOX

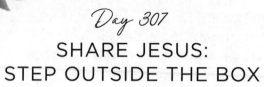

───────── **READ MATTHEW 9** ─────────

KEY VERSES: *As Jesus was having dinner at Matthew's house, many tax collectors and "sinners" came and ate with Jesus and his followers. When the Pharisees saw this, they asked Jesus' followers, "Why does your teacher eat with tax collectors and sinners?"* MATTHEW 9:10–11 NCV

UNDERSTAND:

• What is Jesus' answer to the question posed in Matthew 9:11? Read Matthew 9:12.

....

....

....

....

• Who are the tax collectors of today? Who would your friends be surprised to see you associating with?

....

....

....

....

....

....

....

....

APPLY: We are called to live in this world. While we are set apart as believers, we are still to be "in the mix." If we isolate ourselves and associate only with one another, how will others come to know the healing salvation of Jesus Christ?

In these verses, the Pharisees are shocked to see Jesus eating and spending time with those they considered to be "sinners." In fact, we are all sinners. These tax collectors needed Christ. They needed rescue from a selfish and sinful life. Jesus stated that healthy people do not need physicians, but rather those who are sick need physicians. He gave wonderful analogies, and this one fits so well here.

Just as Jesus walked and talked with those who were the outcasts of society, those everyone knew to be sinners, we are to go and do likewise. Who in your community needs Jesus? Step outside the box. Jesus did.

PRAY: *Lord, help me not to isolate myself among only other believers. While I know I must choose close friends who are Christians so that I can remain encouraged and strengthened, I also know I must not hide away. Give me opportunities to get out into my community and share Your love with those who need to know You. Amen.*

Day 308

DEARLY LOVED IN
GREAT DETAIL

─────────── **READ MATTHEW 10** ───────────

KEY VERSES: *"Are not two small birds sold for a very small piece of money? And yet not one of the birds falls to the earth without your Father knowing it. God knows how many hairs you have on your head. So do not be afraid. You are more important than many small birds."* MATTHEW 10:29–31 NLV

UNDERSTAND:

• What does it mean to be as shrewd as snakes and innocent as doves in verse 16?

....

....

....

....

....

....

• What person in your life knows and loves you the very best? How does it make you feel to praise God for knowing and loving you even better?

....

....

....

....

....

....

APPLY: Jesus was sending out the twelve disciples and calming their fears. He urged them not to be afraid of anyone who could kill or destroy the body but not the soul. Find peace tonight in this passage, trusting that God is watching over both your body and soul so protectively. He will never let any lasting harm come to a soul saved forever by Him. Plus, He knows every single detail about you—far, far better than even your closest loved ones—right down to the number of hairs on your head. Your family and friends surely know and love you, but they can't possibly know and love you like your heavenly Father who created you. Praise Him tonight like this: "You made the parts inside me. You put me together inside my mother. I will give thanks to You, for the greatness of the way I was made brings fear. Your works are great and my soul knows it very well. . . . Your eyes saw me before I was put together. And all the days of my life were written in Your book before any of them came to be" (Psalm 139:13–14, 16 NLV).

_____

_____

_____

_____

_____

_____

_____

_____

_____

_____

_____

PRAY: *Heavenly Father, help me not to fear anyone or anything. I fear only You with deep respect and love. You know and love me far better than anyone else, and I trust that I am constantly in Your protective care. Amen.*

Day 309

YOUR RANSOM IS PAID

—— READ 1 PETER 1:13–19 ——

KEY VERSES: *For you know that God paid a ransom to save you from the empty life you inherited from your ancestors. And it was not paid with mere gold or silver, which lose their value. It was the precious blood of Christ, the sinless, spotless Lamb of God.* 1 PETER 1:18–19 NLT

UNDERSTAND:

• Are there limits to what you would give to pay a ransom for someone you love? Why or why not?

....

....

....

....

....

....

• What does the ransom that God paid for your new life say about the value He places on you?

....

....

....

....

....

....

....

APPLY: You've probably never thought of your salvation in terms of a Liam Neeson film from the "Taken" franchise, but the apostle Peter's ransom analogy gives us a new way to think about our salvation.

Satan laid claim to humankind way back in the Garden of Eden when Adam and Eve ate the forbidden fruit. And each of us has followed in their footsteps, giving in to our own selfish desires and sinning. But even before we thought of God, He thought of us and put up the priceless treasure of His Son's life for ours.

Can you imagine the delight Satan must've taken in such a trade? Our worthless souls for the sinless Jesus! But the Father knew that was not the end. Final victory was His—and ours—on the third day when Jesus came back to life!

PRAY: *Jesus, when I think of how Your precious blood paid the ransom for my life, I am humbled to the point of tears. I don't deserve such generosity, such love, such grace. But You willingly went to the cross to finish the nasty business of Satan's claim on my soul. My heart is Yours. My soul is Yours. Make me more like You. Amen.*

Day 310

BROTHERLY LOVE

READ 1 SAMUEL 18

KEY VERSE: *Then Jonathan made a covenant with David, because he loved him as his own soul.* 1 SAMUEL 18:3 ESV

UNDERSTAND:

• Can you remember the name of your earliest childhood friend? What drew you to this person? Are you still in touch?

....

....

....

....

....

....

....

• Why does God care so much about our relationships with others?

....

....

....

....

....

....

....

....

APPLY: Have you ever had a friend who was so close you were practically the same person? You laughed alike, talked alike, sometimes even dressed alike. That's how Jonathan and David were. These two BFFs were inseparable. Where one went, the other would follow. The boys grew up together and, as boys are wont to do, probably got into lots of mischief together. As they grew, they became mutual protectors in the game of life. The words *He's got my back* were surely their motto.

Maybe you've had a friend like that. The two of you did everything together. Good, bad, indifferent. . .as a duo you could handle anything. Chaos, laughs, tears . . .you bonded over anything and everything.

When you find a friend like that, you've found a real treasure.

The world focuses so much on romantic love but very little on friendship. The Bible, however, highlights friendships such as the one between Jonathan and David so that we never forget—brotherly love is critical to our survival. We were created for relationships, after all.

PRAY: *Lord, I'm so thankful for brotherly love. I don't know where I'd be without the close friendships I've had over the years. I'm so grateful, Father. Amen.*

Day 311
I'M LONELY

---------- **READ PSALM 23** ----------

KEY VERSE: *Even when I walk through the darkest valley, I will not be afraid, for you are close beside me.* PSALM 23:4 NLT

UNDERSTAND:

• What connection between loneliness and fear, if any, do you feel in your life?

....

....

....

....

• What does it mean to you that the Lord is your shepherd? Can you grasp that concept?

....

....

....

....

• Do you believe that God is close beside you, no matter how dark life may seem? Why or why not?

....

....

....

....

APPLY: Loneliness is not the same as solitude. Solitude is a sense of joyful engagement with ourselves and with the Holy Spirit that we experience while being alone. It's good for us. Loneliness, however, is destructive, not only emotionally and spiritually but physically as well; scientific research has found that lonely people suffer more physical illnesses.

Life is full of dark valleys, stretches of time when for one reason or another, we feel very alone. It might be a work situation. . .a family crisis. . .the death of a loved one. . .a serious illness. . .or merely the sense that we have no one with whom to share both the good and bad of our lives. God does not want us to be lonely though. Not only does He want us to find ways to connect with others, but He also wants us to know that He is always with us.

PRAY: *Thank You, shepherd of my soul, that You are always with me, guiding me through even the darkest valley. Give me all that I need to nourish my soul—including the companionship of others—so that I can be all that You want me to be. Amen.*

Day 312
LIGHTEN YOUR LOAD

──────── **READ MATTHEW 11** ────────

KEY VERSES: *If you are tired from carrying heavy burdens, come to me and I will give you rest. Take the yoke I give you. Put it on your shoulders and learn from me. I am gentle and humble, and you will find rest. This yoke is easy to bear, and this burden is light.* MATTHEW 11:28–30 CEV

UNDERSTAND:

- Where can you find true rest?

....

....

....

....

....

....

- When have you carried a heavy burden? What was it? Are you carrying one today?

....

....

....

....

....

....

....

APPLY: Living in a third-floor apartment can be a real challenge. Trying to carry groceries upstairs is always fun. Usually, the third-floor dweller will attempt to carry too many groceries at once. Loading herself down like a pack mule, she ascends the stairs, plastic shopping bag handles digging into her arms. Often, an apple or canned good will escape and cause quite a commotion, bumping and bouncing its way back to the first floor.

This scene sounds humorous but all too familiar when we really think about it. Don't most Christian women you know go around overloaded? Maybe not with groceries but with all sorts of worries and baggage.

If you are carrying a heavy load, know that God stands ready to help you. You were not created to bear such burdens. He offers you a light load. He tells you to cast your cares on Him because He cares for you (1 Peter 5:7).

PRAY: *Lord, thank You that in You I can find true rest. Take my heavy burden. I lay it at Your feet. Please replace it with a light load. Help me to trust You to take care of my worries, guilt, and every other burden I have been trying to carry on my own. In Jesus' name I ask. Amen.*

Day 313

OVERPOWERING HOPE

───── **READ 1 THESSALONIANS 4:13-18; JOHN 11:1-44** ─────

KEY VERSES: *We want you to know for sure about those who have died. You have no reason to have sorrow as those who have no hope. We believe that Jesus died and then came to life again. Because we believe this, we know that God will bring to life again all those who belong to Jesus.* 1 THESSALONIANS 4:13–14 NLV

UNDERSTAND:

• Why did Jesus say He was glad He was not there when Lazarus died?

....

....

....

....

....

....

• What does it say about Jesus that He wept even though He knew He was about to raise Lazarus back to life?

....

....

....

....

....

....

....

APPLY: Are you grieving today? Maybe you have recently lost a family member or friend, and the pain and sadness feel nearly unbearable. But even while you cry and ache and miss them in this life, you can have hope that overpowers the grief. If your loved one trusted Jesus as Savior, they will be brought to new life again like Jesus. You will see your loved one again and spend eternity together in heaven. That is an incredible comfort—and it should motivate us to share the good news of Jesus. Just like God does, we should want all people to be saved from sin and have the incredible hope of the resurrection.

PRAY: *Heavenly Father, I'm grateful for the hope You give us that because Jesus rose to life, so will all who trust in Him as Savior. Please comfort me in my grief, and comfort all who are grieving. Help me to share with many others that the one true hope of salvation and resurrection is found in You alone. Amen.*

Day 314

YOU CAN TRUST HIM

─────── **READ PROVERBS 3:1–12** ───────

KEY VERSES: *Trust in the LORD with all your heart; do not depend on your own understanding. Seek his will in all you do, and he will show you which path to take.* PROVERBS 3:5–6 NLT

UNDERSTAND:

• In what areas of your life is it easy to trust God?

....

....

....

....

• In what areas of your life is it difficult to trust God?

....

....

....

....

• When have you trusted God and clearly seen the path He wanted you to take?

....

....

....

....

....

....

APPLY: What decision are you facing currently? Our lives are made up of big decisions and small decisions—some require a choice right now and some must be thought about, debated, and weighed.

Your loving Father can and wants to give you wisdom in every decision. No choice is too trivial, no problem is too big, no challenge is too insurmountable for Him to guide you through it.

Today, whether you're facing a big decision or not, pray and ask the Holy Spirit to come alive in your heart. Seek out His truth in scripture, and ask Him to make His will obvious to you. Then talk to mature Christian friends who you trust. The Lord is faithful to show you which path is His, and you can step confidently forward as you follow Him.

PRAY: *Lord God, I admit there are times I'd rather trust my gut than trust You. When I'm in danger of relying on my own wits to make a decision, remind me that Your will is what I want to follow. Make the pathway ahead obvious and cleared of obstacles so that I will walk confidently ahead. Be the King of my heart today and every day, Father. Amen.*

Day 315

A GREATER PLAN

──────── **READ EXODUS 2:1-10** ────────

KEY VERSES: *Then Pharaoh's daughter went down to the Nile to bathe, and her attendants were walking along the riverbank. She saw the basket among the reeds and sent her female slave to get it. She opened it and saw the baby. He was crying, and she felt sorry for him. "This is one of the Hebrew babies," she said.* Exodus 2:5–6 NIV

UNDERSTAND:

• Moses' mother took a great risk, placing her baby in a basket in the river. What if things had gone a different direction? What other outcomes might have occurred?

....

....

....

....

....

• Moses would have led a completely different life if Pharaoh's daughter hadn't taken him in. Has your life ever changed because of someone's intervention?

....

....

....

....

....

....

....

APPLY: Oh, the things a mother will do for her child! Moses' mom was no different from any other when it came to protecting her own. But, because of the times she lived in, desperate measures were called for. In order to keep her baby, she had to give him up. God honored her plan, and Moses' life was spared.

We live in a similar age, where Christian parents often have to go to great extremes to protect the innocence of their children. Temptations abound, vying for a child's heart and mind. Everything from TV to video games to cell phones grabs their attention from a young age.

God has a greater plan for your child than you can imagine. So do all you can to protect him from the temptations of this life. Make sure he's safe and strong. Yes, sacrifices will have to be made. But giving your child the best possible upbringing is worth all the trouble. That's what love does, after all. . .it sacrifices.

PRAY: *Thank You for the reminder that children need to be guarded and protected, Lord. I don't want the little ones in my world to succumb to temptations. Help me lead and guide, Father. Amen.*

Day 316

I WANT TO RUN AWAY

―――――― **READ JONAH 1** ――――――

KEY VERSE: *But Jonah ran away from the LORD. . . . He went down to Joppa, where he found a ship. . . . After paying the fare, he went aboard and sailed for Tarshish to flee from the LORD.* JONAH 1:3 NIV

UNDERSTAND:

• Why do you think Jonah ran away from God? Why was he so unwilling to go to Nineveh?

....

....

....

....

....

....

• If you feel like running away from your life, have you considered that you may also be running away from God?

....

....

....

....

....

....

....

APPLY: Sometimes we all need to run away. Even Jesus needed times of escape. But there's a big difference between running away *to God*, as Jesus did, and running away *from God*, as Jonah did.

Jonah's story shows us what happens when we try to escape God's will. Thinking we can flee whatever demands we're unwilling to face, we end up somewhere far worse! We're not likely to be swallowed by a giant fish, but any circumstances where we're cramped, in the dark, and miserable might be a lot like that whale's belly!

There's an interesting detail in this story though—Jonah was in the fish's stomach for three days and nights (verse 17), the same period of time that Jesus was in the grave. This hints at something important: even though we run away from God, all is not lost. God uses even the graves in our lives—the slimy, smelly, dark fish bellies—to transform us. He can resurrect us into a new life, a life aligned with His love.

PRAY: *God, when I want to run away, remind me what happened to Jonah. Thank You, though, that even when I insist on fleeing from You, You give me another chance. You send a whale to swallow me—and then You bring me back to serve You anew. Amen.*

Day 317

HOLINESS

———— READ ROMANS 12 ————

KEY VERSE: *Therefore, I urge you, brothers and sisters, in view of God's mercy, to offer your bodies as a living sacrifice, holy and pleasing to God—this is your true and proper worship.* ROMANS 12:1 NIV

UNDERSTAND:

• What is holiness and why is it important?

....

....

....

....

....

....

• How does one offer her body as a living sacrifice to God? What does this look like?

....

....

....

....

....

....

....

APPLY: Romans 12 is a powerful chapter that admonishes the believer to be humble, to love others, and to seek holiness before God.

As women, it's easy to get caught up in outward appearance. Our society is consumed with style and fashion, exercise and fitness. There is a new diet plan every week, it seems! While certainly physical health is important, Romans 12:1 points out that holiness supersedes even physical health.

When you live your life in humility, serving others, using your gifts, and showing love, you please God. Is it more important that you have the latest hairstyle or fashion trend or that you do what is right and live at peace with those around you? God sees the heart. Seek to be holy. Ask Him to help you.

PRAY: *Lord, help me to live out Romans 12 today. Give me the strength to cling to good and to stay away from evil. Strengthen me that I might use my gifts to bring You glory and honor. Help me to seek holiness that I might please You, Father. In Jesus' name I pray. Amen.*

Day 318

SO DEARLY LOVED

READ ROMANS 8:18–39

KEY VERSES: *Nothing can ever separate us from God's love. Neither death nor life, neither angels nor demons, neither our fears for today nor our worries about tomorrow—not even the powers of hell can separate us from God's love. No power in the sky above or in the earth below—indeed, nothing in all creation will ever be able to separate us from the love of God that is revealed in Christ Jesus our Lord.* ROMANS 8:38–39 NLT

UNDERSTAND:

• What is causing you to groan the most these days? How does this scripture passage encourage you even while you groan?

....

....

....

....

....

• Have you ever felt separated from God's love? What caused you to feel that way? Do you believe the promise in this scripture that it's impossible to be separated from God's love, no matter what hardship you're going through?

....

....

....

....

....

....

....

APPLY: Sometimes you might find yourself or a loved one in a situation so hard and so confusing you have no idea how to even begin to talk to God about it or ask for His help. In those times, you can be so grateful for the Holy Spirit and the promise in Romans 8:26 (NLT) that He helps you in your weakness. He goes to God for you with "groanings that cannot be expressed in words." He pleads for you according to God's will. How amazing to know that you are so incredibly loved that the Holy Spirit is begging for what is best for you and that God is working everything together for good for those who love Him and are called according to His purpose. The final treasure of this passage is the powerful promise that assures you that absolutely *nothing* can separate you from God's love. Close out your day with total confidence of how adored you are by your heavenly Father. Even as you sleep, trust that you are being prayed for by the Spirit and you are constantly connected to God's love.

....

....

....

....

....

....

....

....

....

....

PRAY: *Heavenly Father, let me relax in Your amazing love for me tonight. Thank You that nothing can ever separate me from it. Help me to remember that even while the problems of this world seem overwhelming and agonizing, You are working out Your perfect plans in the midst of them. I am Your dearly loved child, and I trust You! Amen.*

Day 319

SEEKING GOD'S WORD

READ PSALM 119:1-16

KEY VERSES: *How can a young person stay on the path of purity? By living according to your word. I seek you with all my heart; do not let me stray from your commands. I have hidden your word in my heart that I might not sin against you.* PSALM 119:9-11 NIV

UNDERSTAND:

• How does spending time in God's Word add to your life?

....

....

....

....

• What verses have you hidden in your heart through memorization?

....

....

....

....

• How has God's Word helped you "stay on the path of purity" (verse 9)?

....

....

....

....

....

....

APPLY: There are some items that have a knack for getting misplaced. Phones, glasses, car keys, remotes—these things are all essential, so when one is lost, we take the time and effort to seek the missing item until it's found, sometimes up-ending a house in order to find it!

Once you experience the power of God's Word, it becomes an essential part of your life. And when life gets busy and you're not spending time in the Bible, you feel that missing piece. Seeking His wisdom with your whole heart by opening scripture is one of the best ways to stay in tune with God's heart. When we study scripture, we're allowing the Holy Spirit to awaken and speak to us, encourage us, and convict us of areas in our lives where we need to change.

Keep seeking God's Word, and you will find your loving Father was in front of you all along!

PRAY: *Almighty Lord, I am grateful for Your Word. Let Your scripture take root in my heart and soul. Help me to commit more and more of Your wisdom to memory, and let it come to mind when I need it and when I can encourage someone else. Amen.*

WRITTEN ON THE HEART

—————— READ ROMANS 2:12–16 ——————

KEY VERSES: *They show that the work of the law is written on their hearts, while their conscience also bears witness, and their conflicting thoughts accuse or even excuse them on that day when, according to my gospel, God judges the secrets of men by Christ Jesus.* ROMANS 2:15–16 ESV

UNDERSTAND:

- If you've ever been in a legalistic church or relationship, you know how tough it can be to break free. Where do legalists get it wrong?

....

....

....

....

....

....

- How has God written His law on your heart?

....

....

....

....

....

....

....

....

APPLY: Old Testament believers didn't have the benefit of a Savior. They were operating under the Mosaic law, laid down in the book of Leviticus. This law gave regulations for *every* aspect of life. No matter what you were going through, there was a law for it. Only one problem—no one could actually follow those laws to a tee.

Enter Jesus, the fulfillment of the law. He came to do what the law could not—save us. When we accept Him as Lord and Savior, His sacrifice on the cross covers every law we've ever broken. Best of all, when we walk in relationship with Him, He writes the law on our hearts (meaning, He takes the positive attributes of the law, mixes them up with grace, mercy, and forgiveness—and pencils them on our hearts).

Gone are the days of legalism. No more slaps on the hand for messing up. Now we long to serve Him and live by His precepts out of a deep, abiding love for Him. What a remarkable plan!

PRAY: *Lord, thank You for writing Your laws on my heart. I could never keep up with all the Levitical laws, Father. I would fall short at every turn. But You sent Your Son and redeemed me from the curse of the law so that I might live in freedom. How can I ever thank You, Lord? Praise You for the cross! Amen.*

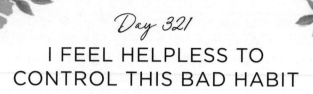

Day 321

I FEEL HELPLESS TO CONTROL THIS BAD HABIT

READ ROMANS 7:19–25

KEY VERSE: *For the good that I would I do not: but the evil which I would not, that I do.* ROMANS 7:19 KJV

UNDERSTAND:

• How did this bad habit begin? Did you think it was something that would give you pleasure?

....

....

• Does this habit now seem like a dead body you're forced to carry on your shoulders (verse 24)?

....

....

• How does this habit keep you from living your life the way you want to live?

....

....

....

• If your habit is truly destructive—such as abusing drugs or harming yourself or others in some way—you need to seek help from outside yourself. Ask God to lead you to the professional help you need.

....

....

....

APPLY: Haven't we all felt the way Paul did when he wrote these words? No matter how much we want to stop a certain behavior, we can't seem to shake it off. We make up our minds to never do this thing again—and then we turn around and do that very thing. It's so frustrating! We feel helpless and hopeless.

It may be that in our own power we're unable to break this habit. We need to understand, though, that God does not condemn us for the hold it has on our lives. If we surrender it to God, acknowledging that we are powerless to stop this behavior, God will be pleased. And as we trust Him, we may be surprised to find that He has brought people or circumstances into our lives we could never have imagined and which achieve what we thought could never be done: they set us free.

PRAY: *Lord, I ask that You deliver me from this bad habit. Show me the steps to take. Remind me that Your love for me is undiminished, no matter how powerless I am to control my own behavior. Amen.*

Day 322

OLD VS. NEW

───────── **READ 2 CORINTHIANS 5** ─────────

KEY VERSE: *Therefore, if anyone is in Christ, the new creation has come: The old has gone, the new is here!* 2 CORINTHIANS 5:17 NIV

UNDERSTAND:

- What guilt do you often attempt to hold on to from your past even though Christ has given you new life?

....

....

....

....

....

....

- How are we to regard other believers—based on their past or on their identity in Christ? What is our identity in Christ?

....

....

....

....

....

....

....

....

APPLY: Our sin was laid upon Christ, the only sinless man, the Son of God. He died for us, once and for all, and if we have trusted in Him as Savior, we are forgiven.

So why do we live weighed down in the muck and mire of a not-so-pleasant past? Do you find it hard to fully let go of the sin you committed prior to asking Jesus to be your Savior?

You are in good company. It's a natural tendency. Still, we must recognize that we are not the same anymore. The old person has gone. The new has come. God sees you not as you were but through a Jesus lens. And through that lens, He sees you as righteous. Don't waste precious energy toting around an unnecessary load of guilt. Lay it down today. Once and for all. And use that energy to spread the gospel to those who do not yet know the Savior.

PRAY: *Lord, lift the burden of guilt I so unnecessarily cling to. Remind me that through Jesus Christ, I am seen as righteous, forgiven, free, and—best of all—new! I am not the woman I was before I came to Christ. The old has gone, and the new has come. Amen.*

Day 323

USE YOUR TIME WISELY

———— **READ ECCLESIASTES 3; EPHESIANS 5:1–21** ————

KEY VERSES: *Look carefully then how you walk, not as unwise but as wise, making the best use of the time, because the days are evil. Therefore do not be foolish, but understand what the will of the Lord is.* Ephesians 5:15–17 esv

UNDERSTAND:

• What things most tempt you from doing what you should be doing?

....

....

....

....

....

....

• How are you actively disciplining yourself in regard to those things, and what blessing and reward are you noticing as you do?

....

....

....

....

....

....

....

APPLY: It's far too easy to get distracted or be lazy about doing the good work God has for us to do. There are just so many opportunities and options in the world! Those things aren't necessarily all bad, but we need plenty of prayer and discipline to prevent them from getting in the way of what's most important in our lives. Most important should be what Jesus said the greatest command is: "'You must love the Lord your God with all your heart and with all your soul and with all your mind.' This is the first and greatest of the Laws. The second is like it, 'You must love your neighbor as you love yourself.' All the Laws and the writings of the early preachers depend on these two most important Laws" (Matthew 22:37–40 NLV). And so, we continue to ask Him to show us how to live carefully and wisely, making the best use of the time to use our gifts to glorify Him in what He has planned for us.

PRAY: *Heavenly Father, please help me to keep Your great commandments first in my life—loving You completely and loving others as myself. Then help me to manage my time and days wisely to bring the most glory to You. This is a prayer I'll need to keep praying repeatedly. Thank You for hearing and helping me. Amen.*

Day 324
WAITING EXPECTANTLY

---------- **READ PSALM 27** ----------

KEY VERSE: *Wait patiently for the L*ORD*. Be brave and courageous. Yes, wait patiently for the L*ORD*.* PSALM 27:14 NLT

UNDERSTAND:

• What are the things in life you consider worth waiting for?

....

....

....

....

....

• Why is waiting so hard?

....

....

....

....

....

• Is it possible to wait without worrying? Why or why not?

....

....

....

....

....

APPLY: God's timing is perfect. Even when we believe this fact wholeheartedly, waiting for Him to act at the right time is difficult. Scripture encourages us again and again to wait patiently on our Father, who knows everything and is in complete control, and to pray earnestly while waiting. Psalm 27:14 goes further by giving us an action step while we wait: be brave and courageous.

What does this mean on a practical level? It means during seasons of waiting, we can live every day having full confidence knowing that God *will* act. We can anticipate that He will do something in a delightfully surprising and altogether perfect way. With courage, we can stand tall and say to ourselves and others, "God's got this handled."

What are you waiting on today? Keep praying, asking for God to act in that situation, and also ask for a dose of bravery to lift your spirit. He will fill you with courage and the eager anticipation of the answer to your prayer.

PRAY: *I don't like to wait, God. Even when I trust in Your perfect timing, I struggle. I worry. I fret. I want to take control of the situation and force my will. Give me patience. But today I'm also asking for courage. Make me brave to live in the confidence that You have this well under control and that You're lining up all the details for Your will to be done in my life. Amen.*

Day 325

A STRONG FOUNDATION

——— **READ MATTHEW 7** ———

KEY VERSES: *"Everyone then who hears these words of mine and does them will be like a wise man who built his house on the rock. And the rain fell, and the floods came, and the winds blew and beat on that house, but it did not fall, because it had been founded on the rock."* MATTHEW 7:24–25 ESV

UNDERSTAND:

- A good foundation is key. Think of a time in your life when you entered into a project or situation that wasn't well founded. How did that project end?

....

....

....

....

....

....

- Why do you suppose God cares so much about foundations?

....

....

....

....

....

....

....

APPLY: "The wise man built his house upon the rock. The foolish man built his house upon the sand." Maybe you sang those words in Sunday school, as millions of children did. Perhaps the words conjured up images of houses along the seashore, the sandy-bottomed ones cratering from within.

God has always been in the foundations business. He wants us to be rooted and founded in Him, as unmoving as a house built on stone. This can only happen if we stay in His Word and spend time with Him, growing and worshipping.

Would you say that your foundation is strong? Have you made it a point to pour into the foundations of others? Or are you content to watch them float along, like a house on shifting sand? If your "home" is in need of a new foundation, today's the day. Go back to basics. Read the Gospel of John and go from there. Ask God to rebuild you from the foundation up.

PRAY: *I want to have a solid foundation, Lord. I don't want to shift to and fro with each passing wind. If there are unstable areas of my life, shore them up, I pray. Rebuild me from the foundation up, Lord. May I stand tall and strong for You! Amen.*

Day 326

DEATH SCARES ME

—————————— **READ JOHN 11:20-43** ——————————

KEY VERSES: *"I am the resurrection and the life. The one who believes in me will live, even though they die; and whoever lives by believing in me will never die. Do you believe this?"* JOHN 11:25–26 NIV

UNDERSTAND:

- Martha and Mary felt comfortable reproaching Jesus for what looked like a failure on His part. Have you ever felt as they did? Have you ever thought, *If only God had stepped in and stopped this from happening! Where was He?* Did you feel free to express those feelings? Why or why not?

....

....

....

....

....

- Why do you think Jesus wept, when He must have known He was about to bring Lazarus back to life?

....

....

....

....

....

....

APPLY: People in earlier times lived with death much more closely than we do today. Modern medicine extends our lives and heals diseases that once killed so many people. Today, death seems unnatural to us, like something we should all be able to avoid, and yet that is clearly not the case. Death is an inescapable reality. It's the great mystery that we all face—and it's only natural to fear the unknown.

In this story from the Gospel of John, Jesus doesn't deny that death is real. Its reality makes Him cry, despite the fact that in a few moments He will bring His friend back to life. We too will mourn and cry when death touches our lives—the pain is inescapable—but at the same time, we can hear Jesus' words: "I am the resurrection and the life. The one who believes in me will live, even though they die."

PRAY: *Thank You, Jesus, that You used Lazarus's death to teach all of us that You are the Lord of both life and death. I'm still afraid—but I know that whatever happens, You are with me. Amen.*

AVOID COMPLAINING

READ PHILIPPIANS 2

KEY VERSES: *Do everything without grumbling or arguing, so that you may become blameless and pure, "children of God without fault in a warped and crooked generation."* PHILIPPIANS 2:14–15 NIV

UNDERSTAND:

• About what or whom do you complain most regularly?

_____

_____

_____

_____

_____

• Are you argumentative? If you are not sure, are you brave enough to ask someone close to you if they consider you an argumentative person?

_____

_____

_____

_____

_____

_____

APPLY: Paul calls the Philippians to lay down their selfishness in the first part of Philippians 2. Then, in verses 14–15, he instructs them to be found blameless and pure by avoiding complaining and quarreling. It's a tall order when he asks them to "do everything without grumbling or arguing." Everything?! This would mean that even when someone mistreated them, they should not complain. This seems to imply that even when they are clearly right, they need not stir up an argument.

Even though this letter to the church at Philippi was written many years ago, it sure hits home today! As you move about your day today, avoid complaining. Say no to quarreling. See if it makes a difference in how you feel when you lay your head down on your pillow tonight. There is peace to be found in following this sage advice from the apostle Paul.

....

....

....

....

....

....

....

....

....

....

....

PRAY: *God, set a guard over my lips today. When I begin to grumble or argue, help me to stop and remember how blessed I am. Give me the mind of Christ. Help me to use my words to encourage rather than discourage those around me. Amen.*

Day 328

SO THAT OTHERS CAN HEAR YOU

────────── **READ ACTS 16:16–40** ──────────

KEY VERSES: *They were severely beaten, and then they were thrown into prison. The jailer was ordered to make sure they didn't escape. So the jailer put them into the inner dungeon and clamped their feet in the stocks. Around midnight Paul and Silas were praying and singing hymns to God, and the other prisoners were listening.* ACTS 16:23–25 NLT

UNDERSTAND:

• Do you feel like you've ever been judged or even imprisoned unfairly?

....

....

....

....

....

• What have you experienced during times of choosing to praise God anyway in the middle of suffering?

....

....

....

....

....

....

APPLY: Few of us could honestly say we'd start singing worship songs soon after unjustly being beaten severely and thrown into a dungeon. Yet that's exactly what Paul and Silas did. Hopefully, we never find ourselves in jail, but we can still learn from their experience about how to respond to awful hardship. Choose to praise God anyway, and—this is the key—be sure to worship confidently so that others can hear you. Let the awesome results of Paul and Silas's faithful display inspire you. They were soon miraculously freed from prison and led the jailer and his whole family to faith in Christ. And who knows how many fellow prisoners were listening to them and what additional impact their bold worship had? Only God knows for sure, and hopefully He'll tell us in heaven someday. Meanwhile, especially in the midst of suffering, keep praising and giving credit to God for all good things in ways that others can clearly observe in your life. As you enthusiastically share your faith, trust that God is using you in beautiful and miraculous ways you can't even imagine to draw more people close to Him.

PRAY: *Heavenly Father, I want to choose to praise You in every awful circumstance. No matter what is going on around me, You are still good. You are still loving and looking out for me. You will save and rescue at exactly the right time, according to Your will. I will tell others of Your love and power and saving grace forever and ever. Amen.*

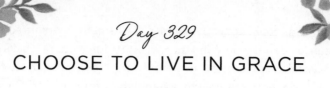

CHOOSE TO LIVE IN GRACE

───── **READ ROMANS 6:1-14** ─────

KEY VERSE: *For sin shall no longer be your master, because you are not under the law, but under grace.* ROMANS 6:14 NIV

UNDERSTAND:

- How did your life change from the time that sin was your master to living under God's grace?

....

....

....

....

- What tricks does Satan use to make you think you are still under the control of your sinful desires?

....

....

....

....

- What does God's grace mean to you?

....

....

....

....

....

APPLY: The world defines freedom as doing whatever we want when we want. It's doing what feels good, what feels right at the time. But while our own evil desires may masquerade as ultimate freedom, sin is really the cruelest of slave masters.

Jesus came to offer us *true* freedom from the bondage of sin. And through His death, burial, and resurrection, Paul tells us in Romans 6:6 (NIV) that "our old self was crucified with him so that the body ruled by sin might be done away with, that we should no longer be slaves to sin."

Sin has a sneaky way of looking for a crack and snaking its way back into our lives. Before we know it, a new sin stronghold has taken root. Examine your heart today. You are free from that cruel slave master! Break free of the chains and live in grace!

PRAY: *Jesus, I long to be free of the sin that so easily pops up in my life. Old habits are hard to break, but I know that Your power is stronger than any temptation I can face. Help me to live confidently in Your grace today and every day. And help me to extend that grace to others who have yet to know You. Amen.*

WORSHIP AT THE THRONE

——— READ REVELATION 4 ———

KEY VERSE: *"Worthy are you, our Lord and God, to receive glory and honor and power, for you created all things, and by your will they existed and were created."* REVELATION 4:11 ESV

UNDERSTAND:

- A day is coming when we will worship at His throne with no distractions, no complications, no pain. What are you most looking forward to when you think of that day?

....

....

....

....

....

- We don't have to wait until we're in heaven to pour out our praises to the Lord. When you think of the phrase "worship with abandon," what comes to mind?

....

....

....

....

....

....

APPLY: What a spectacular picture the book of Revelation paints of the elders worshipping around the throne! Can't you see it now?

Do you picture yourself worshipping alongside them? Are you surrounded by people from every nation, tribe, and tongue? Is the song of worship in one heavenly language or a thousand earthly ones? Does anyone care that hours are passing by as the songs lift and rise then shift to a new chorus?

The truth is, heaven is going to be an amazing place of worship. For there, with all distractions laid aside, we will finally be free to pour out praise uninhibited. Will you sing? Dance? Lift your hands? Only time will tell. But why wait? Let your praises begin right here, right now.

PRAY: *Lord, I don't want to wait until I'm in heaven to lift a song of praise to You. You're worthy of my praise, even in this very moment, Lord. So I praise You! I sing a song of adoration in honor of the King of all kings. Bless You, my Savior! Amen.*

Day 331

I'M SO DISAPPOINTED!

READ NUMBERS 23:19–23

KEY VERSE: *"God is not human, that he should lie, not a human being, that he should change his mind. Does he speak and then not act? Does he promise and not fulfill?"* NUMBERS 23:19 NIV

UNDERSTAND:

• Which disappointments in your life are hardest to bear?

....

....

....

....

....

....

• When you are disappointed, where is your attention? Are you expecting God to do something for you that He failed to do? Or have you been placing your confidence in people who let you down?

....

....

....

....

....

....

APPLY: Disappointment is inevitable in all our lives. People let us down; they promise they'll do something—and then they don't. Things we hope will happen don't happen.

But God promises that He will never disappoint us. When He makes a promise, He always keeps it. He doesn't mislead us. So when He says He'll bless us, He will!

When disappointments start to pile up in our lives, it may be a call to notice where we're placing our confidence. Are we relying on God and His promises? Or are we expecting other people to make us happy in one way or another? Human beings, even the best of them, are fallible. Sooner or later, even the people who love us most will disappoint us. But God never will.

PRAY: *Remind me today, Holy Spirit, to rely only on God's promises. And when You do act, I will give You the credit, saying, "See what God has done!" Amen.*

Day 332

PRAYING FOR OTHERS

—————— **READ COLOSSIANS 1** ——————

KEY VERSE: *Because of this, since the day we heard about you, we have continued praying for you, asking God that you will know fully what he wants. We pray that you will also have great wisdom and understanding in spiritual things.* Colossians 1:9 NCV

UNDERSTAND:

• Who prays for you?

....

....

....

....

....

....

• For whom do you pray regularly?

....

....

....

....

....

....

....

....

APPLY: It's important that believers pray for one another. If you have children, you can see God work in their lives in big ways if you begin to pray for them on a regular basis. Pray for God to give them wisdom and guidance. Pray for them to come to know Christ if they have not yet become Christians. Ask God to show them His will and to give them the desire to follow in His ways.

You can also pray for others in your church, your family, and your workplace. We are a family, the body of Christ, and we must lift one another up in prayer. There is so much power in prayer that we often forfeit simply because we don't ask!

Commit today to praying for other Christians. Lift up their needs to the Lord. Ask Him to work in their lives. Then sit back and watch as God works in the lives of those around you!

PRAY: *Lord, I get so busy that sometimes I forget to pray. I might lift up a thank-you at mealtimes or an immediate need at the end of the day. Often, I drift off to sleep when I'm trying to pray before bed. God, help me to recognize that I am called to pray for other believers and that my prayers truly make a difference. I pause now to lift up to You these special ones who are coming to my mind. . . . [Pray for others specifically by name and need.] Amen.*

Day 333

IF YOU LACK WISDOM

READ JAMES 1

KEY VERSES: *If any of you lacks wisdom, you should ask God, who gives generously to all without finding fault, and it will be given to you. But when you ask, you must believe and not doubt, because the one who doubts is like a wave of the sea, blown and tossed by the wind. That person should not expect to receive anything from the Lord. Such a person is double-minded and unstable in all they do.* JAMES 1:5–8 NIV

UNDERSTAND:

- Do you consider your troubles an opportunity for great joy? How do verses 3–4 and 12 help encourage you in doing so?

....

....

....

....

....

- Do you have any sin to confess and forgiveness to ask for in light of verses 19–21?

....

....

....

....

....

....

APPLY: When we're feeling too much instability and turmoil rather than peace in our lives, we might need to stop and ask ourselves, *Have I been asking for God's wisdom? Do I have faith in God alone and believe that He gives wisdom generously? Am I accepting and applying His wisdom in my life?* Our best source of God's wisdom is the Bible. And James 1 goes on to urge us to never just listen to the Word; we must listen and then *do* what it says. When we follow and obey God's Word and continue in it all our lives, then we will be blessed—and we will have the deep, lasting peace that depends on our never-changing eternal God and not on our constantly changing earthly circumstances.

....

....

....

....

....

....

....

....

....

....

....

....

....

PRAY: *Heavenly Father, I greatly need Your wisdom in all areas of my life. Thank You for Your Word to guide me in it. Today, I ask that You show me exactly the right wisdom I need in my current circumstances. As I read and listen to Your Word, I don't want to forget it. Please help me to sincerely obey and live it out. Amen.*

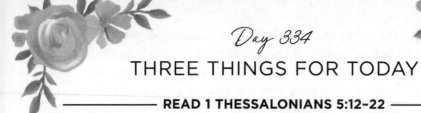

THREE THINGS FOR TODAY

READ 1 THESSALONIANS 5:12-22

KEY VERSES: *Always be joyful. Never stop praying. Be thankful in all circumstances, for this is God's will for you who belong to Christ Jesus.* 1 THESSALONIANS 5:16–18 NLT

UNDERSTAND:

- How would your life be different if you were *always* joyful?

....

....

....

....

- Could you take your thoughts and self-talk and turn them into conversations with God?

....

....

....

....

- Do you think it's possible to be thankful in all circumstances? Why or why not?

....

....

....

....

....

APPLY: How often should we be joyful? *Always*—the apostle Paul doesn't mince words in his letter to the church in Thessalonica. And when can we stop praying? *Never*—again, he makes the expectation clear. He concludes this three-part to-do list just as strong: be thankful—for everything and in every situation.

If it feels like adding these three directives to your stressful daily life is impossible, consider this: if we work toward the attitudes of joy and thankfulness, the frustrations and stresses of the day won't be so monumental. And when we continually talk to God, we have an outlet for the good, the bad, and the ugly of our days. These three things are simple ways to stay connected to the true source of all goodness!

Today, be joyful, never stop praying, and be thankful, and see how God transforms your overall outlook!

....

....

....

....

....

....

....

....

....

....

PRAY: *Father, I admit that sometimes my joy gets buried deep under the daily stresses of life. Restore to me my joy in You. Today I will pray to You with every breath I take. And I will find new joy in You in every circumstance—not just the happy ones but in all circumstances. Thank You for loving me. Thank You for choosing me. Thank You for leading me in Your goodness. Amen.*

Day 335

UNFAIR CIRCUMSTANCES

───────── **READ GENESIS 39** ─────────

KEY VERSE: *But the LORD was with Joseph in the prison and showed him his faithful love. And the LORD made Joseph a favorite with the prison warden.* GENESIS 39:21 NLT

UNDERSTAND:

- Poor Joseph! So many unfair things happened to him. And yet, he prevailed! Have you ever been in an unfair situation? How did you respond?

....

....

....

....

....

....

....

- Joseph rose to an elevated position even while in prison. What can you learn from his story?

....

....

....

....

....

....

APPLY: When you read a story like Joseph's, you start to wonder why God allowed him to go through so much anguish. Tossed into a pit. Sold into slavery by his brothers. Falsely accused. Banished to prison for a crime he did not commit. That poor guy had to jump a lot of hurdles to keep going.

Maybe you've walked a mile in Joseph's shoes. You've been falsely accused. Those you thought you could trust turned against you. They made your life more difficult than it needed to be.

Here's the truth: even when faced with the roughest circumstances, God won't give up on you. If He could take a man like Joseph and elevate him to a position of authority in the prison, then He can take care of you, right where you are. Whatever you're struggling with today, whatever anxieties have held you in their grip, know that God won't leave you on your own. He will give you all you need, even on your hardest day.

PRAY: *Lord, there have been a lot of "unfair" moments in my life so far. Far too many to count. I don't want to lose hope, Lord. I don't want to give in to anxiety. Today I give those concerns to You and choose to remain hopeful, even when circumstances have me down. Amen.*

NOTHING MAKES ANY SENSE

———————— **READ LUKE 1:26–38** ————————

KEY VERSE: *"I am the Lord's servant. May everything you have said about me come true."* Luke 1:38 NLT

UNDERSTAND:

- Can you imagine how Mary must have felt when she was confronted with an angel telling her that she was going to have a baby even though she was a virgin? If something like that happened to you, what would your response be? Would you be able to respond as Mary did?

- When you think of the bewildering, confusing aspects of your own life, can you imagine that God is using these events in some mysterious way to give new birth to His Spirit? What might that mean? Would you be willing to allow it to happen?

APPLY: Comparing the confusion in our lives to Mary's situation may seem inappropriate. But remember, Mary was only a simple young girl at the time the angel came to her. She had no idea how the story would end or the important role she would play. (She would have been astounded if she knew that one day many churches would portray her image!) At the time, she was completely and utterly bewildered. Nothing would have made sense to her.

And yet how did this teenage girl respond? With total surrender to whatever God wanted to do in her life!

....

....

....

....

....

....

....

....

....

....

....

....

....

....

PRAY: *Lord, I don't understand what You're doing in my life. Nothing makes sense to me. But I am Your servant. Accomplish whatever You want in my life. Be born in me. Amen.*

Day 337

WHATEVER YOU DO

——— READ COLOSSIANS 3 ———

KEY VERSE: *And whatever you do in word or deed, do all in the name of the Lord Jesus, giving thanks to God the Father through Him.* COLOSSIANS 3:17 NKJV

UNDERSTAND:

• What all is included in the "whatever" of Colossians 3:17?

....

....

....

....

....

• Have you ever considered that even the most mundane chores can bring glory to God when done in the right spirit?

....

....

....

....

....

....

....

APPLY: Whatever you do. . . That includes a lot of activities, doesn't it? That includes grocery shopping and cleaning the bathroom, driving all over town as a taxi for your kids, and even walking the dog. How could day-to-day chores such as these bring glory to God? It is not the "what" so much as the "how" that interests God. No matter what you are doing, focus on God. Dwell on the blessing of a home when you are scrubbing its floors. Think about the gift of your children when you are carting them around! Leave your cell phone at home when you walk the dog, and spend that time praying and enjoying God's creation.

Whatever you are doing, do it in the name of Christ and with a grateful heart. This is pleasing to God.

....

....

....

....

....

....

....

....

....

....

....

....

PRAY: *God, thank You for the ability to do the mundane chores of my day-to-day life. Thank You for my home and my family and even for the responsibilities You have blessed me with. Help me to honor You in all that I do—no matter how small or insignificant the task may seem. Amen.*

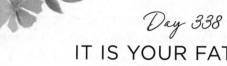

Day 338

IT IS YOUR FATHER'S GOOD PLEASURE TO GIVE YOU THE KINGDOM

———— **READ MALACHI 3:6-12; MATTHEW 6:19-24;** ————
MATTHEW 19:21-30; LUKE 12:32-34;
1 CORINTHIANS 9:6-15; 1 TIMOTHY 6:6-10, 17-19

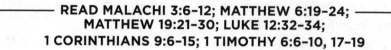

KEY VERSES: *"Fear not, little flock, for it is your Father's good pleasure to give you the kingdom. Sell your possessions, and give to the needy. Provide yourselves with moneybags that do not grow old, with a treasure in the heavens that does not fail, where no thief approaches and no moth destroys. For where your treasure is, there will your heart be also."* LUKE 12:32-34 ESV

UNDERSTAND:

• Based on these passages, what should our view about money and gaining wealth in this world be?

....

....

....

• What ways have you been storing up treasure in heaven? What ways could you store up even more?

....

....

....

....

....

APPLY: Finances can certainly cause a lot of anxiety. So, today's readings are just a handful of the many scriptures in the Bible regarding money, which when heeded can bring financial peace. God's Word is clear that gaining worldly wealth here on earth should not be our goal. In fact, "the love of money is the root of all kinds of evil" (1 Timothy 6:10 NLT). Our goal should be to store up treasure in heaven. How? By giving back to God through good works and with generosity to care for others in need. Let Him reveal where you might need to make changes in your finances and trust *Him* more instead of your own desires and plans. Thank Him for the ways He has already blessed you. Seek out and listen to advice from others you know who are both generous and wise with money. Most of all, remember that everything you've been given is from God, and you are simply a steward of those gifts.

....

....

....

....

....

....

....

....

....

....

....

....

....

PRAY: *Heavenly Father, please reveal to me and correct me where I need to make changes in my finances. I want to honor You with all my gifts and blessings and generously care for others in Your name. Amen.*

Day 339

HOW MUCH GOD
LOVES THE WORLD

──── READ JOHN 3:16–21 ────

KEY VERSE: *"For this is how God loved the world: He gave his one and only Son, so that everyone who believes in him will not perish but have eternal life."* John 3:16 NLT

UNDERSTAND:

• What does the John 3:16 scripture reveal about the love of God?

....

....

....

....

....

....

• What do God's actions reveal about what He thinks of us?

....

....

....

....

....

....

....

....

APPLY: God could've created the world, set it spinning on its axis, and walked away. He could've fashioned humans from dust, and as soon as we messed up our relationship with Him, He could've left us to our own devices—moved on to create something else that maybe wouldn't betray Him. But He didn't. He loves us too much to leave us in our own filth.

He loves the world so much that He gave up the one most precious to Him: His Son. It defies logic, but it's absolutely true. God willingly handed Jesus over to be sacrificed for the sin of the world. Not just your sins. Not just the sins of the people who have already accepted His grace. Jesus died for the sins of the *whole history of the world.*

Love is a powerful force. The love of God is an unstoppable force. Today, live in that all-encompassing love God has for you.

....

....

....

....

....

....

....

....

....

....

....

PRAY: *Merciful, loving Father, Your love is rooted in the most giving, unselfish act in all of history. As difficult as it was for Jesus to lay down His own life, how much harder must it have been for You to give up Your beloved Son to be a human and spiritual sacrifice. Thank You for loving the world so much that You made a way when there was no other way. Amen.*

FLAWED BUT USABLE

—— READ JOSHUA 2 ——

KEY VERSES: *The house Rahab lived in was built on the city wall, so she used a rope to let the men down through a window. She said to them, "Go into the hills so the king's men will not find you. Hide there for three days. After the king's men return, you may go on your way."* JOSHUA 2:15–16 NCV

UNDERSTAND:

- God can use anyone to accomplish great and mighty things. Think of a time when He used an unexpected person to bless you.

....

....

....

....

....

....

- Have you ever walked through a season where you felt unusable?

....

....

....

....

....

....

....

APPLY: When you think of the heroes of faith, the great men and women of the Bible, what names come to mind? Moses? Abraham? David? Esther? Deborah? Paul? Peter? Timothy? There are so many you could list, but you would likely overlook one very important and unusual one—Rahab, the harlot.

Now, it's not typical to see the name of a prostitute in the lineup of biblical greats, but Rahab made the cut because she selflessly aided the people of God when they needed help. She risked everything to protect them. And while many might have judged her, the Lord saw her heart.

The same is true today. There are many amazing people out there. Some might not dress like you or look like you. Others might still be trapped in a sinful lifestyle. But God loves them and longs for restoration. So take the time to talk to the Rahabs in your world. Show them that they have value, worth. You never know—God might just use that person to minister to you in ways you never expected.

PRAY: *Lord, I'm so grateful that You choose to use everyone— flaws, warts, and all. May I never forget that You came for us all and love us all. I praise You, Father. Amen.*

Day 341

I'M SCARED THAT MY MARRIAGE IS IN TROUBLE

READ 1 PETER 3:8-11

KEY VERSE: *All of you should be of one mind. Sympathize with each other. Love each other as brothers and sisters.* 1 PETER 3:8 NLT

UNDERSTAND:

- What makes you worry about the health of your marriage? Is it the way your spouse acts—or is it the way you feel?

....

....

....

- What do you think it means to "be of one mind"? How might you experience that, in practical ways, within your marriage?

....

....

....

- Have you ever thought about loving your spouse as a brother in Christ (even while keeping your sexual relationship intact)? How might that attitude change your marriage?

....

....

....

....

APPLY: Almost all marriages go through times of harmony and happiness, interspersed with times of conflict and pain. Hopefully, the happy times are longer than the painful periods, but no matter how much you love your spouse, it's never going to be easy for two people to live together! Your selfishness will rub against theirs, causing you both pain. You won't always grow, emotionally and spiritually, at the same rate, which means that sometimes one person may feel left behind. The changing circumstances of your lives will bring new challenges to face.

But none of these things needs to threaten the security of your marriage. This passage of scripture gives good advice for building a strong and healthy marriage: don't head in different directions; sympathize with each other; be humble and tenderhearted; don't exchange insults; and finally, search hard for peace—and then do the work that's necessary to maintain it.

PRAY: *God of love, I ask that You bless my marriage. Make it strong. Heal its broken areas. Keep us from hurting one another. Keep us both firmly committed to one another—and to You. Amen.*

Day 342

JEHOVAH-JIREH,
THE PROVIDER

— **READ LUKE 12** —

KEY VERSE: *"Do not fear, little flock, for it is your Father's good pleasure to give you the kingdom."* LUKE 12:32 NKJV

UNDERSTAND:

• What is your greatest concern about the future? Will you surrender it to the Lord today?

....

....

....

....

....

....

....

• Can you name a specific time when God has provided for you either financially or in another way such as physically or spiritually?

....

....

....

....

....

....

....

APPLY: It is comforting to read that Jesus told His disciples not to fear. He called them "little flock." We are part of His flock. If you are a believer in Christ, His promises in Luke 12 ring true for you today just as they did for His followers in that time.

Jesus reminds us that God meets the needs of birds and that we are much more valuable than the birds. He points out that the flowers are nurtured by the hand of God. If God meets the needs of birds and flowers, will He not much more so meet the needs of His children?

Take time to dwell upon all the times when God has provided. Rest assured that He will continue to meet your needs day by day. One of His names in scripture is Jehovah-Jireh, which means "the Lord will provide"!

PRAY: *Lord, thank You for reassuring me that You will always provide for my needs. Just as You have shown up time and time again in the past, I know You will continue to do so. Calm my fears about the future, and replace them with utter trust in Jehovah-Jireh, my provider. Amen.*

Day 343

SMALL PART, BIG POWER

READ JAMES 3:1–12; PSALM 34:13; PROVERBS 18:21; PROVERBS 21:23

KEY VERSE: *We all stumble in many ways. Anyone who is never at fault in what they say is perfect, able to keep their whole body in check.* JAMES 3:2 NIV

UNDERSTAND:

• What ways have you observed the tongue being a fire causing great damage?

....

....

....

....

....

....

• When are you most tempted to use your words sinfully? What practical ways can you work toward avoiding sin in this way?

....

....

....

....

....

....

....

....

APPLY: Did you say everything perfectly in all your conversations today? The odds are that you probably did not. This passage in James 3 is comforting as it reminds us that we're not alone in the struggle to control our words. None of us is perfect at this. It's far too easy to spout off without thinking when angry or hurt. Certain people and certain stressors can trigger us into speaking in ways we know are wrong. Sometimes we simply just get tired and careless. Sometimes we use the excuse that we "just need to vent."

But since God's Word acknowledges how hard it is to control our tongues, should we just give up trying? Of course not. Our words matter—a lot. They have great control and power, like a bit in a horse's mouth or a rudder on a ship. And they have great potential for evil, unfortunately. We should take this passage as a warning to stay vigilant to keep our tongues in check. As Christians, we should not have both praise to God and curses coming out of our mouths. And when we mess up, which we will, we should correct our words and seek forgiveness quickly. Mostly, we should make Psalm 141:3 (ESV) our constant prayer: "Set a guard, O LORD, over my mouth; keep watch over the door of my lips!"

PRAY: *Heavenly Father, please set a guard over my mouth, and keep watch over the door of my lips. I need Your incredible power to help me control my tongue, because I will fail far too often on my own. Please forgive me when I sin with my words, and help me to make things right with others whom I've hurt. Thank You for Your grace that covers me! Amen.*

Day 344
LIVE IN HOPE

— READ PSALM 147 —

KEY VERSE: *The Lord's delight is in those who fear him, those who put their hope in his unfailing love.* PSALM 147:11 NLT

UNDERSTAND:

- Why do you think God delights when we put our hope in His love?

....

....

....

....

....

- Do you have hope today? Why or why not?

....

....

....

....

....

- What situation in your life needs an infusion of hope today?

....

....

....

....

APPLY: Hope is a wonderful, ever-present thing for Christians. When life is good and everything feels harmonious, when the birds sing and the sun shines, we are filled with hope. And when life is in turmoil and everything feels discordant, when the birds screech, the wind howls, and everything feels wrong, still we hope.

Why? Because God has never failed us yet, and He won't start now. God's love is there, holding us up. God's plan continues even when we don't see it or understand it. God's Spirit sustains us as we hold on to hope.

And God delights in our hope. Celebrate hope on the days it comes easy, and ask Him to supply you with an extra dose of hope on the days it comes harder. Praise God for the hope you have in His promises, in His love, and in His care for you. Cling to hope when life feels impossible, but don't give up. Hold on, child. The Father is coming.

PRAY: *Father, thank You for Your sustaining hope. I know I can trust You in all things, and that fact is a great source of comfort to me. I know difficult times will come, but I also know that Your love never fails. Help me to shine Your love and Your light of hope to people around me who may feel hopeless. You have not forgotten them. Amen.*

Day 345

WHEN TIME STANDS STILL

———— **READ JOSHUA 10:1–28** ————

KEY VERSES: *On the day that the L*ORD *gave up the Amorites to the Israelites, Joshua stood before all the people of Israel and said to the L*ORD: *"Sun, stand still over Gibeon. Moon, stand still over the Valley of Aijalon." So the sun stood still, and the moon stopped until the people defeated their enemies. These words are written in the Book of Jashar. The sun stopped in the middle of the sky and waited to go down for a full day. That has never happened at any time before that day or since. That was the day the L*ORD *listened to a human being. Truly the L*ORD *was fighting for Israel!* JOSHUA 10:12–14 NCV

UNDERSTAND:

• "That was the day the LORD listened to a human being." What do those words mean to you?

....

....

....

....

....

• Is God listening to you? If so, how does He respond to your requests?

....

....

....

....

....

....

APPLY: This has to be one of the most fascinating stories in the Bible. Rarely do we stumble across a tale where a human called the shots and God obeyed. It's not that Joshua was bossing God around. He simply took the time to understand God's will and then just spoke with authority as he called the sun and moon to stand still. Might sound like he was a know-it-all, but that's not the case.

Did you know that God likes it when you speak with authority? When you look the enemy in the eye and say, "Be gone in Jesus' name!" you're actually speaking His Word, His truth over the situation. And, like Joshua, you'll see miracles happen as a result.

PRAY: *Thank You for the reminder that I can speak with authority even in the midst of the battle, Lord. I want to see miracles just like Joshua did. Amen.*

Day 346

I'M UNSURE WHICH
PATH TO TAKE

─────────── **READ PSALM 25** ───────────

KEY VERSES: *Show me your ways, Lord, teach me your paths. Guide me in your truth and teach me, for you are God my Savior, and my hope is in you all day long.* PSALM 25:4–5 NIV

UNDERSTAND:

• In what areas of your life do you need God's guidance today?

....

....

....

....

....

....

• How do you expect God to show you the path to take? It's unlikely He will send a direct message to you, speaking in an audible voice or writing you a letter. How else might you be able to perceive God's direction? Where should you turn to seek His will for your life?

....

....

....

....

....

....

APPLY: Again and again, in all the various difficult situations we face, the Bible gives us the same answer: trust in God. Rely only on Him. Surrender everything into His loving hands. That's the only thing that will put us in the position where God can help us.

God always longs to help though. He is waiting for opportunities to demonstrate His love to us. He yearns to show us the path that will lead to our health and healing and happiness. And He will do exactly that. . .if we let Him.

Sometimes, however, even though we may be begging God to show us the path to take, we don't want to hear His answer. Deep inside, we've already chosen the path we'd prefer—and we're afraid God will send us in a different direction. We need to remember that God only wants what's best for us. All His ways are loving and faithful (verse 10).

No matter how many times we rebel against God, choosing to go our own way rather than His, all we have to do is ask His forgiveness. His love and mercy for us are infinite.

PRAY: *Teach me the way You want me to go, God. Guide my path. Lead me closer to You. Guard my life and rescue me; do not let me be put to shame, for I take refuge in You (verse 20). Amen.*

Day 347

THE SAVIOR'S COMING

---------- **READ MATTHEW 24** ----------

KEY VERSE: *"But about that day or hour no one knows, not even the angels in heaven, nor the Son, but only the Father."* MATTHEW 24:36 NIV

UNDERSTAND:

• If the Father, Son, and Holy Spirit are one, then how is it that only the Father knows the time Jesus will return?

....

....

....

....

....

....

• What would you like to be doing when Jesus returns?

....

....

....

....

....

....

....

APPLY: We all await the Second Coming of our Savior, but we do not know the day or the hour it will happen. How is it that even Jesus Himself does not know when He will come back to earth? This is because the Son has submitted to the authority of the Father. It is voluntary subordination.

What will you be doing when Jesus returns? Consider the ways that you bring glory to His name on a daily basis. Do you share the hope you have found in Him? Do you minister to those in need? Do you love those around you? If you are a Christian, you do not need to worry. You are saved and will experience eternal life with Christ. Still, we want to be found serving Him and bringing Him glory rather than dishonor with our lives when He returns.

PRAY: *Lord Jesus, sometimes I imagine Your Second Coming. I look into the sky and picture You coming on the clouds! Help me to be ready and to be found serving You and loving others when You come again. Amen.*

Day 348

READY FOR EVERY GOOD WORK

READ 2 TIMOTHY 2

KEY VERSES: *In a wealthy home some utensils are made of gold and silver, and some are made of wood and clay. The expensive utensils are used for special occasions, and the cheap ones are for everyday use. If you keep yourself pure, you will be a special utensil for honorable use. Your life will be clean, and you will be ready for the Master to use you for every good work.* 2 TIMOTHY 2:20–21 NLT

UNDERSTAND:

• How does verse 13 fill you with peace?

....

....

....

....

....

• Do you do a good job of obeying verse 16? How could you improve?

....

....

....

....

....

....

....

....

APPLY: Timothy tells us we should want to be a special utensil for God to use in the most honorable ways. But what does it mean to do as verses 19–21 describe? How do we keep ourselves pure and our lives clean? Verse 22 (NLT) goes on to instruct us how when it says, "Run from anything that stimulates youthful lusts. Instead, pursue righteous living, faithfulness, love, and peace. Enjoy the companionship of those who call on the Lord with pure hearts." As the NIV puts it, we should "flee the evil desires of youth and pursue righteousness, faith, love and peace, along with those who call on the Lord out of a pure heart." Each of us must ask God how to best apply this in our own lives and circumstances and trust that He will show us where He wants to clean up our lives and correct us. The most rewarding and fulfilling way to live is to be ready for your Master to use you for every good work He has planned for you.

_____

_____

_____

_____

_____

_____

_____

_____

_____

_____

PRAY: *Heavenly Father, please constantly show me what areas of my life need cleaning up. Help me to run far away from temptation and evil. I want to be used in the beautiful ways You created me for. Amen.*

Day 349

WISDOM AND KINDNESS

―――――― **READ PROVERBS 31:10-31** ――――――

KEY VERSE: *She opens her mouth with wisdom, and the teaching of kindness is on her tongue.* PROVERBS 31:26 ESV

UNDERSTAND:

- Who do you know who best embodies the attributes of the Proverbs 31 woman?

....

....

....

....

- When you open your mouth, are wisdom and kindness the first things that come out? If not, what usually comes out?

....

....

....

....

- What situations and relationships can you infuse with kindness today?

....

....

....

....

APPLY: In times of high stress and high emotions, we may be surprised at what comes barreling out of our mouths. We often react too quickly in knee-jerk reactions that can be thoughtless at best and devastating at worst.

But the truth is we have a choice in the words we say. As difficult as it is to train our minds and mouths, we can, like the Proverbs 31 woman, open our mouths with wisdom and demonstrate kindness with our words and actions.

Such training requires filling our minds and hearts with the wisdom that only comes from God's Word. You're doing that when you spend time in the Bible every day. Remember His promises, His kindness toward you (even when you don't deserve it), and His unending forgiveness. Then ask the Holy Spirit to guard your mouth and give you the wise, kind reaction in any scenario. Allow God's love to shine through you in any situation!

PRAY: *God, help me to follow Your example and the example of the Proverbs 31 woman in kindness. Give me the wisdom to understand the difference between kindness and niceness. When the world is fake, make me genuine in my interactions. You are so faithful in Your kindness toward me, and I want to reflect the same to others. Amen.*

Day 350

WALKING IN FAITH

--------- **READ MATTHEW 1:18-25** ---------

KEY VERSES: *When Joseph woke up, he did what the Lord's angel had told him to do. Joseph took Mary as his wife, but he did not have sexual relations with her until she gave birth to the son. And Joseph named him Jesus.* MATTHEW 1:24–25 NCV

UNDERSTAND:

• Can you imagine what Joseph was going through? Which would be the hardest pill to swallow?

....

....

....

....

....

• How do you think Joseph felt whenever someone would say something like "That's a great boy you've got there!"?

....

....

....

....

....

....

APPLY: Joseph was a key player in the story of the birth of the Messiah, but he's often overlooked. Mary we remember. The shepherds in the field? We'll never forget the role they played. The angels? Who else could have made the heavenly proclamation? The wise men, traveling from afar to bring gifts? We are amazed at their journey and their offerings. But when it comes to Joseph—the man who would become dad to baby Jesus—we often forget to mention him.

Joseph had one of the hardest jobs of all. Not only was his reputation at stake (the gossips were surely having a field day), but he had to tackle those weird "This isn't really my son" feelings after the birth. More than anything, Joseph was asked to do something no one had ever been asked to do before—protect his pregnant virgin's image and give her baby a good home. (Try explaining that one to the grandparents-to-be.)

Without Joseph, the plan would have crumbled. Aren't you glad he stepped up and obeyed God? It took a significant amount of faith to believe the angel's instructions, but he did. . .and the story had a beautiful ending as a result.

PRAY: *What amazing faith Joseph must have had, Lord! I'm so glad he responded to the call You placed on his life. Otherwise, the story might have had a very different ending. I want to have that kind of faith, Lord. Amen.*

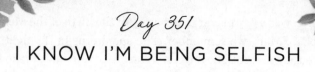

Day 351

I KNOW I'M BEING SELFISH

──────── **READ PHILIPPIANS 2:4–9** ────────

KEY VERSE: *You must have the same attitude that Christ Jesus had.* PHILIPPIANS 2:5 NLT

UNDERSTAND:

• Imagine if Jesus had been a "normal," selfish human being. How do you think His life would have been changed?

....

....

....

....

• Do you consider Jesus to be your role model? Why or why not?

....

....

....

....

• What do you think the world would look like if imitating Jesus became a shared societal norm?

....

....

....

....

....

APPLY: Selfishness makes us want to impress other people with our skills, appearance, prestige, or some other quality, while it blinds us to the reality of others' needs. It makes us think, deep in our hearts, that we're somehow better than others. It drives us to seek our own way, regardless of the hurt it causes others.

Selfishness is woven through the very fabric of our society. As a result, it seems normal to us. Meanwhile, as it hurts our relationships at the individual level, at the societal level it has polluted our planet, created wars and poverty, and driven us to prejudice, discrimination, and divisive factions of one sort or another.

We can't change our entire society, not without a great deal of concerted effort, but we *can* take the first, most vital step—we can allow God to change our own hearts. We can practice the attitudes of Christ.

PRAY: *Jesus, teach me to follow You more closely. Change our world, Lord, I pray—but first, change me. Remake me in Your image. I want to be like You. Amen.*

Day 352

SOVEREIGN GOD

──────────── **READ MICAH 5:1–6:8** ────────────

KEY VERSE: *"But you, Bethlehem Ephrathah, though you are small among the clans of Judah, out of you will come for me one who will be ruler over Israel, whose origins are from of old, from ancient times."* MICAH 5:2 NIV

UNDERSTAND:

• Micah prophesies about a ruler who will come from Bethlehem. Who is this ruler?

....

....

....

....

....

....

• When you read Old Testament verses that predict the coming of the Messiah, what do you think? How does it impact you?

....

....

....

....

....

....

....

APPLY: Have you sung the old Christmas carol "O Little Town of Bethlehem"? Micah, the prophet, prophesied many years before the birth of Christ that a ruler would come from the little town of Bethlehem!

Isn't it amazing that prophets foretold the coming of Christ? God had a plan to redeem mankind all along. At just the right time, God sent His Son to redeem us (see Galatians 4:4–5).

Rest in the knowledge that you serve a great big God. If He is wise enough to craft a plan to save us from sin, is He not able to handle the hurts and hang-ups in your life? Turn to Him, acknowledge His presence, and leave your worries at the feet of a sovereign King.

PRAY: *Lord, help me to trust in Your sovereignty. You are a great Creator. You reign over the universe. You set the stars in their places and call them by name. Surely You are able to manage my little life. I love You. Help me through this day to rely on You in every moment. Amen.*

Day 353
WHEN COURAGE MELTS AWAY

——————— **READ JOSHUA 7:1–15** ———————

KEY VERSES: *So approximately 3,000 warriors were sent, but they were soundly defeated. The men of Ai chased the Israelites from the town gate as far as the quarries, and they killed about thirty-six who were retreating down the slope. The Israelites were paralyzed with fear at this turn of events, and their courage melted away.*
JOSHUA 7:4–5 NLT

UNDERSTAND:

• In what ways has God called you to be a leader?

....

....

....

....

....

• What have been the worst unexpected turns of events in your life? What has God taught you through them?

....

....

....

....

....

....

....

APPLY: Like the Israelites in Joshua 7, we too have had turns of events in life that make us feel like our courage has melted completely away. As difficult as it is, in those times, we must look back and see if our sin contributed to the awful turn of events. Sometimes the answer is "not at all" because it's just the hardship and trials of life or a situation God is using to teach us and refine our faith. But sometimes our sin has led to the rough circumstances in which we find ourselves, and we have to admit that. The hard but necessary truth is, if we disobey God, He's not going to fill us with His blessings and good courage. But there is merciful truth that because of the sacrifice of Jesus, "If we confess our sins, he is faithful and just to forgive us our sins and to cleanse us from all unrighteousness" (1 John 1:9 ESV).

PRAY: *Heavenly Father, please help me to keep obeying You and Your Word and quickly ask forgiveness and make things right when I sin. I want to keep Your courage solid in me. I don't want it to melt away! Amen.*

Day 354

HUMBLE YOURSELF
TO BE LIFTED UP

──────── **READ PHILIPPIANS 2:1–11** ────────

KEY VERSES: *Don't be selfish; don't try to impress others. Be humble, thinking of others as better than yourselves. Don't look out only for your own interests, but take an interest in others, too.* PHILIPPIANS 2:3–4 NLT

UNDERSTAND:

- Other than Jesus, who is the humblest person you know?

....

....

....

....

- What is the biggest challenge you face in living a life of humility?

....

....

....

....

- What is the difference between humility and weakness?

....

....

....

....

....

APPLY: If we're honest with ourselves, we probably care entirely too much what other people think of us. From an early age, we're told to aim to be the best. To achieve. To win. To look out for ourselves first, our loved ones second, and everyone else can worry about themselves.

But the kingdom of God is different than this world. In fact, in many ways it's an upside-down kingdom where the greatest among us are the most humble, the most giving. They're the ones who lay aside their own wishes to bring glory to God. And in the case of Jesus, He gave up everything—including His very life—to complete God's perfect will for humankind.

Today, intentionally put others ahead of yourself. See them as God sees them, and honor as His child each person you encounter. God will honor your humility and lift you up.

PRAY: *Jesus, thank You for showing me the way to humility. When I think I am better than others, remind me of what You did on earth. You lived humbly, with no place to call home. You gave up everything for me. I cannot repay You for that, but I will offer my life as a humble offering to You. Amen.*

Day 355

THE HANDWRITING'S
ON THE WALL

──────── **READ DANIEL 5:1–30** ────────

KEY VERSES: *Suddenly the fingers of a human hand appeared and wrote on the plaster of the wall, near the lampstand in the royal palace. The king watched the hand as it wrote. His face turned pale and he was so frightened that his legs became weak and his knees were knocking.* DANIEL 5:5–6 NIV

UNDERSTAND:

• God speaks in numerous ways, but you've likely never seen Him write on a wall. What's the most unusual way God has spoken to your heart?

....

....

....

....

....

• Why do you suppose God chose this particular way to speak to the king?

....

....

....

....

....

....

APPLY: Throughout history, God has chosen a number of ways to speak to His kids: by appearing in a fiery bush for Moses, by knocking walls down around Jericho for Joshua, by providing a ram in the thicket for Abraham, by providing a child for Hannah. He even used a donkey to speak to Balaam. He's very creative!

Perhaps one of the most unusual ways God ever spoke was through the handwriting on the wall in this story from Daniel. Can you even imagine the terror as a human hand appeared and started to write on the wall, right in front of you? Which would be more important, do you think—what was written or who was behind the message?

Maybe God has spoken in unusual ways in your life—through circumstances, through a friend, through a sermon, or through a particular scripture passage from the Bible. There are numerous ways God can speak to a heart. Keep your eyes and ears open. He's got a lot to say, and you don't want to miss a thing.

PRAY: *You're so creative, Lord! You can speak in any way You choose. I will be listening, I promise. So, speak to my heart, I pray. Amen.*

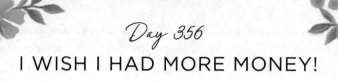

I WISH I HAD MORE MONEY!

——— READ HEBREWS 13:5–8 ———

KEY VERSE: *Don't love money; be satisfied with what you have. For God has said, "I will never fail you. I will never abandon you."* HEBREWS 13:5 NLT

UNDERSTAND:

- Do you think your longing for more money could be something that comes between you and God? Why or why not?

....

....

....

....

- What connection, if any, do you think your longing for money has with a lack of trust in God?

....

....

....

....

- Why do you think this passage ends with the reminder that Jesus is the same yesterday, today, and forever (verse 8)? Does this have anything at all to do with money? If so, what?

....

....

....

....

APPLY: The longing for more money is one many of us share. No matter how much money we actually have, it never seems to be enough. There's always more we wish we could do or have. . .if only we had the money!

We often forget that money isn't anything *real*. It's merely a handy tool that human beings have come up with to symbolize the value of work and objects. In and of itself, it's just paper and metal. And yet, we've allowed it to carry so much— our sense of our own worth, our longing for power and prestige, and our feelings that if we only had *more*, we could fill up the deep emptiness within our hearts. We think that somehow money can keep us safe from life's dangers.

Only God can do that. He knows what we need, and He will give us exactly enough. We can trust Him.

PRAY: *Jesus, money comes and goes, but You always stay the same. You are my only constant source of security. Teach me to rely only on You. Amen.*

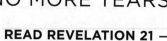

Day 357

NO MORE TEARS

─────── **READ REVELATION 21** ───────

KEY VERSE: *"'He will wipe every tear from their eyes. There will be no more death' or mourning or crying or pain, for the old order of things has passed away."* REVELATION 21:4 NIV

UNDERSTAND:

• Can you imagine a world without death, mourning, crying, or pain?

....

....

....

....

....

....

• What is "the old order of things" that will pass away when Jesus returns and His kingdom is established?

....

....

....

....

....

....

....

APPLY: All we have ever known is the old order. The old order is how life has been since the fall of man in the Garden of Eden. But it is not all we will ever know. There is a better day ahead for those who know Jesus.

God is the Alpha and Omega, the beginning and the end, as was declared to the author in his vision of the Revelation.

Even though things may seem hopeless as you battle cancer or live life with a difficult spouse, they are not hopeless. Regardless of how bad things may get in this world, there is another life to come. You will never shed another tear. You will experience no more pain. God Himself shall wipe away the tears from your eyes. He is in control.

_____

_____

_____

_____

_____

_____

_____

_____

_____

_____

_____

_____

PRAY: *Lord, this life is hard. I get so discouraged. It seems like as soon as things begin to get easier, the world throws me another curveball. I am so thankful to know that this is not the end of my story. In You I am confident of eternity in a much better place. In Jesus' name I pray. Amen.*

THE LORD REIGNS

---------------- **READ PSALMS 97–99** ----------------

KEY VERSES: *The Lord reigns, let the nations tremble; he sits enthroned between the cherubim, let the earth shake. Great is the Lord in Zion; he is exalted over all the nations.* PSALM 99:1–2 NIV

UNDERSTAND:

• What ways have you experienced the truth of Psalm 97:11?

....

....

....

....

....

....

....

• As you engage in discussion of current events, do you help promote to others total trust and peace in God?

....

....

....

....

....

....

....

....

APPLY: It's hard to find the right balance of staying informed about current events without becoming overly anxious about them. The other extreme is to be totally apathetic about them, which is tempting with all the conflict and animosity among people with differing views. So, we need much prayer for God's wisdom and peace in the midst of them, and most of all we need to focus on God's sovereignty. Psalms 97–99 give us a healthy perspective. When we choose to praise God as King of all kings and sovereign Lord over all nations, we can be filled with unwavering peace regardless of any turmoil in the nations, leadership, and politics around us. We must trust that God is in control, and as 1 Timothy 2:1–4 (NLT) says, we also must "pray for all people. Ask God to help them; intercede on their behalf, and give thanks for them. Pray this way for kings and all who are in authority so that we can live peaceful and quiet lives marked by godliness and dignity. This is good and pleases God our Savior, who wants everyone to be saved and to understand the truth."

PRAY: *Heavenly Father, please give me wisdom and a healthy perspective as I try to stay informed about current events in the world around me. I praise You as King of kings and Lord of lords. You will judge all nations with justice and fairness. Please fill me with Your perfect peace as I trust in Your total sovereignty. Amen.*

Day 359

YOU ARE PART OF CHRIST'S BODY

READ 1 CORINTHIANS 12:12-26

KEY VERSES: *So God has put the body together such that extra honor and care are given to those parts that have less dignity. This makes for harmony among the members, so that all the members care for each other. If one part suffers, all the parts suffer with it, and if one part is honored, all the parts are glad.*
1 CORINTHIANS 12:24–26 NLT

UNDERSTAND:

• How can you tell when your church is a healthy body of Christ?

....

....

....

• When have you experienced harmony among the members of the body of Christ?

....

....

....

....

• How have you been cared for by your church family?

....

....

....

....

APPLY: Life for the Christian isn't meant to be an individual or private faith. Yes, we are made to be in a relationship with our Father God, but we live in this world together with other believers. Before Jesus returned to heaven, He established His Church—what Paul describes in 1 Corinthians 12 as the body of Christ.

You are a unique part of your church, made with talents and passions and gifts, and you are cast in a role that only you can play. Body parts must work together and compensate when one part struggles, as well as celebrate and reap the benefits when one part is successful.

How's the health of your church as a whole? Are you doing life together, unified in faith? What practical steps can you take today to get involved in the lives of others?

....

....

....

....

....

....

....

....

....

....

....

....

....

PRAY: *Jesus, I am thankful for my church. We are Your body, made up of flawed individuals, but You bind us together in unity, and we are better for it. Forgive me when I wrongly believe I am better on my own. Amen.*

Day 360

THE ANCHOR HOLDS

──────────── **READ ACTS 27:27–28:5** ────────────

KEY VERSE: *But the ship struck a sandbar and ran aground. The bow stuck fast and would not move, and the stern was broken to pieces by the pounding of the surf.* ACTS 27:41 NIV

UNDERSTAND:

• What a remarkable man Paul was! Even when shipwrecked, he didn't lose his faith. Can you imagine being washed up on the shore of a desert island? How would this affect your faith?

....

....

....

....

....

• Sometimes our faith feels shipwrecked. Think of a time when you felt like that.

....

....

....

....

....

....

....

APPLY: If you made a list of all the things you hoped would never happen to you, "shipwreck" might be high on the list. No one ever thinks they'll go through such an unusual tragedy. Likely, Paul didn't think he would either. But that's exactly the position he found himself in as the ship he was on struck a sandbar and ran aground. In that moment, he had two choices: panic or be present in the situation.

Because Paul knew that God had his back, he remained present in the situation. He never lost his faith. In fact, he stood before the other men and encouraged them to find their courage.

Maybe you relate more to the other men on the ship. Maybe you're more inclined to panic in an emergency. Instead, do your best to follow Paul's lead. Stand firm. Remember, the anchor (Jesus) holds steady, even when winds and waves are tossing you to and fro. Don't let your faith be shipwrecked. Hold tight to the anchor and you'll live to face another day.

PRAY: *Thank You for holding steady, Jesus! I will remain present in the situation because I know You've got me covered. Praise You! Amen.*

MY FEELINGS ARE CONFLICTED

─────────── **READ PSALM 32:8-11** ───────────

KEY VERSE: *"I will guide you along the best pathway for your life. I will advise you and watch over you."* PSALM 32:8 NLT

UNDERSTAND:

• What creates the conflict in your heart? What is it that pulls you in opposite directions?

....

....

....

....

....

....

• These verses imply that joy and praise are directly related to a greater sense of clear direction. Have you ever found that to be true? Can you try it out today to see if it helps you think more clearly?

....

....

....

....

....

....

APPLY: We often feel pulled in opposite directions, like poor Olive Oyl stretched between Popeye and Brutus. Should we do what our hearts call us to do? Or should we be "responsible" and take the safer course? When is it smart to be conservative about money—and when should we be extravagant and generous? What's the difference between giving our children too much freedom and being overprotective? How do we determine when frankness is cruel—and when it's necessary and kind?

Life is so confusing! But God promises to guide us. When we turn to Him, relying only on Him, things become clearer. We can live in the stream of His unfailing love, trusting Him to resolve the conflicts in our hearts.

PRAY: *I praise You, loving Lord, for all You are and do. Keep my heart whole and pure, free of the conflicts that drive me back and forth. Show me the best path to take. Amen.*

Day 362

IMITATE THE HEAVENLY FATHER

READ 2 JOHN–3 JOHN

KEY VERSE: *Beloved, do not imitate what is evil, but what is good. The one who does good is of God; the one who does evil has not seen God.* 3 John 11 NASB

UNDERSTAND:

- What actions indicate that someone knows God personally? How do you know someone is a Christian?

....

....

....

....

....

- Have you been tempted to "imitate what is evil"? How can you keep from falling to this sort of temptation in the future?

....

....

....

....

....

....

APPLY: In the book of 3 John, the apostle John encourages the believers to take care of the "brethren" (fellow Christians) and especially if they are strangers.

How do we apply this to our own lives today? Look closely at your gifts and resources. Do you step outside of your own immediate family to meet the needs of the body of Christ? After all, in Christ we are all part of the family of God.

Do you have room in your home, money in your bank account, or an ability that can help others? Is there a widow in your church whose home is in need of repair? Do you know a fellow believer who could use your help getting a job or finding a place to live? You certainly cannot meet the needs of every Christian brother or sister, but you can meet some of them!

This world calls us to imitate evil. When you imitate good instead, you are imitating your heavenly Father.

....

....

....

....

....

....

....

....

....

....

PRAY: *Heavenly Father, may I always imitate good and never evil. I want to bring glory to Your name as I meet the needs of my Christian brothers and sisters. Sometimes I get so busy serving unbelievers and trying to win them for You that I forget I am called to meet the needs of those within the family of God. Give me opportunities to do just that. In Jesus' name I pray. Amen.*

Day 363

EXTRAORDINARY GRACE

READ MATTHEW 27:32–44;
MARK 15:21–31; LUKE 23:26–43

KEY VERSES: *He said to Jesus, "Lord, remember me when You come into Your holy nation." Jesus said to him, "For sure, I tell you, today you will be with Me in Paradise."* LUKE 23:42–43 NLV

UNDERSTAND:

• Matthew and Mark mention the two criminals crucified next to Jesus, but only the Gospel of Luke gives the details of one's salvation. Why do you think that is?

....

....

....

....

....

• Do you know someone who believed in Jesus as Savior in their very last moments of life?

....

....

....

....

....

....

APPLY: Never forget as you are praying for loved ones who are nonbelievers that God gives every possible chance to come to salvation. When Jesus was dying on the cross, one of the criminals dying next to Him believed in Him and asked Jesus to remember him. And Jesus promised that the criminal would be in paradise that very day when he died. This account shows how full of grace our extraordinary Savior is. He gives grace until even the very last moments of life, wanting everyone to believe in Him and accept Him as Savior. So keep on praying for those friends and loved ones who do not yet trust in Jesus. Keep sharing God's love with them, because He wants to give them every chance possible to spend forever in paradise.

....

....

....

....

....

....

....

....

....

....

....

....

PRAY: *Loving Savior, thank You for the example of the criminal beside You who believed at the last moment. That gives me so much hope for people I know who don't yet trust in You. I will keep on sharing Your truth and love with them. Please turn their hearts to You! Amen.*

Day 364

YOU HAVE THE
PEACE OF JESUS

──────── **READ JOHN 14:27-31** ────────

KEY VERSE: *"Peace I leave with you. My peace I give to you."* JOHN 14:27 NLV

UNDERSTAND:

• How is the peace of Jesus different than what the world defines as peace?

....

....

....

....

• Can fear and peace exist at the same time? Why or why not?

....

....

....

....

• What areas of your life need peace today?

....

....

....

....

....

APPLY: The world defines peace as the absence of war, but as Christians, we know that the peace of Jesus is so much more than that. Within the holy peace of God lies faith that He is in control of every circumstance, trust that He works all things for the good of those who love Him, hope (especially in the midst of difficult situations), and a deep contentment rooted in the joy of the Lord.

How do we experience this peace? It comes down to surrender. We must allow Jesus to be the Lord of every aspect of our lives. When we no longer hold tightly to the control of our desires, our relationships, and our wishes and dreams and instead ask Jesus to guide our steps, that's when real peace takes hold. We realize it's not all on our shoulders.

Breathe in, breathe out. Accept the peace that Jesus offers.

....

....

....

....

....

....

....

....

....

....

PRAY: *Savior, Your peace is what I long for. This morning, fill me with the deep restfulness and contentment that only You can offer. When I try to take back control, gently remind me that the only way to peace is to let it go. Make me an instrument of Your peace to everyone around me today, and energize me as I walk the path You lay before me. Amen.*

Day 365

I WISH I KNEW FOR SURE
YOU LOVE ME, GOD

READ ROMANS 5:6–11

KEY VERSE: *God showed his great love for us by sending Christ to die for us while we were still sinners.* ROMANS 5:8 NLT

UNDERSTAND:

- What experiences in your life have made it difficult for you to believe in the possibility of unconditional love?

....

....

....

....

....

....

- Does your experience of human love limit your ability to understand God's love? How might you come to know God better so that you can believe more fully in His love?

....

....

....

....

....

....

....

APPLY: God asks us to put everything we have and are in His hands. This act of total trust would be nearly impossible if we thought God might drop the things we give Him—or if we suspected He might actually wish to harm us and make us unhappy. But God's love is like no human being's. It wants only our good; there is nothing selfish in it.

Furthermore, it's reciprocal, as these Bible verses tell us. When God asks us to trust Him with our entire life, He has already given us Himself, totally, endlessly, both through Jesus and through the Spirit. We can surrender to Him, knowing we are completely safe and secure. His love will never diminish us or shame us or hurt us. Through Jesus and the Holy Spirit, we can enter a new relationship with God, one that's built on the intimacy of absolutely unconditional love.

PRAY: *Dear God, I may never be able to truly grasp how much You love me—but I thank You anyway. Thank You for sending Your Son into the world. Thank You that through Him I can experience the life of Your Spirit. Thank You for being my most intimate, most trusted friend. Amen.*

CONTRIBUTORS

Annie Tipton loves snow (which is a good thing because she lives in Ohio), wearing scarves, eating sushi, playing Scrabble, and spending time with friends and family.

Rae Simons is the author of more than thirty books. She and her family (along with assorted animals) make their home in upstate New York.

Emily Biggers is a Tennessee native living in Arlington, Texas. She loves to travel, write, spend time with family and friends, and decorate.

Janice Thompson, a full-time author living in the Houston, Texas, area, is the mother of four married daughters.

JoAnne Simmons is a writer and editor who's in awe of God's love and the ways He guides and provides.